#156

Grateful Memories; Ten Years on the Road Taping the Dead

TO
GRAHAM

Last

Boss
Tuom Jumbo

Author Jim Daley

Acknowledgments

I would like to acknowledge the friendships that brought me to this place in my life. My friend Mike Whitley, who turned me on to the first two Grateful Dead songs I ever heard; My friend Don Cartwright who brought the Grateful Dead into our scene and my brother Ray, who went to a few shows with me way back when, and because he's my brother. To Brian McGlynn who has been a good friend, inside and outside the Grateful Dead scene since the day we met in spring of 1979. My friend Dale Curtis, no longer with us, who was the first person who turned me on to live tapes -R.I.P. Finally my friend Rick Colyard, without whom several good friends may never have met. Through Mike, Don, Bob, Tom, Brian and Rick, I have met countless other people who have affected my life in a wide variety of ways, and are just too numerous to mention. Thank you all for being my friends.

To my Mom, whom I love and
miss everyday
May you rest in peace
To my son Denis,
who unfortunately never got to see
Jerry play,
but whose musical knowledge and
abilities far surpass any expectations
I had for him.
May God bless him for the rest of his life

One Great Observation

There was one great scene in NYC when the Dead was
Playing "Radio City" and Garcia and Weir were on
Good Morning America
And they were both dingier than pet coons
and they had some
real scrofulous Deadhead down in front of Radio City and he looked
like he had taken too much of something for too long although he's only
about twenty, and they said,
"Well, what do you do for a living.
And the guy just says,
"Oh, whatever I can do to get by, I spend
all of my money going to Grateful Dead concerts." So quick
they go back to the studio and the straight lady asks Garcia, "What do
you think about somebody who spends all his money going to Grateful
Dead concerts?"
And Garcia says, "What the hell do you think we do?"
Which as far as I was concerned was as clear a description of how it was
with the Grateful Dead and how it was with the Deadheads and how it
was with each other as I've ever heard.
Dead Lyricist John Barlow with David Gans 11-25-82
From "Conversations With the Dead"

Dedication

This book is dedicated to my friend and touring buddy, Bob Smith. He was my driver for 90% of the Grateful Dead shows that I attended. He has also been a very good friend off the road since the day I met him when I was only 18 years old. I lost my licence in 1982 for a DWI and when I quietly asked myself out loud, "What am I gonna do now?" Bob simply told me not to worry about a thing because he was going to pick me up every night for as long as I needed, and drive me to where ever we were going. A promise that he kept with an unflinching and amazing attitude. "Not to worry" was Bob's mantra.

Bob has been a good friend to everybody that he has met over the course of his lifetime. Everyone that I know, that knew him for even a short period of time, was touched by Bob's kind heart and unselfish attitude. Bob always made a point of putting himself in a position to help anybody in need at any time. I think I can safely speak for everyone when I say Bob was truly a great friend and personified what it means to be a Deadhead. Bob is not gone and I don't mean to speak of him in the past tense, but he is unavailable now, and he is still loved and thought of everyday by all of his friends, even though he does not believe it.

Bob now lives in a full care rehab facility without the ability to walk because of a surgical procedure, performed to remove a tumor from an area close to his spinal cord. He was given, in his own words, "acceptable odds" that he would walk again, but that didn't work out. He is paralyzed from the chest down, which complicates his ability to function in life without full time care.

I can't dedicate my book to Bob without giving my friend Tom Fagan an honorable mention. Tom gave me the info I needed to find Bob in Hampton Virginia in 1980, before I even knew who he was, and though I'm sure that I would have met him eventually, it was much better sooner than later.

Introduction

When I started going to see the Grateful Dead, the first thing I realized was that getting there and getting home was a big part of the adventure. Forging new friendships came with the territory as well, and although we know that in everyday life not everyone you meet becomes a friend, out on tour most times they do, if only for a short time. I have friends in Pennsylvania, I have friends in Colorado, I have friends in California. I see them at Grateful Dead shows. All this being said, the biggest part of the adventure for me was the music. I just wanted to be there every time the band took the stage, and walking out with a tape of the show made that adventure even more meaningful. I saw the Grateful Dead play 157 times and of those, I recorded 104. Early on the reason for not recording was usually bad seats or inexperience. Other times it was inconvenient and toward the end it was about tape deck problems. By that time, other people in my circle of friends were taping with new enthusiasm. You could say that the torch was passed, but I would still miss it. The music was always the most important thing to me, so leaving the taping to someone else was an eventual transformation.

These stories come mostly from my experiences on the road, but some key stories of interest from other friends are included. Every Deadhead has his or her favorite story about their first show or the furthest they traveled to see a show or the way the band played their favorite song at a particular show, so I thought a few stories from others would be a great addition. I never realized how many stories I had in me until I started the writing process. By the way, in this story, Grateful Dead concerts will be referred to as shows, as in "Are you going to any shows this coming tour" and "Which shows were your favorite on this tour" and of course, the ever popular, "Can I get a copy of that show from you?" Also, occasionally the Grateful Dead will be referred to as 'Jerry and the boys', or just 'The boys'.

I can say with complete confidence that if I could time travel, (without the ability to actually change anything) I would choose to go back to a time when my friends and I would get together every weekend to party and listen to the Grateful Dead. This still happens two or three times a year for us and it's usually a lot like it used to be for me, except I used to bring the music with me and now that's just not necessary. We are all still 'as one' where the Grateful Dead are concerned. When we get together for a celebration, the Grateful Dead is still our soundtrack. It makes me feel so good knowing that it's still there and it certainly has been a 'Long Strange Trip'

Table of Contents

My First Concert Experience
Englishtown N.J. 9-3-77

This book is about my experiences at Grateful Dead concerts, recording the shows, but the first time I saw the band play, recording the show was not a consideration at all. I didn't even know it would be a possibility. I had no clue about taping or trading tapes, but I did have an inherent love for music. It was in me the way blood is in me, though I had no idea that it would present itself the way that it did. I was introduced to the cassette deck when I was seven or eight by a friend. and when I saw this unique method of playing and recording music I remember thinking; "This is so cool; you can record something, label it and save it for later use. But why would somebody have a need for that. How would that really be useful?" I Guess I found a way, along with thousands of other Deadheads.

So, even though this book is supposed to be about my adventures following and taping the Grateful Dead, I really should talk about Englishtown first because before that, I was just a 15 year old kid listening to the radio. The problem that presents itself here would be that my memory of the event is not what it could be. I remember parts of the day, but not as much as I would like. It was Labor Day Weekend, I've got that. I was turning sixteen in two months. Easy math. The crowd was intense. I've seen pictures. I spent the entire weekend at Raceway Park, where the concert was, and I was essentially on my own.

My brother and Mike worked as Flaggers at the Motocross Track, so we were allowed access to the Pit area on the weekend of the show. I left Friday night with Mike's sister because that was the ride available and I didn't even see my brother until Saturday afternoon. Our parents knew where we were and I'm sure they assumed that we would be together, but they were camping for the weekend, so they had no idea what was really going on. There was an issue with us not being with them, but it wasn't my parents issue, it was my Aunt Judy's issue. I could just imagine the conversation they were having;

"Why aren't the kids here for Labor Day Weekend." my Aunt would ask. "They working?"

"No." Mom would reply. "They went to a concert with their friends this weekend".

"Not that big thing at Englishtown I hope".

"Yes." Mom would answer. "that's the place, Englishtown. That's where the concert is right?"

And this was when the Aunt kinda flipped out. She thought that this was the worst thing that she had ever heard in her life.

"How could you have allowed them both to go to that place with all the drugs and the weirdo's. You know that thing is a catastrophe, right? Biggest fiasco in New Jersey right now. It's all over the news. . . What with traffic jams and the hippies and the alcohol . . .

They're gonna get into trouble! . . .Oh my God!"

I heard this story from my mom the following Monday and I guess just because we were home safe and everything appeared to be normal, they just dropped it and it was never brought it up to us again.

This whole Grateful Dead "thing" started with Mike's sister Pat and her boyfriend Don. Don brought the Dead with him, but for all intents and purposes Mike turned me on to the music. Mike and my brother were just starting to listen to them, in the mix with several other bands and I was in the background. I heard my first Dead song at my house one day in the Summer of '77. It was U.S. Blues from an 8-track tape of 'From the Mars Hotel' that Mike insisted on playing for me. In 1977 8-tracks were cool. Anyway, the chorus of US Blues was exciting and real catchy:

'Wave that flag . . . wave it wild and high. Summer time gonna, come and go my oh my!!'
(Words and Music by Hunter and Garcia)

I liked a lot of different music when I was 15, singing along with every radio hit that was played on the AM dial. Simon and Garfunkel, The Eagles, The Beach Boys, just to name a few. It must have been mid June when we found out, through Mike's oldest sister, that the Dead would be playing at Raceway Park. Since we had access to the pit area, we would be allowed to camp there and it would be a great way to avoid the incoming crowds. We were luckier than we realized at the time. The idea of camping there sounded really cool, but I had no idea how that was going to work out, or *if*. I had a summer job at a restaurant and was saving money to go to Philmont with the Scouts the following year. This I *am* sure of. I don't know what this Grateful Dead thing is all about yet, but I'm willing to roll with it. Although first things first, I have to get the biggest weekend of the summer off, so I was already thinking, 'Good Luck with that!'

This is still the summer of 1977 and the concert was way off on Labor Day. In the world of the Grateful Dead, Jerry just finished with the final touches (editing, producing) on The Grateful Dead Movie, due to hit the big screens June 1st. This is a documentary film about the Grateful Dead concert experience, including a compilation from the last five shows they played at the Winterland Ballroom in 1974. After these shows the band went on hiatus; a self-imposed temporary retirement.

The band was traveling at that time, with tons of equipment, consisting mostly of a P/A system that was literally state of the art and partially invented and wholly designed by Dan Healy and Stan Owsley. Owsley was a chemistry student from Berkeley Ca., who befriended the Grateful Dead at one of their earliest gigs. He eventually stepped into the job of soundman /engineer, picked up the nickname Bear somewhere along the way, and incidently was the mastermind behind the Dead's album, Bear's Choice. Being the Dead's soundman, Owsley took a professional interest in the sound of the PA in each of the venues where the band played. He used his considerable LSD funded resources to tweak it. To that end, Owsley began recording the Dead's performances very early on, from the soundboard and from the audience, so that he could hear what the audience was hearing. It's due to Owsley's persistence and dedication that there is a seemingly endless supply of live shows in the Grateful Dead's vault. His bank roll is also the reason the band was able to tour extensively without worry of starving or living on the street.

Due to their association with Bear, the Grateful Dead became the house band for Kesey's acid tests. These were parties where the band would play and people would show up just to see how much acid they could possibly consume. Jerry said that playing the acid tests was an amazing experience for a musician because it involved so much freedom. They would show up for these acid tests and play if they wanted, or just hang out and check out the crowd. It didn't matter because nobody was there to see them play, they were just added amusement for those at the party. The Merry Pranksters, lead by Ken Kesey, had a sound system set up that was miked at each speaker so it would continually play back to itself, making for a very weird sound(ing) experience.

Now, getting back to the movie real quick; some of my friends went to the Premier at the Ziegfeld Theatre in Manhatten. Luckily for me, it was also shown the following weekend at the Paramount Theatre in Asbury Park. I saw it there with my friend Gregg, who also saw it at the Ziegfeld, but went a second time, so I wouldn't have to go alone. Later in that year, he and I went to a Rock n' Roll Flea market in New York City called The Rock of Ages Festival. This was a memorabilia flea market that was displayed on three separate floors at the Wilshire Hotel. Each floor was dedicated to one specific area of interest, whether it be albums, posters, T-shirts, or simple memorabilia like newspaper articles or back dated magazine issues. I found a complete original edition of the San Francisco Chronicle dated March 8th 1973, the day that Ron "Pig Pen" Mckernan died. Pig Pen, for those that may be unaware, was the original front man for the Grateful Dead when it was more of a straight blues band. I guess it was a good find, and although I don't believe it's worth any real money now, I definitely still have it. How's that!

While I was browsing, I also came across a 'bootleg' album of a Filmore West show from 1971. This was the show when Weir says, "Now now kids, don't fight." And then Jerry adds, "How do you expect us to play when you're screaming." That actually might have been Phil that said that. There was some pretty funny stage banter back then. I was not accustomed at the time to anybody talking on stage and over the years I have realized that there was hardly ever any of that. I also realized later that buying that album was helping to feed the bootlegging industry (now called pirating) so I never bought another one. And even as an eventual taper, I never sold a tape to anybody and gave away tons.

Getting back to the concert situation. (Remember I was talking about Englishtown) One day as I was talking to Dave, another guy that worked at the restaurant with me and he mentioned that he had an extra ticket for the concert at Englishtown. It was only $8.50 so I bought it. Now that I had my ticket, I needed the time off. I was telling Dave that I really wanted to go, but wasn't sure how I was gonna get Labor Day Weekend off.

He said, "Just take it off." I thought, 'Really? Just take it off?' I can't believe I actually had to think about that. . .?
So I devised a plan. (Sounds devious right?)

I said, "Listen Dave, the next time you're talking to Annie, (Kitchen Mgr) tell her that you heard I have to quit, but don't tell her why."

The next time I saw her (within ten minutes) she said, "I hear you have to quit, why is that?"

So I told her, "My parents are going camping Labor Day Weekend. . . and they said that I've worked enough this summer, and if I can't get the weekend off, then I'll have to quit. . so I figured I'd have to quit. . . That's all."

She said, "Don't worry about quitting, take the weekend to be with your family, we will be fine." . . . . Oh Yea. . .!

At that point I had no idea how I was getting there, just that I had a ticket and the weekend off, which was my biggest concern anyway. (Think about how many times we have all been in that situation over the years) Mike's younger sister Chris and her girlfriend were going and the girlfriend's mom was driving, so there's my ride. Chris was only 13 at the time, but her mom figured that her daughter was gonna go, even if she had to hitch-hike to get there, so she allowed the situation to develop. As the story progressed and I was added into the scenario, her mom felt better about the whole thing.

We left on Friday night. Chris and Mary and I were allowed to drink and smoke along the way, just so long as we shared our stash with her Mom. By the time we got close to the Raceway her mom was so concerned about the gas tank running dry, that she was moving slower than the traffic around her. This totally pissed people off and they started driving past us to our right. For those of you that were at the show in Englishtown, maybe you'll recall that there was a large drainage ditch on the right side of the road, so every time a car passed us on the that side, Mary's mom would scream out the car window, "I hope you land in the ditch you bunch of fuckin assholes" and all we could do was duck and cover. We were partying pretty good, but we were still embarrassed by the screaming. Go figure.

The parking situation was so much more than horrible. We were lucky we arranged to be dropped off. People were parking on side streets and lawns. Homeowners were charging $10.00 per car to park on their property. It turned into the largest traffic jam in New Jersey's history. There were 75,000 tickets sold, but an estimated 150,000 people showed up. (The one newspaper headline that I didn't bother to save. . . go figure!) We wound up sleeping on the hood of somebody's car that night and woke the next day to the sound of firecrackers, as they exploded in our direction.

I met up with the rest of my friends that afternoon and as I walked toward the entrance. I saw people all around me dragging coolers, blankets and children along with them. I'm guessing that this was considered a family event by some. I wouldn't have thought so myself, but I'm lucky I'm even here. Coolers? Yea, a cooler would have been a pretty good idea, had I thought of it yesterday before getting in a car with nothing but a ticket in my hand. I was probably the only person there that didn't know where his next meal might be coming from. I had nothing with me, not even a peanut butter and jelly sandwich. No beer – I was only 15 anyway – and absolutely no plan at all.

Still, no problem, not a worry in the world.

I wandered around the very large field that was part of the inside of the racetrack and found the bathrooms on the outskirts of the chaos. I also found a water fountain that was pretty much inaccessible. It was a super hot day, by anybody's standards. At some point someone, maybe the promoter, had the crowd sprayed with a water hose. Felt great, but the accumulated water puddled up around the bathrooms and created a huge muddy pond. No kidding! As I headed that way, I saw that the mud was up to the hippie's ankles (ha ha, hippies! No kidding again.) I'm not sure if the pond was a direct result of the crowd spray or if something else had happened but, I decided at that point, it was a mess that I wasn't prepared to deal with.

Then I ventured up toward the stage to check out the scene. There was nothing going on at that moment on stage, so I became a people watcher for a little while. I've always been a people watcher. People were standing around talking to each other; spread out on blankets hanging with their kids; tie-dyes every where; lots of people lying back napping, waiting for their favorite band, whomever that might be, to take the stage. As I looked around and took all this in, I noticed at least three speaker towers set on huge scaffolding platforms, set up in different places around the field. Beyond that there was a wall surrounding the field that was made up of box cars turned on their sides, from end to end. A strange, yet very original idea. I don't think that it worked very well though. The crowd was definitely overwhelming. It still surprises me even now that I wasn't feeling alone or nervous or anxious at all. Even at 15, (do I have to keep saying that?) being in a crowd of like-minded people, Deadheads, has always been a comfort zone for me. It's a feeling that has followed me through the rest of my touring experience, although I had no way of knowing that day, that I'd be doing this for the rest of my life.

This show at Englishtown was a first for a lot of people in New Jersey. I know this because I have met a lot of them over the years. Some of these became friends, most I would see only occasionally, but the commonality is a forever binding link. One such person does stand out from this crowd though. He was there that day way up toward the front and I may have been staring right at him for a moment, not even knowing. This particular guy has a lot of great stories from the Grateful Dead world, and I will share a few later in my story. Michael had shown up later than the rest of his friends that day, but this had become common place for him and his friends were very used to it. He was there with an icy cold six pack of Heineken, two of them actually and his four parched friends gave him a welcome like it was all for them. He also had, hidden in his cooler, wrapped in foil inside a half a dozen oranges, some crystalized acid. This was liberally shared with those same thirsty friends. A month and a half later I met this acid drenched Deadhead (Fredo) at my friend Mike's sister Pat's house, that she shared with her boyfriend Don. (He's responsible)

The first band that day was The New Riders of the Purple Sage. As I stood there about forty feet from the stage, about three songs in, I heard Panama Red. The only familiar song I remember from this band that day. Within twenty minutes or so, I was back with my friends checking in. Seeing what was up. They had a blanket down and one of them had a cooler with beer and some snacks. Marshal Tucker was on stage by then and they played the only other song I recognized from those two that day; Heard it in a Love Song. I don't think I had heard of Marshal Tucker before, but I was familiar with the New Riders.

I'm not really certain where I was by the time the Dead came on, but more than likely, I was hanging by the blanket that we had laid out, leaning forward on my tip-toes, stretching and squinting for a glimpse of the band that I had ventured there to see that day. The only other image I had of the Grateful Dead actually playing was from the movie that I saw in July and although I didn't recognize many songs the band played, I do remember hearing Friend of the Devil from the first set and Bertha, the opener of the second set. I really wish I had been more musically prepared for the show because every song they played that day was truly amazing. The Bertha alone is definitely one of the most recognizable versions, with a strong guitar opening that included a full piano riff. Ironically, I don't exactly remember it from when it was played, but more from listening to the recording. I do know that it stacks up against many other versions that have been played and to justify my point, another version that comes as close, also very recognizable, is the one from the Manhatten Center; April 5th 1971. This is on the Skull and Roses album and also had a distinctively strong opening and a great middle break. Originally called Skullfuck (mainly by the band members) Skull and Roses, was released as a double live Grateful Dead album and is one of my personal favorites. My Desert Island Disc. I wouldn't be without it.

As far as rest of the set list goes, I remember only those songs that I mentioned before, but they also played an amazing Samson and Delilah and a top ten Eyes of the World. Now this song, Eyes of the World, is one of only a few songs that is appreciated by people who don't even really like the Grateful Dead. You play it for somebody who doesn't know who the Dead are and their reaction would be one of surprise. "This is the Grateful Dead? "Yes, this is the Grateful Dead." I wasn't even an Eyes of The World fan back then. It was just another Grateful Dead song to me. The next time I saw them play it after Raceway Park was at the Spectrum in Philly on January 5, 1979. (also happened to be the next show that I went to. Long stretch between first and second shows) Four shows later on August 12,1979, I went out to Red Rocks Amphitheatre and saw them play it again. These were my first, second and sixth shows over a span of almost two full years. (Before writing this, I never thought about the fact that I flew to Colorado for my 6th Grateful Dead show) The Englishtown version was definitely one of the best, but I don't even remember it from the show. After these three versions, the next really good one (outstanding and really lost in the shuffle, I believe) was at Nassau Coliseum on Halloween in 1979. (Give it a listen back) Picking a favorite version of Eyes of The World is not an easy task for anybody, but I do have some recollection of how I became a fan of the song.

One of the classic versions was played at R.F.K. Stadium in 1973. The Allman Brothers opened for the Dead that day, and the boys opened the second set with a twenty-one minute Eyes of the World. (The studio version is only 5:21) It had a really long jam intro and it sounded like Jerry really took his time singing and jamming through it. Mind you, the rest of the show was quite amazing as well. They played two full sets and were then joined by the Allmans for a full third set. As a taper, I ran across this show early on, but I didn't even get the whole show all at once, just one 90 minute tape. I got it from my friend Brian and after hearing this version of Eyes of The World, I finally started paying more attention to other versions.

All this being said, do I have a favorite? That's still a tough question to answer. I know that those versions I heard at outdoor shows really grabbed me more intensely than those at indoor venues. So, for outdoors the favorite could be City Island in Harrisburg, Pa., in June of 1984, just because it was a great day and a lot of fun, but it could just as easily be Town Park in Telluride, Co., in 1987 because it was a stand alone Eyes, that drifted into drums. I loved it when Jerry would just start to play the opening chords from silence; It was a great feeling. The indoor show that strikes a chord for me (aside from the aforementioned Nassau) is Niagara Falls in April 1984. Coincidentally this one was also a stand alone, into drums. All three of these shows are discussed at length further into the story, so I won't go into them now. Just going over this question in my mind, I realized it would be tough to chose a favorite.

It's still very special to me that Englishtown was my first Grateful Dead experience, because Englishtown is considered to be a classic show in a year full of amazing classic shows. 1977 was really an amazing year for the Grateful Dead. I really wish I had been to more shows that year. (I wish I had been to more shows every year, ha ha!) One thing about Englishtown I thought was peculiar though, was that they didn't play One More Saturday Night at a Saturday Night show. (That one I would've known dammit!). As I glance over set lists from the shows after this one, I see that they played it as an opener or closer at nearly every Saturday night show that they played. I've seen it played at every Saturday night show that I've seen over the years and if they didn't play it on Saturday then they'd most certainly play it on Sunday with an explanation, or an apology. Bobby would be the one to lend an apology. In fact, I have a tape from Cal Expo in 1986, when Weir opened the show with One More Saturday Night, but before the song he said, "We're gonna start off with this one tonight, because we forgot to play it yesterday." The night before they didn't even play an encore. (Thank you DeadBase).

After the show, I went back to the pit area with my brother and friends to crash, this time on the ground in a sleeping bag, but the ground in the pit area was still very hard and uncomfortable. I picked a spot between two cars and I was damn lucky that there was no rain; in fact the weekend was rain free. I think I got a ride home the next day from Mike's sister. I do remember hanging out at home feeling like I had been up for three days, but not really equating it with being the amazing weekend that it actually was. Years later I would appreciate it in just that way. So, here I break it down. This was my first concert experience; I was gone from late Friday night until Sunday afternoon and I actually don't remember how I got home; There were three bands playing at Englishtown; The New Riders of the Purple Sage, The Marshal Tucker Band and the Grateful Dead. And it only cost me $8.50. . . Priceless. . ? Fucking amazing!

The Grateful Dead released this show on Dick's Pick's # 15. Dick's Pick's is a series of official releases from the Grateful Dead's live Archive of shows. Dick Latvala, was a friend of Phil's who, during a conversation with Phil about the vault, was offered the job of cataloging the tapes and it turned into the dream job for a Deadhead. Dick has since passed away, but the series continues in his memory due to his dedication to his craft.

After the Englishtown adventure, I continued along this new musical journey, listening to Mars Hotel and Skeletons From the Closet, but I hadn't considered how many albums were in the catalogue, so I went about looking for another. I wound up with a great one called Bears Choice. On this one Pig Pen covers a tune called Katie Mae by Lightening Hopkins' and another old tune originally done by Otis Redding called Hard to Handle. Weir does Dark Hollow, and Garcia does a very nice acoustic version of Black Peter, just to name a few. What really turned my head, though was a Garcia/Weir cover of Wake up Little Suzie. I already knew this tune from The Everly Brothers, so I started thinking; 'How many other songs this band plays that I'm already familiar with?' What I didn't know was that there was only one original tune on Bears Choice, so as far as covers were concerned, I was in for a real treat. This band covered music from a lot of other artists. David Crosby once referred to the Grateful Dead as the "greatest garage band in the whole world." ('Playing in The Band' by David Gans and Peter Simon) This musical journey was going to be way more interesting that I originally thought. Absolutely!

The next album I checked out was 'Europe 72', the live album from their Europe tour that year. I didn't realize it was a live album when I bought it, only that it was a triple album and there were a lot of songs on it. Upon first listen, I didn't get the jamming so much, but I loved the lyrics. I mean, who writes lyrics like that? Imagine your first exposure to the Dead's lyrics being Chinacat? Real funky lyrics; *Look for while at the Chinacat Sunflower, proud walking jingle in the midnight sun. . .?* Sappy Pop songs on the radio usually sing about love gone wrong. After listening to a couple of live tapes, including the Filmore East show that I mentioned earlier, I was getting hooked on Live Grateful Dead. How could you not love Pig Pen wailing on Good Lovin for 45 minutes. Truly mind blowing. I was really checking out those jams; listening to the instruments attacking one another, sounding at once disturbing and phenomenal; I'm listening to these jams and mentally tracing their destinations, and the more I listened to the flow of the music, the more fun and interesting it was to follow it. Listening to any Dead song roll into a jam and become something bigger than the song, and then roll back to where it had come from, or better yet, to have it become something else completely different was to me, very unique and exciting, drawing me in like a musical magnet. Their music really takes on a life of its own when they're really on, and quite frankly, even an off night can still have amazing moments.

The band took an unexpected break that summer because Mickey Hart was involved a car accident that June. If not for that, Englishtown may not have been my first show. During their unplanned break from the road Garcia and Weir were free to produce and release their solo projects; Cats Under the Stars and Heaven Help the Fool, respectfully. Being a new Deadhead, I picked up both of them, along with the new GD release, Terrapin Station. 'The Fool' had some great tunes on it, originals and covers. We were treated to these songs in the early 80's when Weir toured with Bobby and The Midnites. They were all fun shows. Garcia's 'Cats' had some excellent tunes on it too, including Gomorrah, Rhapsody in Red, and the title track.

I mentioned my friend Gregg before that I went to the Dead Movie with. He was a very friendly, accessible guy, who was also trying to figure out his life. To that end, he enlisted in the Army at the age of 17 with promises of education and placement, neither of which was met, so eventually, through the legal process, he was able to cancel his contract. But before all that happened, while preparing for his departure, he began selling off his personal belongings and since I had some money, I made it easier for him. I bought all of his Grateful Dead albums, plus a handful of others and his stereo speakers, which were huge. They were like part of the living room decor. They really didn't fit in well anywhere. Had I been married at the time the purchase would surely have been denied. I had to make one of them an end table in my room and the other found its home on top of my dresser, laying on its side. They filled my little bedroom with incredible Bass and beautiful sound and moved with me a few times before I finally had to put them to rest, some 15 years later.

Well, as far as concerts were concerned, I was done for a while. I had to get back to my reality, which included going back to High School as a Sophomore, and preparing for my ultimate expedition to Philmont with the Boy Scouts. It definitely did not include figuring out what Grateful Dead show to go to next. I'm certain I wasn't even aware that it was possible to just pick up and go see these guys play again.

Just about a year later they came back East again for another great outdoor show. The greatest show that I didn't make it to. It was at Giant's Stadium in East Rutherford, N.J. in the Fall of 1978, a full year after my first show, and I pretty much blew it off. They were headlining with Willie Nelson and the New Riders. It sounded like a great idea, but it was Labor Day Saturday and I generally didn't have weekends off. The fact of the matter was that I was so new to the job and I had just gotten back from a service break to Philmont, so I didn't even consider asking because it was a holiday. Last year I was working at a restaurant, this time a supermarket. You might guess that I wasn't quite 'on the bus' yet. Looking back now it was an incredibly stupid thing to do, not going to see the Grateful Dead with Willie Nelson right up the street. I should've called out and just hit the road, but at the time I was much too responsible for that, (ha ha) so I missed it.

I eventually saw Willie and Family play at the Meadowlands Arena. (at the time it was known as the Brendan Byrne Arena) Willie is so cool with his mellow tones and lively, exciting jams. 'Whiskey River' and 'Blue Eyes Cryin in the Rain' are two of my favorite Willie tunes. He also has a song called 'On the Road Again', which my friends and I adopted as our theme song for a while when we were hitting shows in the 80's.

"Just can't wait to get on the road again. . .The life I love is making music with my friends and I can't wait to get on the road again. . .
On the road again. . . Like a band of gypsies we go down the hiway....,
We're the best of friends, insisting that the world keep turning our waaay....and our way...is on the road again!! Willie Nelson..*
See, it makes total sense right?

Caught "Dead" in Philly

The shame of it all really, is that I didn't see any shows at all in 1978, and although it is regretful now, I was still in high school at the time, so it's also understandable. 1978, as much as I can recall, really flew by for me. I wasn't tied to a chair watching TV or any such nonsense. I was a very busy 16 year old. Busy with High School and Boy Scouts. The irony in all this, is that the traveling and sightseeing involved with Scouting kept my interest through the age of 18 and likewise, being part of the traveling circus that is the Grateful Dead touring experience peaked my interest in much the same way. I never complained about the travel time involved with getting to all those places we visited in Boy Scouts nor did I ever consider it a crazy idea to drive for three hours to see two or three, sometimes even just one Dead show. It's just what you do. All this being said, I was supposed to see 4 shows in 1978, but they were canceled due to health problems. Not mine though, as you read further.

The Grateful Dead had shows scheduled for the Spectrum in November that were part of the Fall tour that year. They were also special to me on a different level because my birthday fell in the same week. Though not quite on my birthday, it was definitely close enough. This tour started out in the Midwest and continued through the Northeast, then headed down to the Capital Center in Maryland, before hitting the Capitol Theatre in Passaic, N.J. Jerry hadn't been feeling well on the second leg of this tour and at the Capitol he sounded very sick. We listened to the show on the radio and could really hear that he was struggling. This Capital show was a Friday night and the Spectrum shows that we were going to were the following Monday and Tuesday. On that Sunday afternoon, on our way home from church, the monkey wrench came swinging through my birthday plans, as I heard the announcement on the radio that Jerry Garcia was sick with bronchitis and the shows had to be canceled for the following week. He also said that they would reschedule those shows for sometime after the New Year. Ugh!!., I remember being so upset. I was so looking forward to those shows the week of my. birthday and now. . . No shows! There were also shows scheduled for Madison Square Garden and those were cancelled as well.

While these shows on the East Coast were not happening, it was announced that Winterland was closing down and that the Grateful Dead would be the last band to perform there. The Winterland Ballroom was an ice skating rink in the 60's, and legendary concert promoter Bill Graham took over the building after experiencing some success at the Filmore West, (formerly the Avalon Ballroom) and produced some amazing shows there. Because Bill Graham enjoyed a personal relationship with the Grateful Dead, they were invited to close the place. Since The Grateful Dead recently played a gig on NBC's Saturday Night Live, The Blues Brothers; "Joliet" Jake and Elwood Blues (A.K.A. John Belushi and Dan Ackroyd respectfully). were invited to open the show for them. The Blues Brothers came together on SNL as a musical sketch and became an amazing piece of musical history, in my own humble opinion. . . The New Riders were also on the bill to play with them, as they were at the Englishtown show 15 months earlier, except here they were a middle and at Englishtown they opened the show. The Dead played three sets to close Winterland, and included a very special Dark Star and St. Stephen in the third set.

When it came time to reschedule those Spectrum shows they weren't able to book them in succession, so they played the first Spectrum show on January 5, and the second one on January 12. (1979) As it happened, I had to work on the night of the 1st show, but that plan kinda changed unexpectedly for me. Read on. . .

I have this friend that I had been hanging with since my Sophomore year in High School. (Truth be told I've known him since I was 10 years old in Little League, but that's another story.) So, I get a phone call at work at about 4 in the afternoon, and it was my friend Joe on the line. He told me that they were leaving for the show soon and asked when I could get off work. I told him I had to work until 7 pm and then he suddenly blurted out that my mom was in a car accident and I felt my heart fall through my chest.

"What?" I said.

Then he said, "Not really Jimbo, but tell them that. They'll let you go." Oh, now is that a friend or what? I swear to God, (I hate to swear to God) if I ever wound up in jail way back then he would definitely not be bailing me out. He'd have been sitting right next to me. That's my friend Joe.

To set this up; The skies were very overcast. It brisk and wintery on this particular day and by now it had already started snowing, so the story worked really well. I went with my first feeling, when he told me about the accident, and I brought that feeling to the manager in charge and he just let me go. Not even a question. I felt sooooo guilty the next time I went in to work because of the possible questions and the story and the lie. But guess what? No one said a word. Not even the guy that I told about the accident, so I was happy. Then again the bastards didn't even ask me how my mom was.

Assholes!. . . Just kidding.

I went right home to get changed and grab my ticket. Joe and his sister picked me up about fifteen minutes later. As we were driving to the show, I was sitting in the back seat of Maureen's little Subaru or whatever, taking in all this little excursion had to offer and I looked at my watch. "Yup, 6:00. Still supposed to be working. Thanks Joe. Can't believe you did that." "Hey no problem dude. I'd do it again."

Yup. Kinda weird. I have no doubt.

We were taking Rt. 70 West all the way to I95 N and then up to the Walt Whitman Bridge. This was my first and also the only time I would ever go this way. I remember one time coming home this way, but that was because somebody in the car with us lived in South Jersey so it made sense. This made no sense, but I'm not driving.

It continued snowing and had slowly developed into a huge storm. I remember it being much worst in Philadelphia, so we were in for a blizzard of a night. The snow continued to fall during the show and as we left and walked out to the parking lot, we found that all the cars were covered with the white stuff. This presented a problem for a bunch of tripping Deadheads trying to find their cars. Oh, what fun that was!!

After this experience, we decided it would be best to always park in the Pantry Pride (Supermarket) parking lot. This way we would always have at least a point at which to start looking for the car in the event of any misguided brain activity and /or subsequent surprises from Mother Nature we may encounter. We also figured it might be a good idea to count the spaces to Market Street and all the spaces to the side of the building, and to be aware of any other landmarks in the immediate area and any other damn thing that we could possibly think of without looking absolutely ridiculous!, to be certain that this kind of thing would never happen to us again!

After we found the car we made our way to the main road to start our long trek home. We immediately realized that the roads were all fucked up and no one seemed to know where they were going. (First time tripping in a snowstorm, so glad I wasn't driving) We did the only smart thing we thought we should do. We pulled into a hotel parking lot and decided to get a room. I wasn't really financially prepared for the room idea, but I went with it. We all walked into the lobby of this very nice hotel, looking like we had just been through the psychedelic windmill searching for answers to the world's problems (or just an ice cold beer) and we were confronted by 'Hotel Management'. This big fat guy (picture the guy that caught Arthur Bach stealing a tie in the movie 'Arthur') with 20 lbs. of keys hanging off his belt. He comes walking over to us and says,

"If ya's are lookin fer da Grateful Dead, dey aren't here" (His grammar was really questionable)

To which we replied, "Actually, we would like a room."

(Did we really want a room . .? I don't really know. *I'm* not in charge here.)

So then he says, "Look guys, we have no rooms available and we're trying to keep the lobby clear right now, so you really need to leave." We pointed toward the snowstorm out the front door, but he told us again that we really needed to leave. . . ."Sorry fellas".

Side story; The next night Joe went with his brother Tom, my friend Mike and Neebs, who was another friend of his and a very interesting thing happened. They stayed at that very same hotel we walked into the night before and Joe shared an elevator ride with none other than Jerry himself. Joe was of the right mind at the moment to ask Jerry to sign an autograph for him, the funny part was that Jerry's pen didn't work, so he looked at Joe and said,

"Hey man, I guess my pen don't write on your kind of paper. Sorry. Maybe next time" and he walked off the elevator at the next stop. So cool.

The Garden shows were sandwiched between those two Spectrum shows on the 7th and 8th and then two more Nassau Coliseum shows were scheduled for the 10th and 11th. Madison Square Garden shows were rescheduled for the 7th and 8th. We took the train up to Penn Station for both of these. The Party train, it was called. We could drink beer all the way to our destination. That was fun and different. I had second level seats for the first night and almost third level for the second. The first night stands out for me because during the first set I ran into my buddy Charlie. We shook hands, he asked me to hold out my hand, then he dumped a puddle of the best liquid acid in my hand and me, without question, I lapped it right up. "Have yourself a great time Jimbo" He said, and then kept on walking. We had been friends for while now and this scenario that I've described was not the first and would not be the last, in a long list of, "Have yourself a great time Jimbo" moments. By the middle of the second set, the boys were rockin Not Fade Away into Black Peter and I had to find my seat. Thankfully, I was hanging with my two best friends Mike and Patty, and as the stage bounced back and forth from end to end upside down and sideways Patty spoke to me in her usual soft comforting tones and relaxed me to the point where I could actually get up out of my seat again and enjoy the rest of the show. I don't think she even realised what she was doing. She just does this thing and can put anybody at ease. She knew where my head was at immediately and made it no issue at all. I hope everybody out there has a friend just like her. And Mike by the way.

Toward the end of the show I saw Don hanging out, because Mike and Patty had caught a ride up there with him and Pat, Mike's sister. I asked My friend Don if he might have some room in his vehicle (Station Wagon) for me and he says, "Are you serious Jimbo? Everytime you ask you will always have a ride dude. Fare warning though, you'll have to sit in back and it's already crowded back there. I'm sure you'll be fine" "No Problem." I said. It was also raining on the way home and the driver side windshield wiper was broken. Don had to lean over to the passenger side of the car to see, so when he approaches a toll, he has to roll the window down and then the rain was pouring in. Everything was fine though. In my state of mind it was just another thing to contend with. Helped to bring me down a bit too. Yup. I would be fine

The boys played Nassau Coliseum next, on the 10th and 11th and then played the second rescheduled Spectrum show. The second show at the Spectrum included an old song called Nobody's Fault But Mine, which we figured was to reference the shows that needed to be re-scheduled because of Garcia's illness. Another interesting tidbit I just remembered about the second night at the Spectrum was Dancin in the Streets. It was an amazing version. At some point during the song, the floor was opened up like general admission. There was *no longer* an aisle and the guards were *no longer* concerned about it. It seemed like Dancin' would go on forever and during the jam a guy came dancing over toward me and asked,

"Hey man. What song you think they'll do next?"

To which, I replied, "Right back into Dancin, man." for whatever reason, I didn't know. What the hell do I know anyway? About 20 minutes later (maybe it was 2 minutes. . . again, it seemed to be endless to me) that's exactly what happened, and this guy turned back toward me, gave me a very enthusiastic high five and then just kept on dancing. Don't know who he was, but he was wearing a tie-dyed peasant skirt. (first time I had seen that action) Just a moment in time. . . .

At this time in my life I wasn't going to concerts. I was only going to see The Grateful Dead play and I was so excited about the whole aspect of seeing the Grateful Dead play numerous times that I was making notes on the backs of all my ticket stubs. What number show it was for me, and any highlights of the shows as we rolled along. I thought it would be a fun way to remember each show and what songs they played. Really wish I had kept a diary, can you imagine?. I only made the notes for the first couple of tours, probably my first 15 shows and after that only if something really special happened. First time played. That sort of thing. It was always about having fun.

An Epiphany in the Rockies

$\mathcal{I}$n 1979 the focus of the band turned to Brent. He was the new guy, so no matter how much you might want to ignore it, it was impossible. Brent took 'the reigns' from Keith Goddchuax after he and his wife Donna Jean left the band, citing irreconcilable differences. With his masterful work on the keyboards and his falsetto voice, Brent fit in with the band really well and although he endured the moniker of 'the new guy' unfairly for years after he joined the band, he actually contributed a lot of great material to their repertoire, including covers and originals. So after seeing Keith and Donna for only four shows, and not really remembering much about their presence at Englishtown, I was now being introduced to the new guy. This was fine though because we were all new to the scene and now so was Brent. So let's get this thing going.

In the spring of 1979 my friend Joe (same guy that I went to the snowy Spectrum show with) and I had been hanging out a lot. We would go for bike rides down to the beach every nice day and hang out there until I had to go to work. We were talking about our plans after graduation. Plans that I really didn't have yet. Joe's idea was to move to California, establish residency and go to college for free. I thought that'd be a good idea for me too, since I was on the fence. I decided I would give my job notice and then tell my mom and dad my plans to move to California. The plan, if I can call it that, ended there. Quite frankly, my dad wasn't hearing any of it, (maybe that was my mom?) and for some reason, I didn't push it. I was kind of upset, but maybe the idea of leaving home scared me just a little bit too, I really don't know. When I told my dad that I had already bought my plane tickets he said, "Well, you had better think about getting *that* money back." His decision was final.

So, while moving to California was definitely off the table, I did have an alternate plan. I went back to the man in charge of my life and asked this time, if it would be cool if I just went out to Colorado to meet up with Joe and see the Grateful Dead at Red Rocks. This time the answer was yes. My only problem was getting to the airport, but that turned out to be no issue at all. Joe's sister Maureen was perfectly willing to drive me because she was so excited about me seeing her brothers. As I stepped on to the plane I was greeted by many familiar faces. My friends Pat and Don along with Bill, Fredo, Ziffel, Wayne, and his friend Mike were all on board. I didn't know any of these people were going to Red Rocks or that they would be on this flight, but there they were and it was amazing. Our plans were made without each other's knowledge. I'm guessing that because I was so young at the time and my plans revolved around my friend Joe, I never gave it a thought that other friends might've had the same idea.

The flight was great. The shows were August 12th, 13th, and 14, so I flew out on the 11th and Joe and his brother Tom met me at the airport that night. They were driving a VW Bug with a bad transmission and essentially no back seat. Even though I was real excited to be there, I was exhausted from jet lag so I crashed big time once we got back to the motel. Happens to everybody I suppose. We got up early enough to get breakfast and then headed on down to the Amphitheater. . . on a mission. None of us had tickets for these shows, so that was our mission. We drove down I-70 West to exit 259 and headed down to the Park entrance to check out the ticket situation. The Amphitheater is a natural rock formation inside Red Rocks National Park. I didn't even realize there was a Park involved when I first heard about Red Rocks. It really is a marvel.

When we got there we found that there were several Deadheads already lined up with signs in their hands indicating the need for tickets, so we were kinda bummed. We loaded ourselves back into the little Bug we had arrived in and drove up the hiway discussing our options. What we decided was to drive back up to the exit ramp where we had just gotten off because that's where everyone else would have to come from as well. It was the only way in, or at least the most direct way, so we stayed where the traffic would naturally have to flow and began our long wait.

It was very early in the day, so we held our position for quite a while before a single car made its way down the exit ramp. It drove right by. It was a long time before we saw another car; again, no tickets! Then several more all bearing the same bad news. The first car that actually had tickets pulled over and sold them to another ticket less Deadhead that was standing among our group. There was only had one extra and it was gone like that. (snap!) As a small amount of luck breezed by me, another couple pulled up just a few moments later and I got one for myself for $75.00 bucks. (That was a lot back then) I wasn't really prepared to spend that much money on tickets, but I had the cash with me and tickets were few and far between, so what choice did I have? He originally wanted $80.00, but he took $5.00 worth of pity on me. My next two tickets came a little easier, and a little cheaper at $120.00 for both. Tom and Joe did fairly well and then we were done. It took only 4-5 hours to complete our mission. By this time it made no sense to go anywhere, or do anything else except wait for showtime, so we went to the lot and copped a squat, *if* you know what I mean.

The first night they opened with Promised Land, which I was not real familiar with but at this point didn't much matter. They also included a sweet Fennario and Lazy Lightening Supplication, which became rare in later years, and my first Chinacat, which was really cool because

I'd been listening to it a lot from the *Europe '72* album. The one thing you have to worry about at an outdoor show became a problem the first night. With touches of light rain throughout, there was some talk about moving the next two shows to McNichols Arena. This is an indoor complex located across the street from Mile High Stadium where the Bronco's play. I wasn't too happy about the change of venue, but my attitude wasn't doing me any good and I was still pretty psyched about hearing Chinacat, so I sucked it up. Early the next morning it was confirmed that the shows would be moved and I was really disappointed. To make matters worse, there was no rain on the way in the second night. I really felt gypped because I flew all the way out here to see the Grateful Dead play at this beautiful outdoor place with gorgeous views of Denver from the mountains and now I had to sit inside.

That night inside McNichols Arena, while staring at the stage from my position in the crowd, I had an epiphany. Yes, I was really disappointed about the move inside, but when it came right down to it, I could be anyplace in the world and I'd still want to be right where I was. It didn't matter that the show wasn't outside. What mattered was that I was there to see the Grateful Dead. This was my moment of clarity; The moment I felt I became a Deadhead.

After this personal revelation, I wanted to go to as many different places as I could to see them play. I really loved traveling to different parts of the country and this made for a great excuse to hit the road. I said before, the best part about being involved with the Scouts when I was younger was being able to go to different places and experience new things. Following the Grateful Dead was a lot like that, except in this case we were simply following a big party across the country. As my story continues it will become more apparent how true this is, for those not familiar with the experience.

What made the first night at McNichols even better was the announcement right before the second set opener. Bobby stepped up to his mic and thanked the crew for moving the equipment so diligently and then said, "You all might like to know that it's raining like crazy outside right now."

I said to myself, "Thank you Bob! That's cool!"

The second night at McNichols Brent debuted a new song called, *Easy To Love You*. As he began to play, we all sat in great anticipation, thinking about how it was going to come off. Well, it came off like a Grateful Dead song, you know? Brent was cool.

Putting The Music on Tape
For the First Time

One of my favorite Garcia songs is Loser. I could list a dozen more very easily, but for my purposes right now, Loser is the one. Jerry pours his heart out when he plays any song, but when he plays his own tunes, it's a little more heartfelt and he makes his audience really feel it. Garcia's album *Compliments*, where this song was originally released, might just hold the best versions of each of the songs that are on it. Bird Song, Deal, The Wheel, Loser, Sugaree, and To Lay Me Down were all superbly done for a studio take on Jerry's work. I bring up Loser now because Jerry played an amazing version at Nassau Coliseum in 1979, and because this show also holds another distinction for this Deadhead. This was my first time recording a Grateful Dead show.

First off, this being Halloween Night the freaks were out in force and the freak show, of course, starts in the parking lot. Nassau Coliseum had the tightest security I'd ever seen in my limited experience, which come to think of it was minimal. Uniondale Long Island, provided cops on horseback for parking lot security and under-cover cops in tie-dyed t-shirts for drug control. Isn't that excellent! (Bastards!) Everybody was

thoroughly searched on the way in, but taping equipment was not the issue. A baggie of weed here, a sheet of LSD there. That's all the security
people needed to make them happy. Second, basically everybody in our
group of friends was at this show and we were all able to sit together. We
had floor seats, about four rows in front of the soundboard.

I had been thinking about taping shows myself, since I started trading tapes. For me, I was always most relaxed and comfortable after I got
in with my recording equipment and was all set up, ready to tape. This
being my first, it was especially nerve racking. I had my deck packed in a
framed back pack, (leftover from Boy Scouts) wrapped in an old blanket
from home. My poles were shoved in sideways and very obvious. It was so
obvious that I was carrying something large in my pack that I thought for
sure I wasn't getting in with it. My friends Mike and Jeff each took some
batteries and a patch cord, just to help out a little as I proceeded through
the frisking check point inside the front doors. With my fingers crossed
and my pack on my back I approached the guard. The guy patted me
down, then inspected my pack and asked me what was inside. He wanted
me to open it. I fiddled with the straps and played real dumb, taking my
time while telling him that it was camping equipment. He saw the line
building behind me and gave up, or just gave in, not sure which. I was
kind of surprised that he didn't push the issue, but just as happy that he
didn't, and mostly relieved just to be inside.

So taping was a bit of a headache for me in the beginning. But it was
mostly in my head. I had already been to out to Red Rocks by now, so I was
feeling really comfortable in the scene. Just being able to tell someone that
I didn't know that I had been out to Colorado this past summer was a pretty
big deal for me. Almost like I was qualifying myself. – I don't know how true
that statement really is, but I know I wasn't throwing it around like a badge of
honor, ie; a backstage pass, but I was personally proud of it that's for sure – As
far as the actual taping was concerned, my biggest problem was that I had no
mentor. I knew of people that were tapers, but I wasn't close enough to any of
them for it to make a difference. I was mostly alone in my thoughts. I really

had to wing it, but I knew what I had to do. First I went out and bought a tape deck. My first was a Sony TC 158-SD, a very nice high quality tape deck. I've seen it around, in professional settings over the years, so I know it was quality. Next, I went out and bought a single stereo microphone from Radio Shack. (I did look around a bit before I settled for Radio Shack, trust me. I just didn't have a trust fund like many other tapers) I also had to find a mic stand. I couldn't find the type of mic stand that I had seen at shows, but later on I was thinking that they may have been using lighting poles, since lighting poles will extend higher into the air than a basic mic stand. Anyway, I couldn't get that together in time for the show, so I wound up using a wooden pole about ten feet long that I cut up into ten pieces. I drilled holes in each end and put them back together with metal dowels that my dad made for me. Oh and by the way, I had no base for my stand, so I had to wedge it between the chairs and tape it together (McGyver style) with duct tape. Sometimes it worked and other times. . .It just didn't.

I used this set-up for at least eight to ten shows and it worked just fine. I'll never forget this show on Halloween though and I'll tell you why. Everybody in the audience was standing on their chairs when the show started, so I had my microphone set about five feet above the crowd. When the first set was over and we sat down, my mic stand was then about twenty feet above the crowd. I didn't bother to take it down, because I didn't consider that it might be a problem. Soon someone from the soundboard came over to me and asked that I please take it down, at least during the break because they had record executives from Arista there, and they weren't very happy about people taping. After that nothing else was said.

After taping my first 8 shows using my one stereo mic, I had to figure, "there's got to be another way." I couldn't keep taping this way because the mics that other tapers were using were so good, that I had to check them out. (I met a lot of guys out on the road who were either rich kids or drug dealers so they could easily afford nice mics) Coincidentally, by this time my aforementioned Sony 158 that I loved, had been stolen from a friend's house where I left it, so that opened the door for me to buy a new one. This was right around the time when the Sony D-5, which everybody had, was being replaced, or rather upgraded, to the D-5M. Everybody went out and bought the D-5M, even the Grateful Dead got them as Christmas presents from Sony that same year, so another no-brainer. The M was for Metal. It was a new way of recording at the time. A Metallic particle recording surface replaced the Chrome that we had been using. The deck itself only weighed 6 lbs. and was about the size of a large Gideon's Bible. (The first show I taped using my new D-5M was College Park, which I will talk about in a minute.) So, armed with a brand new deck, I set out using patchcords to record shows. This was fun and interesting and way it works is simple; The lead tape deck has microphone's plugged into it and then RCA jacks or patch cords go from the output of that deck to the input of the next and so on. Recording this way, I could choose just about any mics that I liked, or try out any mics that I wanted, as long as the taper would let me patch in. A lot of times the only stipulation would be the kind of deck a taper was using, I guess so that it wouldn't present a problem for him or anyone else down the line. Once the guy sees that I have a D-5M, everything is cool. Two problems did arise with this configuration though. First the recording volume from the lead deck can affect the rest, and second, any tape that is flipped during the show cuts off the signal to the others behind it. For the first problem we simply set the recording levels early in the show and leave them alone after. We got around the 'flipping' glitch by holding down the record button during the flip. This way the signal still goes through. Only thing is you can't rewind the tape with the record button depressed, so if ya wanna take up some slack after the flip it has to be done quickly and hopefully between songs. A flip within a jam is usually done precisely as the tape winds to the end. (Quite a science, huh?) Patching into other mics not only made set-up so much easier for me but it also allowed me to use state of the art mics without having to buy them. . . ever! Now I wish I had bought mics because there are no taping sections for bar bands and I really enjoy that now.

About a year and a half later, I got to thinking that I really needed another tape deck of equal or greater quality to make copies at home. My taping friend Tom was a huge proponent of the Nakamichi Brand, so armed with this information and a new credit card with a zero balance, I went to a local stereo store and found exactly what I was looking for.

This was an auto reverse tape deck with a new twist. Normally with an auto reverse tape deck the tape head would shift, ever so slightly, and the tape would change direction simultaneously. This system was only slightly flawed, in that sometimes wear and tear on the gears and the tape head could possibly mis-align the head, making it playable only on that deck. (Now I'm thinking that only a true audiophile would be aware of the significance of this flaw, but whatever.) The Nakamichi that I bought was called uni-directional, auto reverse tape deck. (A whole new concept in auto reverse) Let me explain. The tape sits in a chassis inside the deck, and a series of gears and pulleys push the tape out and then pull it back in again. When the reverse takes place, the tape would actually eject, spin around, and then return to the play/record mode that it was in. It's a great conversation piece, and a really nice tape deck to boot!

Now, back to the mics. The microphone choices were all really good, and varied widely even back then. My favorite from the very beginning was the Sennheiser 421, which at the time happened to be the Dead's choice as well. They used the 421's for their vocals and for their drums. My next choice, which wasn't around all the time was Sennheiser 441's, which was a little higher grade mic. After using these mics for about a dozen shows, I found Nakamichi mics (my preferred brand name) in two different models and four different configurations. Nak 300's were superior to the Sennheisers, and Nak 700's were superior to both of those. . . (I guess depending on who you ask?) Each had the capability for a shotgun extension, which was great for distance taping. There were also Scheopp mics that grabbed some attention and Neumann mics that had other people very excited. I used each of these other mics at different times during my years of taping, but I always thought that the best ones were the 700's. I wasn't even sure why, initially it was definitely the name. My buddy Tom was the first person I ever heard talk about the Nakamichi Brand and I trusted his opinion, but listening back to those recordings told the real story. You know, some people will swear by Chevrolet for their whole life without a real reason. I also liked AKG 741's and used them on tour a lot too.

The mics were normally set up on a T stand on top of the pole and each one is pointed at its respective speaker. But you know what? Sometimes people get a little crazy with mic set ups, and it becomes really funny to watch. (And sometimes it's literally hilarious, bordering on ridiculous!) I once saw a guy out in California that had two mic stands that he placed about 35 to 40 feet apart, each aimed at its own set of speakers. I didn't ask him about it, but a friend told me that he was going for 'true stereo separation'. You know, in theory, it was probably a good idea, but I'd love to know if the concept actually made a difference. Maybe it has the same effect as cupping your hands behind your ears while listening at the show. If you've never tried that you should. It really works well.

In the late 80's the shows were running a little longer than I was used to, so I had to manipulate my tape flips a little differently. I got the following idea from someone else, and it really made sense after I heard the explanation. Obviously you don't want to have to flip in the middle of a jam and interrupt a potentially huge climax. Let's just say the boys are playing a real spacey jam and it starts building into something very obvious like, here comes 'St Stephen', just for example. You don't want that jam cut, you want it seamless just like it is at the show. For this reason, I started putting the drums on side B of tape 1. That would leave way more room on side B of tape 2 for any out of the ordinary, amazing shit, that inevitably makes the taper's section simultaneously light up as everyone checks to make sure their tape is still spinning and has enough room to catch the whole jam. Sounds silly, huh? I know, but I did the same thing. You have to. If the tape you have in the deck happens to be wound a little too tight and the deck suddenly shuts off, you have to be ready to fix that shit right away! All kinds of things happen that shouldn't, but I never really had a problem. No, I actually did have a problem once or twice because of a double encore here and there and I had to go to a third tape because of it, but mostly I was fine.

Here's a nice story. I was listening to my copy of the show in the parking lot after the show and someone stopped and told me about his personal nightmare. He left his deck with someone to watch over and they cut the encore, missed the last three minutes of the show, because the guy wasn't paying attention to what was going on. He asked me if I wouldn't mind fixing it for him right there and then because he said he really had no other source. I told him of course I would. I was listening to it anyway, so why not? He offered me his extra batteries for my trouble, but I was headed home that night anyway and would have no trouble getting new batteries. We just hooked the decks together real quick and played the encore right there in the lot. We drank a beer together and shared some stories and then he was on his way, very grateful.

Trouble Ahead; Taping the Dead

Ahh yes, the taping/bootlegging (always hated that reference) of the Grateful Dead. Most times a very pleasant experience (especially once inside), but not always. Back in the day, as the story sometimes unfolds, there have been moments where an over zealous security guard takes his job a little too seriously, either out of a strong sense of responsibility (God knows why) or out of shear boredom (how can I make this mundane job a little more exciting for just a few minutes) and decides to make an example of a taper. This story involves two very specific incidents. The first one because I had one of those moments that every Deadhead experiences at least once during a show somewhere. And the other because it was a kinda rare song and I didn't hear it again for a very long time.

The first was November 5, 1979 at the Spectrum. I just realized that this was my 15th show. Not really counting purposely here but I thought it was interesting. The taping here was much less than a hassle free experience. Not only did I have to sneak my deck into the show, but in order to do so, I needed to split up the equipment amongst my friends again like on Halloween. You know, honestly I always had a bad feeling about getting my stuff into a show and it was always a bigger deal to me than it was to anybody else. For some reason, the guy at the gate on the way in always made me nervous. Once inside though, I had such a feeling of relief and euphoria. Such an amazing feeling. It made going through that 'other' feeling a little more bearable. So now that I'm inside, I see that I have really bad seats. To be honest, I already knew that I had really bad seats, but I really wanted to record again and the seat sneak was a new thing to me at the time. I mean to say that I wasn't so sure about how other poeple would feel about my taking up space where I obviouosly didn't belong, so I taped from the side of the stage. The view, by the way, is great from there. You might as well be 30 rows from the stage. I was also taping in front of just one set of speakers and the crowd around me was not accustomed to the tapers rule of no clapping or whistling or screaming. . . You get the picture?

So saying, "Please be a little quiet for me, so I can tape the show."
Gets a response of, "I paid for these seats just like you and besides, you're not allowed to tape anyway."

Real quick, in response to that response. Although it was not written in stone yet, we were actually allowed to tape. (This is the reason why once I was inside, I was King!) The Grateful Dead never ever enforced any code of discipline against taping their shows. The venue, should they choose to do so, can gripe all they want about it, but the band never cared. Most people on the outside of our scene would consider this behavior of ours 'bootlegging'. I'm not one of *them*. To me, bootlegging is not what we do, pirating is another thing altogether and what I do, *what we do* is also something completely different. I have met tapers over the years who have referred to their tapes as 'bootlegs', but that would infer that they were intended to be sold, which is not the case. To call it 'pirating' would infer that the music is being stolen for some personal gain, which was also never the case. I'm not a very big fan of either description. We were tapers and tape traders. That was all.

Anyway, I was talking about the Spectrum right? Well, the worst was not over. As I was taping and dealing with uncooperative neighbors all around me, at once someone had to be shown to their seats, in the same row that I was taping from. The security guy shone his light in my eyes and asked me to step out of the row. I went to hand my mic to my friend, but at that point the guy told me I was busted, and to bring everything with me. While I was being escorted away I was pleading with this guy to be cool and look the other way. At the same time, I was busy switching tapes in my deck. I took a blank tape out of my pocket and wound it forward a little bit and handed it over to the guy. I know it sounds like a lot of work, but this guy wasn't paying attention to anything except his fuckin walkie-talkie. Seemed very proud of himself. His only stipulation for letting me back into the show was leaving my deck with security, which I did so I could go back in. The show was always more important to me than taping, and although I wasn't real aware of it at the time, tapes were all over the place and I could always get a copy.

So here comes the second set opener, Althea. I've heard this one as an opening song a couple times and even as an encore once. I do believe that Jerry was really have fun with it in 1980, because while going through Deadbase, I saw that he played it on consecutive nights a lot. The Grateful Dead wasn't in the habit of repeating much over consecutive nights when we were touring. Hell, I've seen as many as six shows in a row with no repeats, but as much as Weir played Lost Sailor and Saint of Circumstance, just about every night on tour after tour, I have to admit that I really never noticed how often Jerry played Althea.

This thought brings me to another stand-out song at this show for me; Estimated Prophet. On the night in question, they played Eyes of the World into Estimated, which was not the norm. Usually it's played the other way around, but what made Estimated so special that night was that I had a 'chemically induced, bird's eye view' of the stage and I felt like Bobby was singing it right to me.

> 'California, preaching on the burnin' shore,
> California, knock knockin on the golden door.
> Like an angel, standing in a shaft of light,
> rising up to paradise, I know it's gonna shii–ine.
> And I'll call down thunder and speak the same.
> And my words fill the sky with flame.
> And might and glory gonna be my name.
> And men gonna light my waaay'
> (Words and music by Weir/ Barlow /Hall).

I never heard these lyrics clearer than I did that night. I was blown away. (If you're a religious person, who does it sound like Weir is singing about?)

The other song that stood out for me here was Casey Jones, but the version I remember most, that remains with me to this day was from two nights before at Nassau, November 2, 1979. This was two nights after the first show that I recorded. I blew off the taping 11-2 because my seats were in section 303. Before they played it Jerry, Bob and Phil stood in a close circle on stage, then Weir stepped out of the circle and said, "This is only a test." Weir stepped back into the circle and then the three of them turned in unison and faced the audience while playing those familiar opening notes. We were on the upper level on right side of the stage so we could see the band very clearly. The sound wasn't all that great, but this was the first time I'd ever heard Casey Jones. After hearing it again two nights later at the Spectrum, I didn't hear it again for another year. That would be at Radio City Music Hall on October 23rd 1980, and after that show I never saw them play it again. It was pretty much dropped from the

regular line-up and I just never managed to be at the right show after
that.

Speaking of encores. Well, I wasn't really speaking of encores, but
what was the worst encore ever?, or maybe just the most played. Maybe it
was U.S. Blues. We heard this song played so often on tour that we started
calling it 'Useless Blues'. (Sorry Jerry, tongue in cheek, of course). It was
the first Dead song I ever heard, but it was played as an encore so often
that it almost became unenjoyable. Though not a complete throw away
because I still enjoyed it as it was being played, as we did with every song
that they played. I love to hear the album version on the radio now because it always takes me back to the summer of 1977 when I heard it for
the first time. U.S. Blues actually closed the first set three times. Once
in 1989 and twice in '90, but in my touring experience it was always an
encore. (Thanks again DeadBase)

'Belushi Blues'...

Robert Hunter had just played at Town Hall in N.Y.C. I went to see him with my friends Mike and Patty (1980). Right before Hunter's show, the Grateful Dead scheduled shows at the Capital Theatre. These Capital shows were very special. With limited seating and perceived high demand, tickets were sold via post card lottery system. We were instructed to mail a post card to the Capital Theatre Box office within a specified time. As each postcard was selected, the person whose name appeared on the card won the right to purchase tickets. The person whose name appeared on the post card could buy the tickets only at the Capital Theatre box office and had to present I.D. This was quite the dilemma compared to the usual Ticketmaster purchase, but was necessary.

Sometimes when you do something nice for a friend, it's just a nice thing to do. Other times it comes back at you in a really great way. My friend Mike was lucky enough to win, (he sent in about 300 envelopes, between himself and his wife) so he was able to buy tickets for one show. I gave him a ride to the Capital Theatre box office because his car was giving him problems. A couple of days later Mike's wife Patty won tickets too. This time they offered the tickets to me because I gave them a ride for their first win. Some would say that this was incredibly generous. I would agree, but I would also add that they are two very good friends of mine, (That's a given) and that they are two of the best friends I've ever had in my life. Mike and I are going on forever, (growing up across the street, it's tough to put a number on it) and Patty I met in High School when I was 15. Mike is my 'bro' and his family is mine. My brother is also married to his sister-in-law. I brought my brother with me to the Grateful Dead show at the Capital Theatre on March 30th, 1980. Mike went April 1st.

These Capitol Theater shows were very special for a couple of reasons. First, the theatre is small, so there was such an intimacy factor involved that even without the lottery system it would have been difficult to get tickets. Second, during the show that my brother and I went to, Jerry and the boys played *U.S. Blues* for the encore and John Belushi, from Saturday Night Live, joined Jerry on vocals. (Belushi Blues) He did a couple of cartwheels across the stage during the jam. It was freakin hilarious. I could see the look on Jerry and Bob's faces while all this was going on, and it was priceless.

My friends and I discovered the comic genius of John Belushi, Dan Ackroyd, Bill Murray, Gilda Radner, Loraine Newman, Chevy Chase and Garret Morris as we watched Saturday Night Live in the mid to late 70's. Together they were an unforgettable ensemble of comedic characters, whose performances and talent were one of a kind and were sorely missed as each of them left the show. These were the *Not Ready for Prime-time players,* lead by comedic stand outs Belushi and Ackroyd. On April 22, 1978, as part of an opening musical sketch, John and Dan became The Blues Brothers. These characters, "Joliet" Jake and Elwood Blues, blew the audience away with their performance of *Hey Bartender,* to open the show. With Steve Martin as the host The Blues Brothers took the stage a second time that night as the musical guest and played a song called *I Don't Know* with the Saturday Night Live Band as their back up.

What started out as a sketch involving two blues musicians evolved into a best selling album, 'Briefcase Full of Blues' and a blockbuster movie, 'The Blues Brothers'. John also starred, in July of this year, as frat boy John 'Bluto' Blutarsky in the film *Animal House*. This was John's breakout role, which lead to world wide exposure and popularity. John showed his acting chops in several films after this, proving he could pull off drama, as well as make us laugh. John's sudden and amazing success took a toll on him in the form of heavy drug use and John eventually was taken from our world on March 5th 1982. John's life was chronicled by Bob Woodward in a book called 'Wired'

Anyway, back to the Capital Theatre. On April Fools day, (1980) the members of the band played a musical joke on their audience. They opened the show playing *'Promised Land'*, with a twist. Weir on keyboards, Brent and Jerry on drums, Billy played bass, Mickey played rhythm guitar and Phil played lead. After the song was over they acknowledged the joke, and played it again on the correct instruments. It would've been so cool to be there for that one, but that's why they had to have lottery. Everybody wanted to be there. On the positive side, I really learned my way around the city of Passaic (for the Capitol Theatre anyway) pretty well before the end of that run. After seeing Garcia there, and then making the two trips for tix and then the actual show, it became a very easy trip to make. Couldn't do it now without G.P.S. though. . .

On April 5th, the Grateful Dead appeared on NBC's Saturday Night Live again. This time they performed Alabama Getaway and Saint of Circumstance.

These events were all a part of our lives at this time, which is really the reason why I even mention them. Being a taper, I found out about the April Fool's stunt through the Dead 'taper grapevine' as per usual and when the boys played on SNL, we made a party of it at a friends house and watched the entire show together. It's just what we did.

Honestly, the only problem we encountered, touring as much as we did, was that we became too familiar with their format. Even though the shows were *always* different, the set lists became somewhat structured. We knew certain songs would usually follow certain other songs. (This may or may not have happened because Brent was learning the material too) For instance, every time we heard Chinacat Sunflower, we were pretty sure that I know you Rider was coming next. Estimated Prophet was usually, but not always followed by Eyes of The World. That kind of thing. He's Gone could follow it just as easily, also drums or Uncle John's Band. Then there was the Scarlet/Fire combination. Almost always in place, but Fire on The Mountain could just as easily come out of drums or space with no Scarlet. Scarlet was played by itself years ago, but not much since my touring started. When all is said and done though, when the Grateful Dead were on stage, there was always the possibility that all this could change. Nothing was standard, preset or 'set in stone' as it were and that's what made the Grateful Dead unique and always worth the trip. The set structure was something that we were all aware of, but it didn't matter that much, or affect our touring at all. I only mention it as an observation, definitely not a complaint. Take a look a Cassidy real quick as another example, (then I'll stop, I promise) which is a first set song that comes with a long, beautiful, flowing jam that could go in so many directions, but always comes back to the source. Weir and Garcia were asked by David Gans years ago about why that song never developed into something crazy like 'The Other One' for example (which, if you give it a serious listen, it definitely could) Weir's response; "We never thought of that, but it sounds like a good idea."

And it's not that big a deal at all, but when you think about the possibilities, which are limitless, you have to wonder. After seeing Bobby and the Midnites in the early 80's, I had to wonder why Big Iron didn't get some first set action with the Dead instead of (just to throw one out there) Me and My Uncle or Looks Like Rain. Oh well. We are left, but to dream.

Spring Tour 1980

*O*n the Spring of 1980, the Grateful Dead tour was in full swing once again. My first road trip, at 18 with my 1967 Mustang was to Hampton Va. on May 2. My friends Joe, Brian and Joe's brother Tom all came with me. There are a couple of ways to get there, but for our first time we decided to take the Garden State Parkway down to Cape May and take the Ferry across the Barnegat Bay. Before going to Hampton, I gave my buddy Tom a call to see if he was going. He had planned to go, and though we were not going together Tom did give me some important info on a friend of his. He told me about a K.O.A Campground in Virginia Beach where we could meet up with his friend Bob, whom I hadn't met yet. That didn't matter to me at the time. I figured that since he was Tom's friend, we would be friends eventually anyway.

He told me that when we pulled into the campground, to pull off to the left and look for Bob's van. It was black and it was brandy new, because he had just driven it off the lot from a dealership in Eatontown, N.J., and drove directly to Virginia. As I pulled into the camping area I looked to the left and all I could see was Bob's van. There was no one else there! It looked like the first hole on a golf course. A long wide stretch of green grass and a black van. It was too late to check in, so I just drove to the site and parked. I introduced myself to Bob and met two more friends right away. Frank and his brother Bob and Bob's girlfriend Alesia. Frank was a nice, easy going guy. Frank's birthday and mine were four days apart so that made for very interesting celebrations during the month of November. Alecia and I are still good friends.

My favorite thing about camping has always been the campfire. I say, get one going and keep it going for as long as we are awake. Luckily, we all agreed on that. We had beers on ice, a grill fired up for burgers, and the Grateful Dead playing right up the street the very next night. We were psyched! None of us had tickets to the show, but this was not considered a problem at the time. It was not a far drive from the KOA at all, just a hop, skip and a bridge /tunnel away. About fifteen minutes. When we got to the Coliseum we stepped into another world, as far as I was concerned. Going to see the Grateful Dead up north by us was a different kind of thing. I guess until now I hadn't really, completely taken in the parking lot scene. There was tail gating for sure, like for football games, but we were surrounded by tie-dyes and friendly, curious Deadheads. We made our way up to the box office and bought our tickets. It was general admission and not really crowded. Like a Deadhead's heaven.

My friend Jimmy, whom I had met through Rick, was in Virginia for the show as well, but not with us. My friend Dale from high school had a tape connection by the name of Claudio, who was down there with Jimmy. The two of them were hanging, outside the coliseum the day before the show and they were approached by one of the crew members and asked if they would like to help out with the setup of the show. They jumped right on that invitation and were paid $7.50 an hour to work and were allowed to hangout backstage with the band. They were also invited to join them for the next show in Baltimore.

The Hampton show started out with *New Minglewood Blues*, from the recent album Shakedown Street. Minglewood Blues was recorded many years ago by the Grateful Dead for their first studio album. It was played very fast, even rushed through, but the whole album sounded like that. It went through some changes over the years and was re-arranged for the 1978 Shakedown release as New Minglewood. Not to be outdone or overdone or whatever, it was re-arranged once again after the album release for reasons that only Weir could answer. When the newer version of Minglewood was first played out at Red Rocks, the guy that was taping called it *Brand New, All new, New new, Minglewood Blues*. Tell me that's not hilarious.

So, now I am becoming more familiar with the Grateful Dead's material and that makes the concert experience so much more fun. Listening to Jerry tune up between songs mostly gives away what the next song is going to be and this became a fun game to play among Deadheads. (Candyman, no Fennario, no dammit, It Musta Been the Roses, Shit! No, Wait!. . . But it was a little easier than that).

Anyway, the first night in Hampton was a Friday, so after the show we went out for a bit, but everything was closed. We headed back to the campground and found another group of campers that Tom had begun a conversation with that afternoon. These guys had a case of Jack Daniels with them. Not the quart bottles, the little guys, forty-eight of them. One of them worked at a liquor store and had slipped it out back door. I think his father owned the place. Anyway, Tom was in heaven. I couldn't really give a shit about a case of 'Jack' because I'm a beer drinker. I'll do a shot for a good time, but it sure wouldn't be that stuff.

The next day we went to the beach. I remember both Brian and Joe making comments about me sitting in the sun with no shirt on all afternoon, and being so white, but I just laughed it off. Well, as it turned out my white Irish skin didn't appreciate being unprotected all day in the scorching hot sun, and paid me back in pain and suffering for the rest of the night. I had chills that started at about 7 o'clock that night, and then I knew I was done. Tom was also a little 'under the weather' so to speak, but Brian and Joe wanted to go out. I was steadfast and couldn't be bothered. I felt a little weird about it because I was on vacation, but when I get burned like that. . . I just need to lay down. They wanted to borrow my car, but I really wasn't too comfortable with that either. I went to bed and let them fend for themselves, or so I thought. I found out that they had found my hide-a-key, pushed my car down a dirt path toward the entrance to the KOA and then started the car. The two of them went into town and had a blast without us. I didn't find out until years later that they had "stolen" my car for a joy ride in Virginia. Anyway we went to the next show, the following night, and I was still very uncomfortable. Bad sunburn.

Next stop on tour for us, was the gloomy city of Baltimore. The streets of Baltimore were dark and vacant except for the crowd of Deadheads lined up outside the Civic Center. That night there was a slight chill in the air, even for May. We had stayed for the weekend in Hampton because it was beautiful, but the further north we traveled the chillier it became. We had no tickets for any of these shows and as I said earlier, at the time, it just didn't matter. Tickets were so available it was ridiculous. It got even more peculiar for me over the years and I'll tell you what I mean. It seemed like whenever I had tickets, either one for myself or extras, there would be extra tickets everywhere, but if I *needed* one, there were none to be found anywhere. Ridiculous when you think about it, right?

When we got to the door and walked through the entrance, I found a big burly guy that looked like he should be bouncing at Scores or Club 54, and he said to me, "What's in the pack buddy?"

"Just camping stuff, man. Just drove up from Hampton. Got no where to keep it right now." "Let's see", he said. (He probably should have told me to put it my car)

He searched me pretty well, actually all he did was repeatedly pat the sides of the back pack for several seconds, felt something very hard, (my tape deck) but didn't identify anything. My deck was the size of a small VCR, and it was wrapped in a large quilted blanket. He gave up searching rather quickly, because any moron could've found it. I guess he wasn't interested in holding up the line. Then he found all those poles that made up my mic stand.

"Tent poles." I said.

So he gave me a look. The kind that said 'Jesus Christ' with his eyes rolling back into his head and then quietly told me to go ahead in.

Brian looked at me and said, "Holy shit!"

Frankly, I couldn't believe it either.

Anyway, we were fuckin late! I didn't have time to set up shit! There was a huge walk way between the lower level seats and the upper deck, so I just pulled out my deck, pushed record and held my mic in my hand. That would have to do until we actually found our seats. We had pretty shitty seats for this show anyway, so I snuck off to the side on the second level and just parked my ass right there. The tapes were half-assed, and sounded pretty hollow and distant, but from where we were, ahh-ha. . . they sounded exactly the way we were hearing it.

The highlights of the show included a cover of Marty Robbins' El Paso and renditions of Scarlet Begonias and Fire on The Mountain. It was all so new to me then, so it was really great to see them play familiar songs. The Civic Center in Baltimore was in the middle of the city. I said before we were very late getting there, so I didn't get to take it in completely, but I do remember that we came around a corner and suddenly we were in line to get in without really trying to find a line. It was situated like an office building would be in New York City, but once inside it was immediately different. There was an escalator right next to the spot where my bag was checked, and the ride up was a short one and then we were right inside. At a show like the Garden in New York, the walk up to the concert hall was much longer than that. There are three escalators to the top level, and there just happens to be a view of the city from one side.

After these shows we went home, checked in with work and family while The Dead went on to Penn State on Tuesday, Cornell University on Wednesday and then on to Glens Falls on Thursday. The next show we went to was in Hartford, Connecticut on May 10. I taped this show with my Sony 158-SD and my single stereo mic for the first two songs, then switched to a three mic set-up featuring two Nak CM-300's with shotguns and a middle 300-CM mix. Seemed to me like a pretty sweet rig, (no shit!) so I figured why not go for it.

Saturday night in Hartford was a rockin show, no surprise there. One of the sweetest things was that there were a lot more hometown folks at this show than at the others. Mike and his girlfriend Patty were there and Don (my favorite hippie) was there with Mike's sister Pat. It was much like being at a neighborhood party with the Dead as our house band. They opened with a nice Chinacat followed by the ever present I know you Rider. This coupling had become the norm, and would remain for the rest of the years the Dead played. Garcia's partner in musical magic, Robert Hunter wrote Chinacat, as he sat conversing with a Sunflower on a bright sunny afternoon. I Know You Rider is a standard from many year's back. I was told that those lyrics were found lying on the street somewhere with no author on it. Sometimes you choose to believe what ya hear and other times. . . you just shrug. They followed Rider with Feel like a Stranger, then Jerry quieted the place with an incredible Comes a Time. (a first for me) This was followed by a continuous jam that included Estimated Prophet > He's Gone into Uncle John's Band, which finished off the first part of the second set, pre drums.

Under normal circumstances, I would be dancing around with no one in particular, seriously, and that wouldn't matter because that's just the way it is at a Dead show. You can dance with the person closest to you or simply dance with yourself. At this show however, I was able to enjoy the company of those people in my life who were actually responsible for introducing me to this amazing music.

The jam between He's Gone and Uncle John's Band was so bright and exciting I could not believe what I was hearing. Uncle John's Band had become a huge favorite for me. It's not a song that got a lot of stage time from my experience, so whenever they played it, it always put a smile on my face. I know I was not alone in this feeling either. It has a very uplifting melody and really cool lyrics;

'Come hear Uncle John's Band, playing to the tide, come on along or go alone he's come to take his children home'. (Hunter/Garcia)

It seemed to me that *Uncle John's Band* was written about the Grateful Dead playing for its audience. That's what I hear. I remember seeing them play it on Halloween night at Radio City in 1980 as an encore and it was so much fun. It's great because it's not a song that is typically rushed through like Johnny B. Goode, for example. If the band is physically shot by the encore then they could rush through any song just to get off stage. (Day Job and Alabama Getaway come to mind) A folksy song like Uncle John's just doesn't get the rush treatment, at least not in my experience. There's a nice middle break where they can cut loose and really jam it out, and to me it sounds like a lot of fun to play. Another highlight of this show was the double encore which, I'm so sad to say, was a rarity for my favorite rock n' roll band. This was a Saturday night and they had just released a single for their new album, so they played Alabama Getaway into One More Saturday Night. It was a very satisfying show.

The Historic;
Radio City Music Hall

R adio City Music Hall in New York City is an amazing place to see a Concert. I know this now from my many experiences there over the years. Looking back to the time when the Grateful Dead played there, I feel very lucky to have seen them play in that magnificient theatre, especially at my young age. I was still very new to the scene at this time and even though the band had been together for 15 years they were all still relatively young. Jerry had just turned 38 over the past summer and he was healthy, just as solid as the guitar he was playing. I was about to turn 20 and I had never been to a theatre as beautiful. I was especially excited to be a part of this experience at Radio City because I had just been out to Red Rocks only a year ago.

After the Spring tour in 1980, the boys were done with the East Coast for a bit as they headed out to the Midwest and then the West Coast for the remainder of the Spring and Summer. The announcement was made soon after about this very special run of shows; something a little different. The thought was to play a single venue for multiple nights, rather than traveling from city to city as per the norm, and their first choice for hometown intimacy was the Warfield Theatre in San Francisco. For them this meant familiarity, convenience and less travel time. They were also able to pretty much nail the sound for the entire run of shows, which was a plus for us. Because the setting was so intimate they thought it would be a great idea to try an acoustic set opener. This was something they hadn't tried in a very long time. Although this format wasn't specifically chosen to commemorate anything, they eventually gave in and called it '15 Years So Far'.

The complete announcement included a fourteen night engagement at The Warfield Theatre. This would consist of three sets each night, and feature an acoustic set opener, followed by two electric sets. The music would vary a little bit from night to night, but not as much as it normally would. Not only did they still have to contend with a new keyboard player in Brent Mydland, who took over for Keith Kodchaux, but they snagged a nice chunk of their workable repertoire for the acoustic set, slightly limiting the electric sets. That being said, the acoustic sets also included a variety of songs that hadn't been played in years, so it was most definitely worth it. These special shows that were scheduled on the West Coast were also scheduled here on the East Coast. They played two shows at the Saenger Performing Arts Center in New Orleans and then eight shows at Radio City Music Hall in NYC, in October. Which is where we are heading.

Every show performed over the course of these twenty-four special nights, was highlighted by an acoustic set closer of *Ripple*. Ripple is one of those songs that you've probably heard on the radio at one time or another and may not ever have connected it to the Grateful Dead. It's sweet lyrics are beautifully written and when you listen closely, it'll put a smile on your face every time. A positive uplifting message of hope and inspiration;

"If my words did glow, with the gold of sunshine, and my tunes were played on a harp unstrung, would you hear my voice, come through the music. Would you hold it near, as it were your own." Hunter/Garcia

When these dates were announced, a friend of mine and I decided that we would go to the box office in New York City to wait on line for the box office to open. We left on Friday afternoon, parked the car and stood on line overnight to get tickets. I know, it sounds a little crazy to stand in line all night for just two pairs of tickets, but I really did it just so I could say that I did it. You know? This wouldn't be the last time I would wait in line all night to buy tickets though. Through the early 80's we would usually go to a Music Shop in Red Bank, N.J., where the Ticketmaster location was and wait behind the store overnight with wristbands, to buy our tickets. It was a long night of waiting. Sometimes we would go out for a bite when the crowd wasn't too ridiculous. The problem here was that there was a scalper conspiracy going on at this location. We heard that the owner was printing out tickets by the hand full when they became available and then selling the best seats to his scalper buddies for up front cash. The other scenario was that the scalpers had their people in line buying the max amount of tickets and being paid to simply hand them over to the other guy. What really pissed us off was that we believed the owner knew what was going on; even knew that the people he was selling to were scalpers. This made it nearly impossible for anybody else to get good seats, even though we waited all night for the chance to buy them. The guy had a really sucky attitude toward us too. We waited very peacefully, and patiently. Not being loud at all. There were never any cops called or anything like that for any reason, but he would still find some reason to bitch. It was probably because he felt he could just sell all his tickets to the scalpers and make his money, but with us there, he'd have to justify not selling them to us, maybe. This is all just theory by the way. I have no proof of any of it. But just ask anyone from my area about the ticket situation and they'll tell ya the same story.

All of this shit stopped in 1983. That was the year that the Dead established the Grateful Dead Ticket office. Through this system we were able to buy tickets directly from their office by filling out a post card and following some very specific mailing instructions. These included sending the post card within a certain time period. Not before a certain date, so that everyone had an equal chance to get tickets, and then after a certain date the entry would no longer be valid. I always made sure I got my post cards post marked right in front of me at the post office. It really was a great system. I can't remember a time that I was refused.

Early that Fall, my phone starts to ring (and often). My friend Rick called me almost every day, to ask if I knew anyone who needed tickets for Radio City. Every time he called I said, "I don't know, but I'll take them and I'll see." The tickets just kept falling in my lap. Very uncommon for me to be in that position. Of course I wound up keeping all of them. I wasn't thinking I was keeping them at the time, but that's how it worked out. I went to five out of the eight nights and went to work the next morning three out of the five, then I drove straight back up to the city again. Yes, I know, very tiring and what the fuck was I thinking? But it was worth every second.

As a taper, I now find myself in a quandary. I have already been to 26 shows, but I only recorded 5 of them. I love walking out with a copy of the show in my hand, but I was taping with one mic and the huge wooden pieced together pole. It wasn't a great situation to begin with and my Sony was to big to sneak into a place as tight and secure as Radio City, so I opted out of taping this time. I knew that others would be taking bigger risks with greater plans in mind, (and probably a greater end result) so I was content to just go to Radio City and enjoy the atmosphere at this incredible theatre.

When I was just 19, I went to see the Grateful Dead at Radio City Music Hall. It was October 22nd, 23rd, 26th, 27th and 29th, which was Wednesday, Thursday, Sunday, Monday and again on Wednesday. Then there was the Halloween show. Closing night. This show was simulcast to several theaters and or skating rinks that night due to overwhelming demand. This was not the first time a live simulcast was done for a rock n' roll show, (I looked it up) but it was the first time for me. I went to a rink in West Orange, New Jersey with a bunch of friends who were also without tickets. This Halloween show was a huge event at Radio City. It was hosted by Tom Davis and Al Frankin of NBC's Saturday Night Live. They did interviews with the band and a comedy sketch with Brent. They begged Brent to introduce them to the Grateful Dead audience, which he did, albeit unenthusiastically, but he introduced them as Frank and Dave, which was pretty funny. They also interviewed Brent about what might be the reason why the band no longer plays the very popular song St. Stephen. Brent explained that he doesn't know how to play it and he demonstrated by playing a couple of really bad notes on his keyboard. Later, Tom Davis pretended (maybe, maybe not) to have been dosed with acid by someone and said he was tripping really badly, climbing up the walls inside Radio City Music Hall. Tom's relationship continued with the band and eventually took on the task of hosting a New Years show that was Telecast several years later.

The third show that I saw at Radio City was a Sunday night. I went with my friend Joe and had a very interesting ride into the city that night. As we passed the toll booths before the Holland Tunnel, Joe noticed and pointed out to me, a driver on his side of the car that happened to be brushing his teeth while driving. Joe and I had eaten something mushy and purple about a half an hour prior to this, so as if it wasn't already funny enough to see a guy brushing his teeth in tunnel traffic, it was definitely magnified several thousand times at this point. Joe lost himself in the moment though and wound up vomiting in his lap, which made the moment (and the story) that much funnier for me. I proceeded to drive (or rather roll) into the back end of the car in front of me. Great! Now, being in the state I was in, excitable, confused, ecstatic, hilarious, more confusion, and now a bit worried, I jumped out of the car, because the guy in front of me had jumped out his car, to examine the damage. As I did that, my car rolled forward and hit the guy's car again as we were checking for damage! Apparently, I had neglected to put the car in park for my little nervous and tripendicular rendevous with the driver whose car I hit, (ha ha) twice. (Maybe not so funny) Anyway, all was well and we both got back into our cars and sort of drove away. By sort of, I mean we hadn't made it into the Tunnel yet, but we were about to.

For the first set we wound up in the aisle on the far right side of the stage about 35 rows back with a great view of the band. As they were tuning up for the first number, I stood there taking in all my surroundings. This particular night is still pretty vivid in my mind. I could see for twenty feet in all directions. (except to my right cause there was a wall!) Dozens of smiling faces with looks of wonderment, curiosity and anticipation filled the area. We all shared a certain sense of pride to be seeing the Grateful Dead in this historic venue. I've always maintained that it never really mattered where the band played as long as I was in the same room with them, but this place was really different, on a huge scale. As Jerry played the opening chords for Iko, I recognized it right away and was completely blown away. They also played Dark Hollow and On the Road Again, which were also two of my favorite tunes.

During the set break, Joe and I were moved from our position on the wall, so we had to take our seats in the first balcony. We were about eight rows back, and the second set was about to begin. By the way, Joe and I were peeking by now. After a short warm-up jam to start the second set they played Samson and Delilah and then Althea. Next, they started playing Estimated Prophet. Then, as if someone pulled a plug, it crashed to a stop. Then something very strange happened. The band seemed to be trying to figure out what they were going to do next and the crowd spontaneously erupted in a simultaneous request for *Saint Stephen*. For me, it was like a wave came up out of the crowd and broke right on the stage. The whole audience seemed to have the same thought at exactly the same time. Jerry stood there on stage scratching his head as if to say, 'Well, I guess that's what *they* want to hear'. . . . But then Weir stepped up and restarted Estimated and the moment was gone forever. But what a moment it was! I've always wondered if anyone else experienced that moment, the way I did.

The acoustic sets were the highlight of the run of course, and amongst those highlights were some gems. A typical set would include *Deep Elum Blues, The Race is On, I've Been all Around This World, El Paso, To Lay Me Down, Monkey and The Engineer, Bird Song, Heaven Help The Fool (instrumental only), On The Road Again, Rosalie McFall, Dire Wolf,* and *Ripple.* Other song choices in the mix were *Cassidy, It Must've Been the Roses, China Doll, Jack-a-Roe, Dark Hollow, Lil' Sadie,* and *Oh Babe it Aint no Lie.* So, while the acoustic sets did take some songs out of the rotation from the electric sets, it didn't really make much of a difference because the song selection was excellent and there were still three full sets.

These Radio City shows were considered by all to be historic. It was so great to see them in a such casual setting, and many Deadheads (myself included at the time) might never have seen the inside of this amazing theatre, if not for these shows. The acoustic sets had a comfortable feel to them. I felt like they were playing in my living room. For a new Deadhead like me, it was as if a few good friends had gotten together to jam and have fun. (More so now I realized at the time) There was even some casual conversation between songs that was not as noticeable during electric sets.

At the time there was a promotional poster featuring two skeletons posing by Radio City, standing on either side of the building and there was a big stink about copyright infringement. They said it portrayed a bad image of Radio City Music Hall. They didn't think it would serve them very well, publicity-wise. To this end the poster, which was being sold by GD Merchandizing was pulled from circulation. Alas, I never got me one. . .

The thought of driving to Radio City was a little scary at first. I had never driven to the city before, except to get blank tapes from Crazy Eddies on Canal Street, and that was simply in and out, no bullshit. For this little adventure, I wasn't real confident about parking or about my exit after the show. (depending on my relative state of mind) As it happened, getting in wasn't a problem at all. Just straight through the Lincoln tunnel, up 6th avenue take a right at W 51ˢᵗ street where the parking garages are on every surrounding block. On the way out you just hop on 7ᵗʰ, which is a direct route back to the tunnel and since most everybody is heading that way anyway, it was that much easier. Everyone in the city drives like a maniac though, so it's a necessary evil to follow suit. It's actually a lot easier if you don't let the traffic get to you. If you don't like driving on crowded streets or if you're just afraid to, then you're better off with mass transit.

On December 8ᵗʰ 1980, only 38 days after the Dead's last show on this run, John Lennon was shot outside his Dakota Apartment building. He was killed by a deranged fan who believed that it was his job to kill Lennon. John's death was announced by Howard Cosell during a nationally televised broadcast of ABC's Monday Night Football:

"An unspeakable tragedy, confirmed to us by ABC News in New York City. John Lennon, outside of his apartment building on the West Side of New York City. The most famous perhaps, of all of the Beatles, shot twice in the back, rushed to Roosevelt Hospital, dead on arrival. Hard to return to the game after that news flash, which in duty bound, we have to."

I knew I was a Beatles fan, but I couldn't immediately put a face to the name or remember which songs he sang. I was just 19 when John was killed and my musical obsession at that time was the Grateful Dead. However, over the next couple of years I took some time to appreciate John and his musical contributions through the Beatles and his solo career. And as I said, I was a huge fan of rock music since I was very young. You really can't love rock n' roll and not be touched by John Lennon's music. Lennon's political rally's toward world peace in the 70's lead the Nixon Administration to target him for deportation. They believed that John's protests, coupled with his friendship with George McGovern could cost Nixon his re-election. He was therefore ordered deported in March of 1973. That order was overturned in 1975 and by 1976 John received his Green Card. After Nixon's resignation, Ford showed very little interest in continuing the battle.

John Lennon's senseless murder was a slap in the face of humanity. The man who dedicated his life to making beautiful music and chasing a dream of world peace was gunned down just as he was getting back to the business of making music, while enjoying his casual lifestyle and relative anonymity on the streets of New York City.

East Coast 1981

This tour started out in Chicago in February and then hit the Stanley Theatre in Pittsburgh, but if there was one show to see on this tour, the next one on our itinerary might just have been it. The show was at the Cole Field House at the University of Maryland Campus in College Park, Maryland on March 7,1981. We had seats in the 17th row, 'dead center' (no pun intended) and it was the start of something really special for us. The first set was very long and included an amazing Bird Song, which among the versions of Bird Song that I have heard over the years stands out easily as a favorite. It lasted almost twenty minutes. (17:10 thanks to Archive.org for that) I wanna say it was the first one I saw played, but I think it's more like the first one I was really able to fully enjoy because of our close proximity to the band. The second set opened with an electrifying, upbeat Iko, or as I prefer, Aiko. I like the spelling much better. I think the (A) gives it character. So you've got your first set Bird Song and your second set Aiko among the highlights so far for me, but what I mean to say is; what I'm trying to tell you here is; you watch the Grateful Dead perform from 17th row center, walk out with a crispy copy of the show, and see if you can pick out only one or two songs that were the best or most exciting parts of the show. I'm gonna call off Jack-a- Roe too. . .and Ok, just to get it off my chest; Dire Wolf, Deal,

Truckin, and of course, the second Grateful Dead song that I ever heard; One More Saturday Night. Come on, from seventeenth row center! Just incredible.

By the way, Bird Song was written by Robert Hunter soon after Janis Joplin passed away. You'll listen to this song differently next time won't you.

> *"All I know is something, like a bird*
> *within her sang.*
> *All I know she sang a little while,*
> *and then flew off"*
> Lyrics by Hunter,
> Music by the Master.

I have to go back to Aiko real quick. They played a re-arranged version of the song at College Park. Though they played it the same way they did at Radio City, it was now electrified and more amplificated. (yea, I know, not really a word, but it's funny) Aiko comes out of New Orleans; a funky street chant, and the chorus goes something like this; *Jocka-moe, feeno, ahna day, Jocka-moe feena-nay*, which loosely translated means "You can kiss my ass!" The boys had played it a couple of times before, but at an understated slower tempo. This was the first time I heard it played this way, with a really upbeat tempo and Aiko became a standard part of the repertoire for the rest of the years that the Dead played. In the 80's the boys were frequently joined on stage by the Neville Brothers during various benefit shows and when that happened they would jam through The Women are Smarter, Not Fadeaway, Daylight Come or Aiko on a continuous basis for as long as everybody wanted it to go on. It always seemed like everybody on stage was having such a blast.

After revisiting my tapes and digging through these particular shows, I see that although I didn't record any Radio City shows, I did record a lot of shows after Radio City. I taped College Park from 17th row, superb quality with a single stereo mic. After College Park we headed home to regroup. The next two shows were at the Garden in N.Y.C., March 9th and 10th by way of the "party train". (New Jersey Transit) I recorded from 11th row using Nakamichi TC-M 700 mics, on the first night and then from somewhere behind the board the second night using Sony mics.

The band filled the air with amazing, tastefully selected crowd favorites and added one on the 9th that doesn't get a lot of attention; Beat it on Down the Line. They start this song with Mickey and Billy pounding the shit out of their drum kits for any number of beats from five to twenty-five and then start the song. On September 11, 1985, they pounded out 42 beats before the song for Mickey Hart's birthday. . . That's pretty cool. . .These shows from College Park forward were all taped using my new Sony D-5M and a variety of different mics.

The Garden shows were always fun and interesting. First because here we are in the city of New York and let's be honest, this is a place that is generally known for its strangeness, so not only are we not looked down upon so much, we actually add color to the landscape. We are the city's rainbow for the afternoon. There were literally crowds of people dressed in tie-dye on every corner surrounding the building and we are not bothered at all. We fill the taverns on every block in the vicinity and throw money at bartenders and waitresses and mostly clean up after ourselves. Once we're inside, it's a different kind of heaven. The security guards love us. I've had conversations with them and they've always said that we were the coolest, calmest, and most fun and well behaved crowd that they've ever had to deal with. After a few shows there, my friend Robin mentioned she'd found a great little place right across the street from the Garden called The Good Old Days Bar and Grill. The layout now reminds me of TGIFridays with different levels for seating, decorative walls and a very friendly atmosphere. I would go up early in the afternoon when I could get the whole day off, and hang out there for a few hours, have some dinner with some friends and then go across the street to the show. It was a great place to hang out before seeing our favorite band, but has since closed its doors to make way for a corporate building. Isn't that just wonderful?

We made it to one more show in Hartford, Conn. a week later on Saturday. It was a one night stand and as usual, it was a blast. In Hartford they played One More Saturday Night for the encore. I think Saturday Night might have been my favorite encore ever. It was the first song that I knew all the words to, so maybe that makes the difference. It also seems just as appropriate (to me) to be used as an opening song, or the end of a show and I've heard it played in both positions. I'll mention it again later, when it turns up as a set opener. Pay attention. Watch for it.

A funny thing happened on the way up to the Civic Center in Hartford. This time, I wound up on 278 N, and the flow of traffic gently forced me off an exit and led me right past Yankee Stadium. As I turned at the next corner, I looked up and saw the marque for the Stadium. I turned around to look at my passengers, shrugged and made a quick U-turn to get myself right back on track. We still made it to the show on time and got tickets in the parking lot for cost. (still not a rarity)

The city of Hartford was jam-packed with colorful, smiling Deadheads, each one on a slightly different mission. Some looking for tickets; some looking for a quick bite to eat; others selling their wares, trying to make a buck or two for the next show or their next ticket, or just wandering aimlessly, searching out new friends to hang with, or a joint to share. A lot of entrepreneurial Deadheads were selling home-made jewelry, handmade tie-dyed t-shirts and the like, and some would make food for the hungry passerby. There was always some kind of tail-gating going on at shows and that was a great way to socialize and meet new people.

As the Grateful Dead invaded any particular city we would become great material for the local press. While the local business' would enjoy an economic boost, because of the traveling circus aspect of a Dead tour, the press had their own personal field day, as it were. The reviews of the shows were usually mundane, written by someone who either didn't know about the Dead or really couldn't care less about them. (same guy) Once in a while it became human interest, but it seemed that a lot of the writers only wanted to point out that the Grateful Dead were "aging hippies" and would include pictures of Deadheads who basically looked homeless, yet very happy. And sometimes, you get shown the light in the strangest of places if you look at it right, you know what I mean? Of course, one good drug related story would surely sell more papers than a simple review of the show, or an interview with an older traveling hipster. (Holy Hipster!) In later years, when things began to get out of control they were given more opportunities to write about drug busts and the infrequent overdose.

This subject brings me to yet another quick Jerry story. He was interviewed a lot over the years about one thing or another, and one particular time he was asked about the drug use among Deadheads. Whether or not he accepted any responsibility for it. I honestly forget where I read this, but I know I read it somewhere. Jerry impishly skirted the drug question 'as a whole', (accepting responsibility?) but offered some insight instead. In a nutshell (and not verbatim) he said, 'I'm reasonably certain that not all Deadheads take drugs, and just as sure that a lot do. That being said, Deadheads have kinda figured how to take their drugs, as it were, if ya know what I mean.' (wink) That is to say that Garcia was very aware of his influence over Deadheads as a whole, but was very disinterested in influencing anybody to do anything. As far as drug use at shows was concerned, those people that overdosed were mostly looking for the ultimate good time and thought that taking any drug that would get them there, from any source known or unknown, would be the way to achieve that.

Thankfully, we knew better.

Southbound 'Dead Ahead'

For the rest of March this year, the boys hit some venues in London and Germany and then came back to the East Coast. The Grateful Dead were on tour again, (or still) so we were heading back to our famed and friendly Hampton Roads Coliseum in Virginia and what a weekend it was. It was May 1,1981. We got twelve good friends together and planned a trip that started at Shooter's house in Ocean, N.J. We partied until about 9:30 pm and then slept until about 3 am when everybody got up and piled into four cars and convoyed, (that's right, I said convoyed) down to Virginia as one. I had my brother Ray, and my friends Joe and Brian in my little Mustang; 1967, Lime Green, Vinyl Roof, automatic trans, leather bucket seats and a self installed cassette player. We were heading out route 33 west to 66 west to get on the Garden State Parkway from there. When we got close to the entrance, which came up too quickly for me, I went to make the right turn, but couldn't slow down enough for my own comfort, then for some reason, instead of driving past the on ramp and turning around to try again, I went for it. The car's tires started to screech and I was about to side-swipe the curb. I really didn't think that would be a very good idea in the split second I had to think about it, so I straightened wheels toward the curb to hit it more head-on. The car jumped the curb and we took flight! We landed on an unfinished portion of the road and came to a stop. I looked at my brother who was still holding his beer in his hand, then turned around to see Brian and Joe just staring at each other; looking shocked, and absolutely thankful that we weren't all dead.

Joe broke the deafening silence as he spoke, "Holy shit !, Jimbo. Nice landing dude. Does this thing still drive?" (I'm just thinking. . .Holy Fuck!) I started the car and under my breath I said, "Oh, Thank God." Then out loud, "Sorry guys. Everybody Ok?" Then I slowly backed away from the curb, pulled around the small area of construction and back out onto the road. No cops in the vicinity, thank God,(again) and we continued our journey. The Hampton show was great and the camping was amazing, but you just read the best part of that little excursion. Well, not the best part, but the most exciting.

I have to say that the tapes from 1981 have really stood the test of time. As I listen to this show now, it still sounds really good. I recorded using my D-5 and used Sony mics again. I'm not aware of the model type because I didn't write it down. Apparently though, Weir had been playing Lost Sailor and Saint of Circumstance enough at this point that I referred to both as 'Lost Bobby' and 'Saint Bobby' respectfully. He played both songs at so many shows in a row that it was big news amongst Deadheads one night on tour in 1981 when he didn't play either one. We had fun with random stats whenever possible.

Anyway, Hampton was always a fun place to go see a show and it being general admission made it that much better. We all stayed overnight in Virginia and then headed straight to Philadelphia for the Spectrum show on the 4th. I didn't tape the Spectrum shows because I had sucky seats and sneaking down to the floor was not a consideration for me at the time. My deck was there the second night though. The set list was great and the quality of the music was absolutely phenomenal. I know, I know, I know I say that a lot, but this time. . . I really mean it!. . .

The first set started with Don't Ease Me In, typically a set closer, but it was a fine choice to open. The second set opened with my new favorite combo, Chinacat Sunflower > I Know You Rider > Samson and Delilah. This Samson was, dare I say better than the one from Englishtown. Seriously, listening back to the tapes, Samson from the Spectrum rocked and was the best version I had heard up to that point and still stands up to most others that I've heard live. Maybe Fox Theatre Atlanta Ga., 5-19-77 stacks up as well, *"Ok, I want everybody out there to take part in an exercise, a simple exercise, I want everybody to stand up, turn around and put your hands in the air. Don't try anything funny cause I've got you covered. . . Thank you. Thank you very much."* Bob is such a comedian, isn't he?

The next song at the Spectrum show was To lay Me Down. And you know how sometimes you just can't compare. . .

Sometimes there are just no words to describe. . .

Let me just say that the attention that this song received, not only from Jerry, but from the entire house that night was indescribable. Sometimes there are just no words, but I'll try. Jerry had the entire crowd in his control; Completely mesmerized. That is to say that he had everybody's complete attention. It was breathtaking and heartfelt. Enough said?

I don't know. . .

This Spectrum show comes with a great back-story. I loaned my D-5 to my new friend Fredo, (pronounced Fray-doe) whom I'd met in 1977 at Pat and Don's house in Spring Lake Heights. He had the unique experience of traveling within the Dead's circle for a little while. He had the best connection for speed, acid and pot that anyone knew. (See The Oldest Deadhead I know) I first met Fredo shortly after the Englishtown show in 1977. Don kept telling me over and over again that Fredo was on his way, and that he had his copy of the Englishtown show with him and we were gonna listen to it. It was all very exciting. This was my first show and although it was broadcast on the radio, I hadn't heard a tape of it yet. While we were waiting for him to show up, Don told me that his real name was Mike, but I didn't know him by that name. I only knew him as Fredo. I was never actually introduced to him as Fredo, so I would refer to him that way, but when I spoke to him I would call him Mike. I figured that nickname was reserved for those friends of his that had known him for a much longer time than I had. I'm pretty sure now that I was really over thinking the whole thing.

On this particular occasion (the Spectrum show) Fredo called me and asked if he could borrow my deck to record the show. I didn't really know him that well yet, (quite surprised by the phone call actually) but his connections to my current friends were very deep and came with a lot of respect, so the answer was gonna be yes. It would be as if Jerry asked me himself, sort of. (I also probably figured that this favor could also become an interesting friendship and great tape source) Fredo intended to patch my tape deck into a new [bass box] system that was designed specifically for the Sony D-5M by veteran taper Barry Glassberg. The tape from this show was absolutely superb for an audience tape. I mean you could tell it was an audience tape, but there is an ambience about it that is tough to describe. The one bummer about it was that he was five songs late—those songs were fixed for my copy—but the rest of the show had amazing sound. The China/Rider was crisp and clean and was executed with the precision of a Swiss Watch. . . You could hear it like there was no one in the hall.

When I went to pick up my tape deck from Fredo, a couple of days after the show, I asked him if he had anything interesting from Jerry Band that I might not have heard, like an Eleanor Rigby or something like that. (I had heard somewhere that Jerry had played it) He told me that he had a tape that he'd just made for an old friend of his that I could have because the guy never picked it up. As he was searching for it, he said that he had drawn some pretty 'trippy' artwork on it and he wasn't kidding.

He asked, "How does this look to ya?"

It was crazy colorful, wildly artistic and imaginative. It looked like it started in the center and then kind of exploded in all directions, without an actual picture but a design, possibly from a psychedelic universe. (From inside his head)

I said, "Wow, how high were you when you did this?"

"I don't remember; probably very."

He told me that it was his best effort in years, as far as creativity was concerned, but he was willing to part with it because I had loaned him my D-5 and he really appreciated it.

By the way and FYI, the show he gave me was Kean College 2/28/80, when Jerry played *After Midnite* into *Eleanor Rigby* back into *After Midnite*. This was one of those shows that wasn't really in circulation at the time, so no one had it except for a few people. The fact is that in my crowd, no one had it but me and that was way cool. When my friends heard this one they were blown away, for that matter so was I. As most people know by now the middle break where 'Eleanor' gets going, Jerry catches fire. . . It's smokin. (Metaphors on top of metaphors!) I'm sure that if Paul McCartney ever hears it, he'll be blown away by it too. It was an amazing jam and was eventually released by Rhino Records and the Garcia Estate, entitled; After Midnite

When I picked up my tape deck from Fredo's house we had a surprising, yet very interesting conversation about it. He mentioned to me that I really should get a cover for it, or make one or do something to protect it. I couldn't agree more with the actual concept of protecting the deck, it was just a matter of figuring out how. What should I use to cover it? Should I use a bag, and if I did, how much protection would that actually provide? I went home and brain stormed a little, gave it some real deep thought. What am I gonna use? It should be soft on the inside. Protective on the outside? . . Canvas would good protection for the outside, but a simple cloth, like a towel wouldn't work for the inside. I asked my Mom if she had any ideas. Once I told her what I was trying to do, she got real interested in my little project. She told me that she had an old quilted sheet that she wasn't using anymore. It was a quilted, fitted sheet/mattress protector. I folded it in a variety of ways before it came to me. I used the quilted sheet for the inside, by cutting it to fit my deck, measuring three inches over on each side, (allowing for batteries and an AC cord) and four more on top just in case I needed it. Then I folded it in half with the good, soft side out and sewed around the three sides, leaving the top portion open. (Sewing was a skill that my grandmother taught me when I was very young) Then I turned it inside out and proudly checked out the first part of my new bag. It looked really good. It was sewn very tightly, by hand and pretty much square. During the process, I asked my Dad if he had a canvas bag anywhere around. He brought me an old Army type of duffle bag that wasn't being used. I took this canvas and cut a piece from it, slightly larger than the cloth bag I had just made. I took the better looking side and folded it into itself, then sewed along its edges, leaving the top portion open again. I turned this inside out very carefully (this was not as easy as the cloth bag) pushing the corners out completely. Then I pushed the cloth bag deep inside the canvas one, so it fit tightly. I used waxed twine (the kind most often used to tie up newspapers) to lace the top of the outside bag to the inside bad, folding the canvas bag over the cloth one first. Then I sewed the two bottom corners through both fabrics to keep the bag from coming apart at the bottom. The final part was stitching velcro across the top of the bag, so I could keep it closed when I wanted it closed, but I left the ends open about a half an inch on each side for the strap that attached to the deck. I must admit it turned out to be an excellent bag for my deck. It had enough room in it for my AC cord, batteries at the bottom and room enough for two blank tapes, which could be slid in behind the tape deck. (This so that the tapes wouldn't scratch the clear plastic door that closed over the tape). I still have my D-5 and the bag that I made for it, but the deck hasn't worked for years. It needed a new motor and several other smaller repairs that I couldn't afford to fix when it first broke. In the Fall of 2009 I finally got it fixed and I was so happy.

As we sat there listening to music and exchanging ideas for my tape deck and talking about the Garcia Band show that he was giving me, he pulled from his pocket some amazing Speed. Crystal, brown, moist, nasty looking speed and offered me a line. I wasn't prepared for this moment by any means, but I was familiar with the concept by now so I said, "Sure." I snorted it up. It burned and my eyes teered up and I felt immediately exhilarated. About two weeks later I got another call from Mike that went like this, "Are you interested in any more of that crazy amazing music that I turned you onto last time you were here?" I said, "I think I definitely would be. Why what's up?" "Just come down now if you could, but stop before you get here and call to let me know you're here. Ok?" "Sure enough. Thanks." I drove down, stopped for the call and showed up a few minutes later and bought a small amount of the best Crystal anybody had ever seen, from the one guy that would have the best of that kind of thing on hand.

Now getting back to the tour. I was on vacation this particular week and the next show was on May 5th, 1981, in Glens Falls, New York. I wasn't sure how I was going to get there, but I knew that Mike and Patty were going with his sister Pat and her boyfriend Don. Their friends Mike and Brian were going too. The result of my initial phone call was very disappointing. Pat told me that there wasn't enough room for me in the car with six people and personal stuff, so I was out of luck. Man, I was so bummed. I had a ticket and the time off, but no ride. I could've taken my own car, but I really didn't want to drive the old Mustang all the way to Glens Falls alone. So I'm sitting in my living room staring out the big front window. So bummed out. Then phone rings again. I went to answer it with a really hopeful feeling. It was Pat calling back to tell me she couldn't possibly leave me home and that they'd make room for me somehow. I was so excited! My Mom was sitting at the kitchen table, listening to this story unfold and she was very happy to see my relief.

Up in Glens Falls the Dead played one of my favorite surprise combos. I already discussed my love for Uncle Johns Band and Truckin is a song that we all love to hear, with it's anthemic cry of *What a long Strange Trip it's Been*, with the lights shining brightly while the crowd goes wild. Well, in this particular instance Truckin was followed by the unexpected surprise placement of Alabama Getaway. This song is mainly a set opener or an encore up until now, so it was very exciting. The way it was thrown into the mix during such a fantastic jam gave us all something to wake up our minds for the moment. We were all very high at this show, with help from some high intensity psychedelics and the most fucked up thing happened after the show.

Somebody stole a bunch of original design t-shirts that Pat had with her to sell in order to make some traveling money. This was the first time I ever experienced anything really negative on tour. This was a rare isolated incident for us. Someone decided it would be a good idea if we split up on a corner outside the Civic Center and headed in four different directions to look for the shirts, with the intention of meeting back there in ten minutes.

Oh. . . My. . .God!

As we all started walking away, I'm thinking that my brain is definitely not in gear for this particular task, but I went with it. I turned to look at both sides of the street, but was definitely not very sure of any one thing at this point. I wasn't real excited about the short adventure I was about to embark on, but it was genuinely a beautiful night to hang out. I walked for what I thought was ten to fifteen minutes, tough to tell when you can feel your heart beating throughout your entire body and you're feeling the presence of every human being that you get close to. I looked around, checked out the crowd; Lots of people walking around; waiting for friends to catch up; wondering what they were gonna be doing for the rest of the night. (God, can this be over) After what I thought was enough time, I turned around to head back, and hoped to God that the corner would still be where I left it. Maybe this was all a sick joke, being played on me by my friends to see just exactly how fucked up I actually was. Well, let me just say that I was *just fucked up enough* to think that I was being fucked with. But I kept walking. . . and walking, . . and hoping. . . and when I finally got back to the corner, they were all actually waiting for me, but none of us had any luck on our mission. No shirts. . .

Following all the drama we headed toward our hotel, which was really nice. They call it The Holiday Inn. There was an indoor pool that was open for our enjoyment so we took full, unsupervised advantage of it. There was a hot tub too, but I swear that sucker must've been turned up to about 500 degree's. Our friend Mike was sitting in the tub for most of the time we were there just soaking it up and loving it. I put my big toe into it and found it was way too hot for me. I was content to just relax in the pool, which was bathtub warm. It's a funny, very peculiar kinda feeling to be immersed in very comfortable, somewhat warm water when you're tripping. Altered States, anybody?

Mike was hanging with Brian for most of the night and had hooked up with a couple that said they had some amazing hash to smoke. Brian caught a ride back to the hotel with this 'hashish totin couple' so they could find their way without a bunch of confusing directions. Over the course of the next half hour, this couple passed out on the bed, but it was before whippin out the amazing hash that they had spoken about. So what's a room full of smokeless heads to do when there's hash to be smoked but the 'mule' is passed out. I guess you search the mule and smoke the stash that had been promised. That's what we did.

(Here's where things get uncomfortable)

After we smoked, we all started talking about the fact that these people were still here, passed out in this hotel room that was roughly the size of a broom closet and we figured *someone* should wake them up and ask them to leave. (Party was over, they should go right?) I was actually quite comfortable on my section of the floor, so I was keeping my mouth shut. They talked their friend Brian (whom I really didn't know) into telling them they had to leave because let's face it, he brought them there in the first place. It was never the plan for them to stay over, but in their defense, we didn't get back to the room until almost 2:30 am. Listening to him tell them they needed to leave was really awkward for all concerned. I'm pretty sure that had it been me with Bob at Glens Falls that year, we wouldn't have found ourselves in that position. We never picked up stragglers. But if it had *ever happened*, we would've let them stay.

The one thing that sucked about this trip was the loss of a very special tour jacket. I left it behind in the Hotel room there. We were heading for home when I realized that I didn't have it with me so we drove all the way back to the Hotel to pick it up, only to find that it was already missing from the closet in the room. I was really surprised that it was gone. It had a beautiful painting of 'Ice Cream Kid' on the back of it. The maid should've figured that someone might be back for such a nice piece of artwork, even though it was on a scrappy looking jacket.

The Ice Cream Kid is part of the artwork from 'The Europe 72' album/CD. It's not that I couldn't find it in the room. I actually hung it up, uncharacteristically, in the closet and then left without it. Also, it wasn't actually a jacket, though I wore it that way. It was an Army shirt, something you could pick up at a surplus shop. It was an extra large, which was a little bit too big for me and the sleeves had been torn off, which made it kinda cool looking and topping it all off, it was really comfortable. It was a perfect canvas for a painting. I went to Peddlers Village, up the street from me, because I knew a guy that did portraits there. I didn't know it at the time, but this guy was going to be famous. The Artist's name was John Bass, and his niche` was painting landscapes at lightening speed. The funnier thing is that my friend Brian's mother worked for Bass at the time and I found out much later that she was the actual artist for my Ice Cream Kid.

On May 7th 1981 the Grateful Dead appeared on NBC's Studios The Tomorrow Show with Tom Snyder. They played *On the Road Again, Dire Wolf, Deep Elum Blues* and *Cassidy*, a nice little quiet acoustic set as Tom stated, and he was so grateful, no pun, that he made a point of mentioning it to Jerry.

"Thanks so much for the quiet acoustic set guys." He said, "I really appreciate it. A lot of bands come in here and blow us out with the sound and it's nice to hear some nice casual music. Thanks so much." Bob and Jerry were the only band members there and it was a very entertaining interview. Jerry has a great wit that'll make anyone laugh and Bob's boyish charm is always very evident. During the interview, Tom picked up on a statement that Weir had made recently about the band, describing themselves as "misfits who play for misfits". Jerry and Bob both raised their arms up against one and other and proudly proclaimed. . . "Misfit power". . . By the time they played their next gig in New Haven Connecticut, the "Misfit power" bumper stickers were everywhere. . . . Naturally!

The boys actually played the first of three nights at Nassau the night before, but we didn't make it. Instead, we went to the second and third nights at Nassau to finish off the local tour. After that they went on to New Haven, Conn. for the 11th and 12th of May. On the 12th they dedicated He's Gone to Bob Marley, who passed away the night before. Then they played one show in Providence. (Sorry I missed that one. . . Fun show) Then we caught up with them at the Rutgers Athletic Center (The RAC) in Livingston, N.J. on the 15th. This building, home to the Rutgers Scarlet Knights, is an 8,000 seat basketball arena designed to keep crowd noise at a deafening level, so the sound levels were immense. It also had a glass ceiling and there was a storm brewing outside so we were able to see lightening flashing across the sky above us. It was a somewhat small venue, but it was very open, you could even call it spacious. We could walk practically anywhere that we wanted to go and no one would say a word. It seemed as though there weren't very many people there, but I remember it being very crowded. (That's like a Yogism) It made me wonder why there weren't more general admission shows. This was a show that brought everybody together; The beach bums and surfers in our wonderful beach town, plus most of the Deadheads that I was hanging out with at the time, all got together for this one. In fact one of those surfer dudes was taping that night, so I blew it off to just have some fun with no obligations. It worked out well for me.

This place also stands out in my memory because of the slightly new arrangement of Eyes of the World they played that night. I can describe it only by saying that it had six extra notes tacked onto the already familiar melody. As they started playing it, I ran up the stairs that lead to a large open balcony that surrounded the back area of the gym so I could see Jerry playing the new melody and really enjoy it.

A Big Decision; What To Do?
We Knew What to do...

The band played only three more shows on the East Coast at the end of 1981, and then went off to Europe again. These were the shows that included the now legendary Melkweg shows in Amsterdam. More on that later. The shows they played beforehand were on the 25th of September at the Stabler Arena in Pennsylvania; the Buffalo War Memorial on Saturday the 26th, and then the Capital Center in Landover, MD on the 27th. Talk about a road trip. The Stabler is in Bethlehem Pa., about 100 miles to the West of us; Buffalo, N.Y., is about 400 miles North of us and the Cap Center is 200 miles South. We did the math and chose to go to Buffalo on Saturday and then make the trip to the Cap Center on Sunday. The only thing we missed at the Stabler besides an extra long first set was a Might as Well opener, which at the time was just being dusted off, or in layman's terms, re-introduced to the bands repertoire.

The set list in Buffalo was exceptional, opening with Shakedown > C.C.Rider, which was very sweet. They love Each Other, Cassidy, and then Jack-a-Roe, which I never get tired of hearing. On the Road Again, which was reintroduced at the Warfield and Radio City shows as an acoustic song and then Ramble on Rose, Looks like Rain, and Brown eyed Women. Then closing out the set with an extended Let it Grow jam that flowed nicely into Don't Ease Me in. I taped in Buffalo using AKG 1000's, but apparently they didn't sound very good because I see on my liner notes that I re-recorded them from my friend Dave's copies, which made mine 2nd generation audience. I guess my master copies sounded really bad. The Buffalo War Memorial was kind of hollow sounding, much like Nassau Coliseum. I guess that would explain it.

The second set was the best; Playing > Bertha > Estimated > Goin Down the Road Feelin Bad > drums > Not Fade Away > Morning Dew back into Playin in the Band > One More Saturday Night. The encore was Johnny B. Goode. This is a great example of why one would travel for hours to see this band play just one show. It was always worth the travel and the adventure, because the people were always all there for the same reason. But why would we go all the way to Buffalo to see just one show? Because sometimes the music is bigger than the band. It's not just a concert, it's six separate musical talents on a stage in one universe. "There is nothing like a Grateful Dead Concert". If you get it, then there's no further explanation necessary. It was over 400 miles of pavement between home and the great city of Buffalo and more than worth every mile. Of course, we had to leave right after the show to cover the 470 miles to get to Landover in time, but again, see the aforementioned reasoning.

The Capital Center show opened with three first set openers. Jack Straw, Alabama Getaway and Promised Land. The first set included It Must've Been the Roses, which never got enough stage time for my money. Second set included a new one for us, Man Smart/Women Smarter. It was done by Ricky Riccardo on the 'I love Lucy' show a very long time ago. We were laughing about the Ricky Riccardo reference after the show. We just called it Women are Smarter. I found out later (cause I looked it up!) that Harry Belafonte made the song popular in 1956. We also heard Bob Dylan's It's All Over Now Baby Blue, for the first time at the Cap for the encore. My seats were so horrible here that I didn't even bother to bring my deck in with me. At times the end result is just not worth it, and Deadheads have been aware for years that the Capital Center sounds like crap too. Enough said.

These last three shows were quite a haul even for the veteran touring Deadhead. The fact that we are willing, even eager to travel, sometimes for days to see this band play even one show was foreseen somewhat. There is a great story in a book by Blair Jackson that I would like to share you, my readers. I'd first like to mention that I have read most of the books available in this category and Blair's book, *Garcia: An American Life*, is chock full of excellent Garcia stories and one of these was very telling of Garcia's future. Blaire tells the story of a much younger Garcia that would do odd jobs for cash with his friend David and Jerry would always have his guitar with him. One day as they were leaving, he started strumming and singing while they were walking. It was summer time in Palo Alto, and there were some kids outside playing in the street. After walking for a while Dave turned and saw that there were a bunch of kids following them and they were dancing around, having a good old time. When Jerry saw them he stopped for a minute to observe and they were all over him to keep playing. Jerry loved the reaction. Little did he know, he'd eventually have tens of thousands following him everywhere he went, just to see him play. And another. . .

In 1964, Jerry and his friend Sandy Rothman, who were both heavily into bluegrass music at the time, set out on the road to checkout some bluegrass shows and record them, learn the craft, and try maybe making a living at it. They traveled most of the way across the country before Jerry decided to head back home. Jerry found inspiration that he would carry with him through the rest of his life, and influence the music that he would eventually play. Jerry and his friend were 'bluegrass heads' and apparently wanted to check out the scene and record their experiences. Who does that sound like? It's no wonder then, that Jerry had an understanding and appreciation for the tapers, and their interest in bringing the music home with them.

Jerry always said, "Once we're done with it, it's theirs."

They played for the enjoyment, not because it was required for album sales. (what album sales?) There was no other obligation. As far as letting anybody record was concerned, there is the theory of saturation. You let everyone tape your performance, the market is saturated with the material. If everyone has it for free, then who can actually sell it? Along with that is the unspoken code among Deadheads that no one sells tapes for more than the price of a blank. In fact the blanks were so cheap in the 80's, (average price in bulk, of a single Maxell UD-XLII was .99) that it never gets mentioned during the trade off. I personally gave away a tons of tapes. I genuinely enjoyed sharing what was essentially shared with me. So among Deadheads there was no worry of 'pirating' or 'bootlegging'. By the way, along with the touring, most Deadheads that I know also supported the band by buying their albums when they were released. You have to realize that by the time 'In The Dark' came out, we had been listening to the Dead play Touch of Grey for about 5 ½ years, and obviously, everyone went out and bought it anyway. . . Hello!

Blair Jackson, by the way, was also the co-creator, with his wife Regan, of the Grateful Dead mag, The Golden Road. Any Deadhead that subscribed to it was well informed about anything and everything Grateful Dead for years. The Golden Road included a special section on songs that the Grateful Dead played that were originally done by other artists (yes cover tunes) and the origins of those tunes. There was also an entertaining section that covered TV and movie sightings. I had a movie sighting published in an early issue. Thanks Blair. I still have all my issues in mint condition, in a nice collectors binder.

East Coast Tour 1982

The first show on this tour was in Durham NC., at the Cameron Indoor Stadium April 2, 1982. Our tour started the next night at The Scope in Norfolk, Virginia. The first thing we noticed when the show started was that Jerry and Phil were at different sides of the stage. It was the big news in '82! Jerry was to Bobby's right and Phil was way over where Jerry used to be. At first I thought it might just be a goof, but later we heard what it was all about. Bob moved his speakers to the front of the drum risers to bunch up the players to hear everyone better. It seemed to work out that playing in closer proximity to each other was a better idea than just playing on the same stage. They found that they could actually hear each other in real time rather than just following along with the jam. This idea was so helpful that Jerry and Phil figured it would help them as well. Phil could hear the drums better from the far left so that helped him to keep time better. That's the best explanation I could figure from what I read.

This was the 4th consecutive tour that Bob and I did together, along with one or two other friends that were able join us for more than just a couple of shows. We were doing at least five or six shows, I should say five or six cities each time the boys came close to us and then an extensive road trip much further away whenever that opportunity would present itself. (I loved taking a plane to see Jerry and the boys) This tour had some pretty interesting set lists, but in later years we would see a more structured set list. By structured, I mean we heard the Scarlet / Fire and the China/ Rider. That kind of thing. But on this tour, songs were put in real different places where set openers and closers was concerned, not to mention encores. For example: The Women are Smarter is a first set closer in Philly, but in later years it was almost always placed within the first three songs of the second set, at least pre-drums. Well, let's move on, or rather back to the Scope.

I remember thinking when they first announced this tour, how weird it was that the boys weren't playing at the Coliseum in Hampton this time around. "What the hell is the Scope?" I asked Bob. We figured out where it was and how long it would take to get there, so no big deal. I taped every show on this tour, but I had to use my single stereo mic occasionally because if I didn't have floor seats I wouldn't be able to find a patch for my deck. The Scope offered a unique taping opportunity though. The guy I was patched into that night had one Nakamichi mic and one Shore mic. (I don't really remember that configuration, but that's what I wrote on my tape case.) The sound in the Scope Coliseum wasn't the best to deal with, but the tapes came out pretty dam good. We drove home right after the show because we planned to have a full day off between there and the Spectrum and Bob said he would rather just get home and wouldn't mind driving half the night to get us there. Sunday was our day of rest and prep for Philly.

The Spectrum shows were the 5th and 6th and this time we had two unexpected guests with us. Our much younger friend Patty (only by 5 years) and her girlfriend Anno. They grew up together in upstate New York and had known each other since Kindergarten. Patty moved to the shore when she was a little older, but kept in touch with Anno through-out her whole life. I met Patty at one of my garage parties when she was dating my new friend Shooter and I met Anno when she came down to visit Patty and came to Rick's for a party. Ok, that part is over.

So here we are, all ready to take off to Philadelphia when Patty and Anno suddenly decide to jump into the van. Patty had no money, but was armed with about 100 Jerry Garcia posters her x-boyfriend had left behind. It was a promotional poster, not in circulation at the time, from a gig that Jerry had played a very long time ago. Shooter had printed a bunch of these posters (about a thousand) and had been selling them in larger quantities to anyone that wanted to make a little money for tour. She was able to sell enough of them for ticket money and travel expenses. Patty's mom knew where we were going, but apparently somebody neglected to make that all important phone call to Anno's mom and dad. (They still say they were kidnapped) So, two shows at the Spectrum, a couple days off for us while the band went up to Syracuse and then over to Rochester. We then caught up at Nassau Coliseum for two shows, on the 11th and 12th. We were having a blast, and the excursion was even more fun with our unexpected guests.

On April 10th Jerry played a solo acoustic gig at the Capital, so we quickly scoffed up tickets for that. It was a quiet acoustic set with a break followed by another. I read recently that Jerry had terrible stage freight when he did solo gigs, but you'd never know it. He always played sweet and soulful. Probably had his eyes closed the entire time.

Now we go back to the Spectrum. The first night we saw a Jack Straw opener, El Paso and then Deep Elum Blues. The second night brought about a great first set; Twelve songs starting off with Cold Rain into Promised Land, and included Jack-a-Roe, All Over Now and Might as Well, not to mention the mid set appearance of Big RxR Blues. What a great set! Never thought it would end. Second set started off with an extended Shakedown Street, *"Don't tell me this town ain't got no heart"* never a disappointment at the Spectrum. Oh yea, the one bummer about this show was that I was forced by unrelenting circumstances, to hold my lone stereo mic in my hand for the entire show, while taping from my unlikely spot at the side of the stage, at just about an even distance with the soundboard. Though unhappy about the taping situation, it happened to be a great view from there. Shakedown was followed by the Lost Sailor Suite, which is what we called the pairing of Lost Sailor and Saint of Circumstance. We really thought that's what it was called. They were meant to be together, much like the Weather Report Suite on Wake of the Flood. Then there was a pretty amazing Terrapin Station and an incredible Dew. The tapes actually sound pretty phenomenal. Twenty-eight years ago (at this point) and holding up really well.

The parking lots, by now were steadily growing, yet still under control. Not so many ticket less Deadheads yet, but plenty of vendors selling everything from veggie burgers and veggie wraps to cheese burgers and hot dogs. The specialty grillers were the best though. These people would wrap just about anything that even sounded a little healthy in a falafel wrap and hawk 'em like crazy. This was before the rest of the world discovered how great fajita wraps are. Of course, just as many sold beer or soda. This was also before the bottled water revolution. Dam, if I knew then what I know now about consumer demand, I would no longer have to work for a living.

The first night at Nassau was Easter Sunday. This is a time when my family had a traditional dinner at the same wonderful restaurant every year. Salad, Italian Bread, followed by the best Pizza on the planet. I remember having to leave our Easter dinner a little early that year to meet up with Bob and get to Nassau on time. The best part was having that week off from work, but telling my Mom and Dad that I was leaving at 4:00 to go see the Dead was just a thing for me. The holiday was very important to my Mom, but she was also fine with me leaving when I did. I spent the better part of the day with them. Just so happened that the better part of *my* day was about to begin . . . (Now that's not nice! Just kidding!)

The Easter Sunday show opened with a strong Mississippi ½ step > Franklin's Tower into an unexpected El Paso. I always liked hearing that song. It was one of the few that was definitely not overplayed, at least not from my perspective. It was also one of a few songs that I could play for my Mom that she would recognize and appreciate from my standpoint as well as her own. My parents exposed us to the Country crooners of their time, with Marty Robbins definitely among them. It was also unexpected because we just heard it a few days earlier. The second set opened with Bertha > Samson, not a common pairing, then Brent played his Good Time Blues, 'gonna get to ring that bell, . . cause right now I feel like hell'. Jerry did He's Gone and Weir followed it with Truckin into drums > NFA > Black Peter > Around and round > Good lovin, then Don't Ease Me in for the encore. You see here that they followed Not Fade with three songs and an encore. Definitely not the case in later years.

The next night they played 18 songs without a repeat in the bunch. The show opened with Aiko > Minglewood, with a Fennario and a Bird Song into C.C.Rider, ending the set with Deal. The second set featured an exceptional Estimated Prophet > Uncle John's Band, a nice pairing in any book of set lists and Uncle John's has always been a favorite of mine. The encore was a rocking cover of (Can't get no) Satisfaction. Rock n' Bobby. Yeah! We stayed at a hotel up in Nassau for the first time because we were headed up to Glens Falls next. Our friend Tom F. had a room at the Hempstead Holiday Inn with a friend of his, so we all crashed there. The Holiday Inn was connected to the Coliseum by a walkway tunnel, so staying at that Hotel meant we didn't have to venture out into the night air, either before or after the show.

When we started out on our adventure with Patty and her girlfriend, our original intention was to give Anno a ride home. We never intended to get anybody in trouble, (after all, everyone *knew* where *we* were) but our little side trip to the Spectrum and Nassau with our two friends was not received well by Anno's dad. The first I heard that her parents didn't know where she was, was when we got closer to her place. The way I looked at it, that was essentially on her not us, so once we arrived at her destination, we kinda expected to be able to crash there, (normally they would have insisted) but we were shown the door with this thought:

"Guys, normally you'd be more than welcome to stay here, but she's (with the pointed finger) in a lot of trouble so you can't stay this time, but please come back soon."

I personally didn't know Anno's parents at this time, but I can attest to their sincerity because I've been a very welcome guest in their home several times since then. On our way out the door Bob and I were both a little concerned about where we were going, but Rick told us about Patty's sister's house which was right up the street (about 10 miles) and knew where we needed to go. Patty's sister Kate was home, but on her way out for the week, which apparently wasn't a problem. She directed us downstairs and gave us blankets and told us to have at it. We set up our blankets on the couch and watched some TV and fell asleep. It was a good crash and we needed it because we were all spent.

In the morning we found a note from her that will always stick in my mind. "This is 'stop over in New York State Kate', saying thanks for coming and see you guys soon." Made us laugh for a few minutes. Kate was very cool.

My friends Mike and Pat drove up to Nassau too so when we split for Glens Falls, Mike gave Patty a ride back to Jersey. On their way Mike's rear tire on the passenger side flew off the car and everybody freaked out, except Mike. He held it together and pulled to the side of the road with no complications. They wound up staying at Mike's sister-in-laws house up north for the night and made it home safely in the morning. On April 13ᵗʰ '82 Bob Weir and Jerry Garcia appeared on David Letterman's Late Show at NBC's Studio's where they played acoustic; *Deep Elum Blues*, sat down with Dave for a segment and then played *Monkey and the Engineer*.

The show in Glens Falls was on April 14ᵗʰ 1982. Bob was driving and after we dropped Anno off, it was just me Rick and Bob. We were on the Taconic Parkway, moving with the flow of traffic, at about 85mph. We were driving a big black van with no windows and a huge wooden bumper that said Grateful on the far left, for passing of course, and Dead on the far right, to complete the obvious slogan. Apparently, it could have said, "Please pull us over and search us", because that's what happened.

We were pulled over by the State Police of New York for speeding in a crowd of vehicles that were all speeding. We exited the van as per request or demand, whichever you prefer, and were searched. My friend Rick, who was tripping at the time, was in the back of the Van taking a piss in a jug and when the door was opened a handful of empty beer cans fell out onto the pavement. (Nice welcome invitation that was!) As he was about to step out of the Van, a buck knife that Rick was wearing on his belt drew the attention of one of the officers, so he subsequently drew his firearm and Rick was now face to face with the wrong end of a gun. The knife was confiscated, if only temporarily and the gun was returned to its holster. Whatever it takes to keep that thing wrapped up is just fine.

The van was torn apart, the couch in back almost pulled out, the cooler emptied of about only 8 beers, as we were about to pull off the main drag and get more. The man in the uniform with the mirrored sunglasses looked at my friend Bob and said, "You mean I should believe that you guys are headed to see a Grateful Dead concert, and you got no pot, no cocaine, no heroine, no drugs at all." (Heroin?, This guy was definitely way off !)

The Man spoke primarily to Bob, and we (myself and Rick) primarily kept our mouths shut. Bob spoke up, "Officer, not everyone who goes to see the Grateful Dead does drugs sir."

To which, Man replied, "I guess you're gonna get some when you get there."

Then, "No sir, we're just gonna pick up some beer later, is all." There was not much more interaction than that. Bob wasn't thrilled about being put in this situation, but seriously, there was no real need for anybody to be worried. (Except Rick was peaking by now)

Now, by this time there were two other State Police cars, one in front and two behind our van counting the one that originally pulled us over and there were three other cops (beside our personal friend in blue) standing around looking at each other scratching their heads. I guess they all figured that this would be a great way to spend the first part of their day, 'the big Deadhead drug bust'. Everybody gets their names in the paper and big pats on the back and everything. But we sidestepped that inconvenience and really kinda pissed everybody off. I had never seen a cop so. . . frustrated and disappointed. We saved him a ton of paper work obviously, but he'd have gotten that big pat on the back if he had found what he was counting on finding. The fact was, we weren't real worried because we had nothing on us and we all knew it. Once we realized what they were hoping to find, we were pretty relieved. It had a calming effect knowing we weren't really in any trouble. They obviously could've busted us for the beers, but there was only two open containers among the four of us and since that wasn't this guys objective, we really lucked out. We pulled off the next exit, counted our blessings after being let go and replenished the cooler. He didn't even give Bob a speeding ticket and that was the cause for the stop in the first place. 'What a maroon!..What a colossal maroon!' (I love Bugs Bunny)

As we pulled out, back onto the Taconic, we decided to pick up a fellow traveler who was without wheels. The way our day was going could we possibly be pulled over again? Well, our luck changed for the better when said traveler pulled out a 'fatty' and we all indulged a little and relaxed a bit. When we got to the Civic Arena parking lot, we had some fun answering questions. It seemed that there were a bunch of Deadheads behind us on the Parkway that were concerned and/or amused by our plight, and that gave us a chance to laugh off our frustration and once again revel in the reward of not being busted for anything. Some Deadheads may also remember this show for the bad acid that was going around. There were some bogus sheets at this show and a vigilante crew of Deadheads apparently caught up with these guys and turned them over to the cops. Strange sounding as that is.

The area around the Civic Center in Glens Falls was much like Hartford. It was in the middle of the city and the parking lots were spread out over a larger area. This was fine, but it wasn't real conducive to tailgating. We did a lot of wandering with beers in hand. Of course everybody was wandering with beers in hand because of the concert, so public consumption wasn't really an issue and the atmosphere in that regard was casual.

At the show that night they played a really nice version of *Deep Elum Blues*. Although they played it for us at the Garden first a year before, the 'Deep Elum' at Glens Falls sounded more solid to me and it made me smile and dance. Maybe it was the venue, maybe it was our seat location. I don't know, but it was different. Up to this point I had been using my Stereo mic a lot because my options were limited with the tickets I had. At this show however, I had options. Plenty of options. I was patched into a pair of Sennheiser 421's initially, but I started a conversation with Mark from Westchester N.Y., and subsequently switched over to his mics. Nakamichi 300's with shotguns. A real nice mix that included a specially designed bass box for the D-5.

By the end of the night, Mark asked me for a favor that kinda surprised me. Something happened to his master while we were taping, so he asked me if he could borrow my deck for the night and bring back it back for the next show. Since I was using his mics, we had developed a kinship of sorts through the night, so I allowed the thought to process and gave it some consideration instead of just saying no. He told me that he would bring fresh blanks for me for the next shows. Though that was not a deciding factor, I decided to trust my gut and loan it to him. The next shows were in Providence, Rhode Island. He gave me his phone number and address in Westchester, and he promised me that he'd fix both of our tapes and return my deck with the fresh blanks and even batteries for the next night. When I told my friends about this arrangement, they told me I was crazy, but I got some really good vibes from Mark and I felt confident that all would work out.

On the way back to the hotel after this show, Bob needed a cup of coffee so we found a Dunkin Donuts and parked the van. We were all really pretty stoned from the show and maybe you can already imagine what's it's like to be around sober people when you're drunk. Imagine then for a moment what it might be like to be pretty stoned, on whatever it is that you might be stoned on, and trying to tell the young lady behind the counter that you really want a donut. I tried but the words weren't quite coming out like that. I remember distinctly having to annunciate very clearly (mostly for myself) so that I'd be sure of what I was going to end up with. I was trying to say, "Can I get a Chocolate Honey Dipped donut please?" without falling over my totally dried out tongue. It was too funny. Then the poor young lady behind the counter (at 3 am mind you) has a bad case of acne going on, and she's just doing her job when she asks, "How can I help you?" and we were, or I was, trying to be very adult about the whole thing until I stepped out of the store.

I said, "I'm sorry, but did anyone else find that ridiculously funny?" I swear, once we started laughing, we couldn't stop. We started rolling down the highway still laughing. Not a real nice story I know, but what the fuck!, still funny as hell even as I'm thinking about it. They finally changed the name of that donut to Chocolate Glazed. Lots of good that does me now. . .ha ha

Next, here comes an uncomfortable scenario. The ticket that I had for the show in Providence was obstructed view, Section 224 at the side of the stage. So I had to keep walking up stairs, passing every section while showing my ticket to all these usher people and one after another kept saying, "No keep on going, keep on going." Luckily for me though, once I got through the door that they would let me go through, I stepped over forty dozen rows of seats and across whole sections of people until I got to the floor section, where I casually stepped over the 4 foot security wall that lead me to the floor. The security people didn't give a shit about tap-ing, and once passed the inside hallway nobody seemed to care who was sitting where. I easily made my way over to meet up with my buddy Mark who was already setting up. He had brand new Metal tapes, Energizer batteries and a big smile on his face. It was a 'man hug' moment. What a bond! The show was great, but it didn't even matter what they played. I had found a person in a crowd of strangers that I was able to put my trust in and it really worked out great. I knew this guy for three hours and trusted him with my D5. I trust very few with my deck, so believe me, to trust someone with it that I barely knew was huge. I used Mark's mics again, Nak 300's with shotguns. Those mics were really great for distance. 700's are a little sweeter, but you can't always be so choosy. This show started off with some crazy mixed up sound problems, but had another long first set of eleven songs including a really sweet Fennario and Beat it on Down the Line and Cassidy.

The next two shows were in Hartford and they were actually quite surprising shows to say the least. We were in section 122 for the first night, (pretty descent seats, but not for taping) but it was somewhat easy to get to the floor, so down I went. The first night was filled with great musical choices, including El Paso, (again?) Jack-a-Roe, Shakedown Street, and a composition known as Spanish jam, (part of the standard Dark Star jam a long time ago), and then One More Saturday Night. Over-all, as usual, a great show.

The next night was a little different for a couple of really weird reasons. First, my seats were in nosebleed heaven. Not a great place to tape from, but apparently I wasn't the only taper relegated to the 400's (seat section) that night that couldn't get to the floor. The sound was Ok from up there and I also considered the fact that I could eventually get a better copy of the show anyway, so what did it matter as long as I was inside sharing space with other tapers. It started out like a real party atmosphere. The songs were all upbeat and the band sounded great. The second set started off with a killer Cold Rain and Snow > Samson and Delilah. (Alright children it's time for your Sunday sermon now) I'll tell you we could feel the whole band playing even from all the way up in Dead's heaven. Ship of Fools was followed by Playing in the Band and that lead to Eyes of the World, into drums. The date of this show was April 18th 1982 (in case I wasn't clear) and it was the anniversary of the 1906 Earthquake that destroyed parts of San Francisco. (Is everybody with me now?) Phil started playing this really off the wall space jam on his bass and then stepped up to the mic, and started telling us a story. And here we go. . . . . Go Phil!

"The Barbary Coast, 1906. The wicked place in the world....ha ha...
ohh yea...Nothing but sin and no salvation..." (a little growl, then)...
"woo, hoo, hoo.. lots of fun, hey..."

(At which point the three of us that were taping bent over with our
flash lights to make sure the tapes were still spinning and that there was
plenty of room left for whatever the Fuck was about to happen.)

This was followed by a whirling, . . spacey, . . crazy jam with drums
and percussion instruments and weirdness. Some of the strangest examples of spacey weirdness that I had ever heard.

"Yea, San Francisco, the Pearl of the pacific, The Jewwweeelll. . .
The ring of fire! . . .Hang on, hang on. . . Until. . . until. . . I say, . . I
say . . . I say, . . .until. . . That one fateful day. . ."

The instruments sounded like they were just clanging together and
Phil's bass was turned up so high that it was rattling the place. Even our
seats in the upper deck felt the tremors. Everyone was freaking out and
couldn't believe what Phil was doing. It was amazing and chilling and
scary and fun all at the same time. He wasn't done yet, though....

"San Francisco in ruins"....

This trippy space lent itself very easily to The Other One, which
came up next..Then Black Peter > Sugar Magnolia, back into Playing in
the Band, which originated before the drums and then they finished off
Sugar Mags with Sunshine Daydream. What an exciting night. Not only
did Phil hit some amazing heights, but the not too often seen Playing
Sandwich or Reprise, which is what it's commonly referred to, was
thrown out there (or in there). I wasn't so disappointed now about not
going to the Baltimore Civic the next night cause "what could possibly
top this?"

What could top this you ask? . .(we asked) Phil did it again, except this time he did a spacial jam with Edgar Allen Poe's "The Raven" in the middle of the space. "Quoth the Raven. . Nevermore"

Poe died on October 7ᵗʰ 1949 in Baltimore. Maybe Phil heard a reference to it that day somewhere, or maybe he'd been planning it for this place, who knows. Some people though it was Poe's birthday or the day he died, which prompted the tribute, but neither is true.

Fuckin' Grateful Dead, man!

I continued taping shows and trading with other Deadheads. It became a way of life for me and all involved. It was our reality away from. . .Our reality. I never quit my job for it, none of us ever did (none of us that actually had jobs) and we never got arrested. We were 18 to 21 years old at the time, hitting the road and touring like crazy people, so not getting arrested for anything stupid was a really good thing, and surprising too!

Great bunch of Friends

This chapter is about those friends of mine who kept me company on the road. It was pretty much the same core group of adventurers. The mix would most certainly change depending on who was free to hit the road at any given moment, but the travelers that remained faithful were myself, Bob, and Rick. The following makes up the who, where and when. I don't know for sure, but I think my group of friends were unique in that we all came together via our mutual love for the Grateful Dead and a we all went to shows together whenever we were able to, all 15 of us. We were also genuine friends with no pretension and I think that's what made it truly unique. In any given group of friends there is almost always some underlying tension or attitude among one or two, but there was none of that what-so-ever in our group. We were all genuine friends and were always there for each other.

In the Fall of 1977, after attending and surviving the Englishtown extravaganza, I returned to high school as a Sophomore and a changed human being. I was used to casual/neat for school, but now I was wearing Grateful Dead t-shirts a lot. Not everyday, but most. I thought it was great to wear just a t-shirt to school after going to Catholic School for eight years. Catholic School made deciding what to wear everyday a no-brainer. In public School deciding what to wear was a new adventure every day. One of those days when I was wearing a favorite Dead shirt, I met a guy named Dale. (God bless him. . RIP bud. . .) He sat in front of me in one of my classes and because of my shirt we started talking about the Dead. He was real friendly and we talked for a long time, given that we were in class at the time. The next day he handed me a tape of a Dead concert, which I brought home and listened to on my little portable cassette player. It was a pretty shitty sounding copy of a show from Tuscaloosa Alabama, May 17th 1977. (Yes, this was most definitely my first live Grateful Dead tape. How do I not remember a tape from Tuscaloosa?) The next day, he brought me a show from Binghampton, May 9th 1979, which sounded better, but not fantastic. Of course, I had nothing to compare these tapes to except albums, so to me it was just so cool to have them to listen to. The next tape he brought to me sounded really good though. This was what got me hooked. This was a classic performance from the Filmore East in New York City on April 26, 1971. This was a soundboard with a few generations worth of bad recording equipment all over it, but it still sounded really, really great. This show is a favorite among tapers and tape collectors, which most of us are now very aware of. I got a much better copy of this Filmore show some years later. As for Tuscaloosa, I always wondered if there was a better copy out there and to that end, The Grateful Dead released that show in the May '77 Boxed set, which is the reason I bought it!

When my tape collecting adventure began, it wasn't easy getting good quality tapes from people, because I didn't have anything to trade. I pretty much had to rely on the occasional give away from a kind hearted soul. That's one of the reasons I never made people 'actually' trade with me. If I had something that somebody wanted all I needed was a blank tape and some patience and I'd just do it. This could be for a friend of mine or a friend of a friend. Another reason was that I enjoyed making copies for people just to see a smile. Eventually I had a bunch of tapes within my grasp, which could make it difficult to decide what to listen to at any given moment. So, when somebody wanted something specific, that would give me a reason to dig something out. Mailing lists were another thing altogether. I had a couple of friends that would hand out their address at shows along with promises of copies of the show, but I could never wrap my head around that. I was far too lazy, once I got home, to bother with mailing anything. I did do it once, maybe twice when I was first starting out, but soon I started getting real honest with people and just saying no. I never considered my attitude about it being mean, I was really just being honest. Unless you have a lot of patience for that sort of thing it just becomes a headache.

I really find it so funny that our music sources have changed so drastically since I was a kid. I used to carry around a box of tapes and my D-5 everywhere I went, so I could DJ the party and (secretly control the room) listen to whatever was new and interesting. Now the music is just so available that it's no longer necessary. Everybody that wants it has an ipod and a collection of CD releases from the Dead's vault. Do I miss those days? Absolutely, but I do have a nightmare story about them good ole days.

I've seen the bumper sticker a hundred times, but it was always on a car. I swear if I had seen them for sale anywhere I would've bought a bunch and stuck 'em all over the place, because you know what? Mean people absolutely do suck! Thieves are worse. When Rick showed up to my first garage party, he brought with him four people; Jimmy Belles and his brothers Tony and Bobby from Avon and another friend named Eddie. Eddie was from the surfer crowd in Belmar. (This was something a little different for us) Eddie lived on 12 avenue in Belmar, two blocks from the beach. The house from where my first tape deck was stolen. Without this event, however fucked up it was, I would've never been able to buy my D-5M. (Even fucked up shit happens for a reason)

By 1980 some of my friends were already married. Two that are prominent in my story are Mike and his wife Patty. They had a house in Spring Lake Heights that had a great party yard in back., and this was the one bad memory from that house. I was pretty much the house DJ at that time. I'd bring my tape deck sometimes, but usually just a box of tapes. Cassette tapes of live Grateful Dead shows, (naturally) usually my latest acquisition or just something that I was really into at the time that I wanted to share. The box held only 24 tapes, so I had to be somewhat selective. At this particular party, there was a small group of unknowns that were hanging out. I'm not even sure why they were there, but as the night flew by and the party was winding down, I noticed that my tape box was not where I'd left it. Those strangers that were hanging out were also gone. The story was that two of them had orchestrated the theft together. One handed the box of tapes out the bathroom window to the other. They thought it would be cool to steal some Grateful Dead tapes. This was extremely upsetting to me.

I honestly can't remember anything in my life, up to that point, having that much affect on me. Even my DWI in 1982 was just something that was bound to happen to any one of us. The way we all drove before, after and even while drinking back in those days is laughable, even scary in comparison to today. The DWI wasn't so devastating that it hurt me. I just "Finally got caught!" With the tapes though, I remember being really pissed off and upset and hurt like never before. That first night after they were stolen I remember talking to my mom about it and crying' Asking why would someone would steal something from another person. She didn't have an answer for me, but it definitely helped me a little to talk about it. I could never understand the reasoning behind that. Does a person ever consider their own feelings when they steal. How they would feel if they were violated like that. It's really so personal that unless it happens to you, maybe it just doesn't register.

To get to the heart of the story, I need to go back to 1979-80. Through my friend Dale Curtis (and his friend Claudio) who started me trading tapes, I met my friend Brian. From the time he and I first met he has been one of my most consistent friends. Over the years, we have traded tapes and kept in touch, even throughout my marriage when most friends at least temporarily part ways. While I was usually the guy in charge of the tunes at our parties, he was always good for a "tasty morsel" as he would put it. I would have a full box with me and most often he would have one or two tapes with him that I didn't have and they would always be great choices. He and I have been through a lot together and have remained really good friends through all these years. Brian was the person responsible for returning those tapes to me.

Through a series of conversations we figured out that one guy, a friend of a welcome guest at Mike's house, was primarily involved in the theft. When I heard his name I was shocked, I recognized it from my younger school days. We found out where the guy worked and three of us went there and paid him a visit. It was me and my friends Mike and Jeff. When we confronted him he denied knowing anything about it, but we could tell that he was lying. His face was surprised and scared at the same time. We told him that the tapes had better find their way back to me or we would be back. It was all so out of character for me to do something like this. I'm so non-confrontational, it was totally bizarre for me to be involved in this gang type of threat. I was there because I had a few very good friends who were willing to back me for this particular purpose, and I will always be grateful for the support that they gave me.

Anyway, here comes Brian's part in this whole stinking mess. A friend of his from his small neighborhood was showing them off to him and Brian had heard that I had tapes stolen from me. His friend was familiar with the guy whom we had confronted a few days earlier that was at Mike's house. Brian called me at about 10:00 one night, probably a week after my tapes were originally taken and couple of days after our little visit. He asked me a couple of questions and then said, "I think I found your tapes." Thankfully he was able to get them back to me un-damaged and all together. I'll never forget that. By the way, Brians mother worked for the artist John Bass, whom I talked about earlier and actually painted the Ice Cream Kid mural on the shirt that I forgot, or left behind in Glens Falls a few chapters ago.

My infatuation with the Dead, going back to the beginning, started when I was out at McNichols in 1979, but my introduction to their music was much simpler than that. Listening to U.S. Blues all those years ago, I felt the lyrics were fun and the music was very different from anything else that I had heard. The other songs we listened to on Mar's Hotel were Loose Lucy and Pride of Cucamunga, but the next song that I actually knew the words to was One More Saturday Night. Later in the same week as I was hanging with Mike at his house, he played that song for me from Skeleton's From the Closet, an earlier Best of album that also included Sugar Magnolia, Friend of the Devil, Uncle John's Band and Truckin. Mike told me the first three lines from the song and then said, "Just listen." It was just me and Mike and we listened to this song.

"I went down to the mountain, I was drinking some wine. Looked up into heaven lord I saw a mighty sign, writ in fire across the heaven, plain as black and white get prepared, there's gonna be a party tonight, uh huh, hey, Saturday Night....uh, huh, One More Saturday Night."
Hunter/Weir

Since that time I have seen the Grateful Dead more than 150 times and I've traveled to twelve different states across the country including Pennsylvania, Maine, Connecticut, Maryland, Florida, Rhode Island, New York, Virginia, North Carolina, Colorado, California, and of course New Jersey. I've seen Jerry by himself and with his own band a bunch of times and Bobby Weir in all his configurations a bunch of times too. I've been on the bus since 1977. Deadheads know that 'On the bus' is another way of describing a fan of the Grateful Dead, other than just being a Deadhead. In Bobby's song 'The Other One' Weir explains it pretty well.

"We were skipping through the Lilly Fields and we came upon an empty space, it trembled then exploded, left a bus stop in its place. The bus came by and I got on, that's when it all began."
Weir/Barlow

That's definitely when it all began, for all of us. And that's the way Deadheads see it. This experience that we are all having at this very moment, started when we got "on that bus". However, I'm not a person who thinks that a you have to go to hundreds of shows to be considered a Deadhead. I don't think you have to go to any shows to call yourself a Deadhead. Take a look at all the people who were never able to witness Jerry on stage with the Grateful Dead. They are just as much "on the bus" as I am and just as much as any one of my friends who spent hours on the road with me. My thought is, being a Deadhead is more a frame of mind than it is a history of travel. To me (and most of the Heads that I know) it's just about loving the Grateful Dead. Even if you've never seen the band play, you can still appreciate them. The jamming on stage and the camaraderie within the audience tells the story.

Now getting back to my friend Mike. His influence on our music appreciation was wide and varied. He introduced us all to Dan Hicks, Tom Waits and Robert Hunter. He was one of the few people I know of from back then that had a real appreciation for Hunter's solo stuff. We would listen to Garcia's Reflections with the Might as Well and Mission in The Rain and They Love Each Other and then go to Hunter's Tiger Rose, Cruel White Water, One Thing to Try and Promontory Rider. Mike, Patty and I saw Hunter perform before I saw Jerry for the first time and I have always loved watching Hunter perform his on songs.

So now these other friends of mine come into the picture. In the Spring of 1979 I made a new friend that would change lives and make every party we had that much more interesting and fun. I was graduating High School in June of that year, so my parents gave me permission to have a party in our garage to celebrate it. We had already hosted a Wedding reception for my cousin just a few months prior, so I knew it could be done. The whole family was invited plus any friends that I wanted. We had a keg of beer and lots of food. The garage was swept out and reorganized. Even my Dad was happy to admit that when the party was at our house the garage was the cleanest that it ever gets.

One afternoon after school, a week before graduation, I was headed toward my bus and I spotted this guy wearing a jean jacket with a Skull and Lightening (Grateful Dead) patch on the back of it.

I walked over to him and said, "Hey man, you going to see the Dead at the Garden."

He said, "Yea man, you going?"

"Absolutely." I said.

So we started talking and I told him about the party I was having and gave him directions, "Right down the street and make a right, you can't possibly miss it."

He said he'd try to make it and then I got on the bus to head home.

Two weeks later he showed up and brought a carload of people with him. New friends, Shooter, Ed, Jimmy and Bobby. I had my stereo set up in the garage and tapes were spinning. My friends and family were gathered together to applaud my accomplishment (High School Graduation). Most of the family filtered out by around 9:30 that night, but most of my friends hung in there until real late. (Or real early) There were probably fifteen of us, including the guys that Mike and Gregg and my brother just met, and we were all Deadheads. What are the odds of something like that ever happening? What an incredible party that was, and it was the first of many.

Soon after, Rick had a graduation party at his house and it was at this party that I met another lifelong friend by the name of Tom. He was an established Deadhead taper. I remembered seeing him out at McNichols Arena in August, standing by the soundboard, arms folded, pretty much motionless, (he was certainly not a dancer) so I introduced myself to him that way. I asked him if he had a tape of the show from McNichols. He said that he did and then I asked him if I could possibly get a copy. I told him it was my first time out to Colorado and I was really excited about being able to get a copy of the show for myself. I didn't get it right away, but eventually I did. There was a soundboard (SBD) copy going around among tapers at the time. Tom's roommate Barry had made a few copies of the show form Tom's tapes and they were floating around pretty freely.

This was something that I didn't have access to yet, but everyone said that the soundboard copy was so superb sounding that it was like listening to a different show, and there is a great story behind this.

The back story: Tom was on tour in the deep south in 1979 at a show in Miami, when he opened up a conversation with Dan Healy and made a connection. Healy saw that he was using his oversized portable Nakamichi 550 to tape. There were only few Deadheads out there using this massive machine. For all its inconvenience, (bigger than most VCRs and it ran on eight D-Cell batteries that sometimes had to be changed between sets) it produced some great sounding tapes. A few times when he had difficulties getting it past the guards he would give up his batteries on the premise that without them, the deck would be useless. Then on the inside he would have friends with extras. I mentioned before that the first time I saw Tom was out in Colorado at Red Rocks, or rather at McNichols Arena in August of 1979. He was standing by the soundboard taping (presumably). During drums, Healy asked Tom if he could borrow his audience master for the night just to see how they compared, because the sound was so good from that vantage point. Given that Healy is the sound engineer for the Dead, he pretty much has to loan him his copy, but Tom figured, 'as long as we're having this conversation, why not go for a trade'. It took him the rest of the show, worrying that he might never get his tapes back, to ask Healy to loan him his copies for the night. He agreed, they swapped and Tom spent the next couple hours tracking down his friend Fredo (my future friend) to borrow his deck without actually telling him why he needed it. He figured that if he told his friend he had Healy's masters, there would be a whole massive mission for everybody to get first gen copies. He didn't want that hassle. He tracked Fredo down, and somehow coaxed the deck away. He copied one tape that night in his room and the left the two decks spinning the second set in the backseat of whatever vehicle he was using for transportation while they ate breakfast the next morning. That night at the second show at McNichols's they exchanged tapes again.

That's how everybody got a soundboard copy of that McNichols Arena 'Shakedown Street'. If you're a taper and don't have a soundboard of that show then you're probably under 30. So sorry. Anyway, during this particular tour there were times when Tom was unable to get that monster of a tape deck into a show or two. One in particular was the Tampa Fla. 12-13-78. Tom decided to take a chance and knock on the back door of the coliseum, just to see who might answer the door. Luckily for him, Dan Healy happened to hanging out with some crew members so when the door opened and he saw Tom, he showed him right inside. Right time, right place. Tom was also short on blanks here and wondered out loud if Healy might happen to have an extra or two at his disposal. No surprise, Dan was able to loan Tom two Maxell tapes that night.

Back to February real quick; This tour was really filled with nice surprises. Early in February 1979, Tom and his friend Tony were heading out to the Mid-West to catch a few shows, but Tony left before him and managed to get to Carbondale, University of Southern Illinois in a blizzard. He had his D-5 with him, but couldn't find anybody in the hall taping. (To this day an audience copy has never surfaced) There was a night off and then they played Kansas City, where Tom caught up with him. Tom didn't have blanks or time to get any so he mentioned his dilemma to Healy and he came through with two for him. After the first show Tony arranged a ride on the bus with members of the sound crew (the band had rented their equipment from Clair Bros. for that tour) and one of the guys from the sound crew noticed Tom's deck and asked for a copy of the show. He handed Tom one tape, assumed blank, labeled Carbondale and Tom stuffed the tape in his pocket and told him he'd be happy to make him a copy. Tom saw that the tape wasn't wound completely to the spool so when he found a quiet moment, he listened for any sign of music and figured out that it was the first set from Carbondale, recorded from the board. He never did make the copy or ever see that guy again, but the story goes on. To this day Carbondale was a mysterious show. The odd sequence of songs, none of the set lists that are available are correct. In Parish's book he talks about Jerry having some kind of meltdown during the show and the band slipped into a drums sequence in the first set apparently to allow Jerry some time to get it together. On the tape it comes out of drums and into Miracle > Bertha, after which Weir says, "short break". It remains a mystery what actually transpired, but the tape that he got from the sound guy that night matched a unique discoloration of the tapes that Dan loaned Tom a few nights prior, so it definitely came from the same box of tapes. Any tapers that have this show, you now know where it came from as well. By the way, since it was obviously the band's copy of Carbondale that Tom wound up with, he eventually mailed them a copy of the tape with a short bullshit explanation. Also the second night in KC, Tom again was not allowed in with his Nak 550, so he and Tony went around to the back door and knocked, hoping for a small miracle and Healy and a crew member happened to be standing by the door, opened it, and allowed Tom in with his deck.

Anyway. If I may go back to Avon where I was. Tom and I met there at Rick's house and a little more than a year and a half later, we started trading a lot. (another story later tells how this came about) Tom had a lot more shows than I did, and luckily for me he was generous. It was very funny really. Everytime I would go over to his place, even for a second to drop in, I would head right to the stereo rack and pick up whatever tapes he had been listening to, like a kid in a candy store and Tom would give me a look, over his glasses. . ."I'm actually on my way out at the moment. See anything you like?" I would reply, "These will do just fine". That went on for what seemed like forever. Rick and I became very close through our Grateful Dead connection and continued to hang out and party and exchange tapes via my sources and his. Tom was slightly less available. With a different circle of friends, we didn't get together as often, but everything changes over time. Tom and I became real good friends through a taping exchange and some occasional parties. However, we also had our first born sons six months apart and with that, it became a more normal family relationship with birthday parties and everything else that goes with that. Rick and I never had that connection.

Truth be told, I am Rick's son's Godfather. A title I hold proudly. Still, I don't see Ricks family very often.

Still, it amazes me how many people I met through my connections with Tom and Rick. When it comes right down to it, I met all those people through my connection to the Grateful Dead. Without that borrowed Steal Your Face jacket on that beautiful sunny afternoon in High School, I wouldn't have spoken to Rick and who knows how long it would've taken for us to meet. But since then, right after graduation, Rick and the friends that I met through him, and those that I was already hanging out with were pretty much inseparable. On any given night a phone call could be made and it would turn into a party. We'd get together every weekend and a couple of times a week and get a ¼ keg every time. We quickly became very friendly with our local liquor store owner. He gave us the tap and never questioned the whereabouts of the kegs unless we had two or three backed up at any given time. We were paying just $21.00 for a 1/4 barrel, when everybody else was paying up to $27.00. We saved a lot of money, and avoided the inevitable mess that comes from cases and cases and cases of beer.

The end of the summer was now coming and I thought it would be a great time to have another garage party. I thought I needed a reason for the party so my parents didn't think it was just to drink beers and listen to Dead tunes, but they were into having my friends over and it was the end of summer! The first garage party I had was in June of 1979 and that was definitely more a family graduation party, but there were a lot more people at this one. It was really more an open house this time, with at least another dozen or so that I didn't even know. The crowd had increased at least that much with just local Deadheads that would be friends of mine for years to come. It was during this, my second garage party, that Don and I made a stronger connection.

I remember The Other One was blasting through my speakers and I was just looking around at the people in my garage when I noticed Don was sitting on the edge of the overhang in what is essentially the overhead storage part of the garage. I climbed the same ladder that he had used and sat down next to him for a few minutes. Before I tell this story, I have to say that the one thing that I've always appreciated about Don was his depth of intelligence regarding most subjects and the absolute look of joy on his face whenever he was listening to the Grateful Dead. So as 'The Other One' was playing I asked him about the lyrics.

"Don, "What are the words there?" *Spanish lady comes to me, she lays on me this Rose*.?"

He said, "I'm not sure dude. Might be *'she lays on me this prose'*

I said, "Sometimes, you just don't know? Right."

He said, "Hey man, as long as you love the Grateful Dead, what difference does it really make, you know? You love the Grateful Dead right?"

"Yea. . .Definitely." Enough said.

My favorite hippy. He's responsible. Responsible for bringing the Grateful Dead into our world. I introduced him to a friend one night and said, "This is my friend Don. He's responsible. Right Don?"

He said, "That's right man!" No explanation was necessary.

These parties were usually kept going into the early hours of morning, (typically fueled by some hallucinogenic compound) and usually one of our neighbors (we knew who it was) would invite the cops around 10:30 or sometimes closer to midnight. No doubt, they would always show up and usually with some sense of humor. You have to know or remember that this was 1979-'80-'81 and that was way before cops really cared about kids drinking on private property, or about adults knowing that underage kids were consuming alcohol. They never checked anyone's ID's or anything like that. They mostly just showed up because they were called and they had to. They would ask us to keep it down so they wouldn't be called again because then they would be forced to do something about it. They were never that concerned. It was a much simpler and happier time. My garage parties happened twice a year for three years before I gave up the idea. Not only did they become too much for the aging neighborhood, but I had also moved out by then so the garage parties, like everything else, came to an end.

I didn't go to bars before I was legal. I didn't have a poker face, so I could rarely lie my way in. There was a local tavern that served me once in a while, but even there the regular weekend bartender eventually asked me for some ID and when I couldn't produce, I had to say good night. In November '79 I turned 18, and at the time that was the legal drinking age in New Jersey. In 1980 the drinking age went to 19 and then three years later, to 21. It didn't affect those of us who were legal before the law was changed though, so once I was legal, I hit the bar scene to check out the local talent.. . . Intoxicadoes.

That's a one word description, and the name of local band that was 'the shit' back in the early 80's. The Intoxicadoes played at a lot of clubs in the shore area back then. The Harbor Inn and the Ship Wheel brings back memories, but we saw them mostly at a bar called Park Place in Asbury Park, N.J., one block north of the Stone Pony. (Park Place burned down around 1985) We would go every Wednesday night for dollar Heinekens and classic rock n' roll. Lead very efficiently by Mr. Billy M. on lead guitar accompanied by Roger on bass guitar, George on rhythm and Leo on drums. Billy is still working the shore area today. These guys played everything that was on the radio; Skynryd, Dylan, Dead, Stone's, Beatles, Pure Prairie League, Jimmy Buffet, and I could go on, but you get it. My two favorites were Amy by Pure Prairie League and Sweet Home Alabama by Lynryd Skynryd. For the longest time I thought that Amy was an original tune. . . . funny! The following they had packed the bar on a Wednesday night almost every week, and that says something.

This was a time in everybody's lives when it was not considered a very bad thing to be driving drunk. For that matter, it wasn't even considered risky. Those of us who were 18 to 21 years old then, remember that you could drive home from almost anywhere you happened to be drinking and only if a cop had a reason to pull you over, would he stop you, and only if you got into an accident, would your sobriety be in question. That's not to say that no one got DWI's then. If you got pulled over for a legitimate reason and you were visibly inebriated (and you didn't have a name you could drop) then they would nail you for sure, but the punishment for a first offense was community service and a fine, not loss of license.

When I was about 18 years old, maybe 19, I was driving down Main Street, between parties during the day, with two friends in the car and each of us had an open beer in our laps, which we were drinking. I was pulled over and we were asked to get out of the car, so we carefully put our beers on the floor at our feet and stepped out of the car.

"So, where you guys heading?" One of them asked.

I just shrugged and said, "A friends house."

Then the cop says to his partner, referring to me, "You think he needs a haircut, or is he standing on a tilt?" They both laughed. Ha ha. . .

The cops searched the car (just barely) and quickly found the beers on the floor.

Again looking right at me he asked, "You think that it's wise to drink, while you're driving?"

We looked at each other and realized that we weren't in a whole lot of trouble, so I said, "We didn't want to throw them away, so we just took them with us."

He said, "Well, dump them out now, and be more careful from now on." He told me that he stopped me for a bad taillight, but he let me go with just a warning. Boy, how the times have changed. The whole incident lasted about ten whole minutes and I don't think I was even a little bit nervous.

We followed the Intoxicados through the bars of the Jersey Shore for a long time and after a while they just kind of disappeared. That left us with no other choice than to have our own parties and provide our own entertainment until we heard about another bar band that was making the rounds. My friends and I caught up with these other guys quickly. A Dead coverband called Thunder Mountain Boys. We became friends with these guys by shear repetition. Whenever we showed up at one of their gigs, they would always announce our presence and then the party would start. They referred to as "The Belmar boys".

The Belmar Boys primarily consisted of myself Mike, Patty, Gregg, Jeff, Ray, Shooter, Rick, and Brian. I remember one night we showed up to the Brighton Bar in Long Branch and we were kinda late. As they finished the song they were playing, Terry stepped up to his mic and said,

"I guess the party can start now. I see the Belmar Boys have finally made it.

Welcome guys! Here's some Grateful Dead for you"

Their repertoire included a little bit of everything; Jimmy Buffet, Van Morrison, Lynryd Skynryd, Paul McCartney, Rolling Stones, Beatles, Marshal Tucker, Charlie Daniels and of course the Grateful Dead. They even had a couple original tunes that they played once in a while. In fact for the longest time I thought Pencil thin Mustache was theirs. There were several bars in the Shore area where they played on a regular basis, but the most memorable events were what they called wetdowns. These wetdowns were fire department sponsored events, (essentially fund raisers for whatever was needed for the company at the time) where the band volunteered their time and talents to raise money for the fire company. It was called a wetdown because they would take their fire hoses out and wet the new trucks down for the first time to christen them. The main source of fund raising was simple enough. Buy a plastic mug for just $5.00 and drink all afternoon for free. There was a 50-50 drawing for cash and a 'big wheel' for low key, in-house gambling. These were the best outdoor parties of the summer.

Aside from the wetdowns, one of the most memorable gigs they ever did was a biker rally that was organized one Saturday afternoon at the PortHole in S. Belmar. We had a table outside in the back where the band was playing and the bikers shared a couple tables facing us from the other side. We were just a bunch of Deadheads getting drunk and listening to our favorite Dead cover band and suddenly somebody started a chant that bounced back and forth between us and the biker dudes. . . "Your side sucks" was the chant that started and we were just screaming at each other at the tops of our lungs. The band got involved a little bit, with a little impromptu background music, but for the most part it was just us and the bikers. At first I felt a little intimidated by the whole 'biker motif' that was staring us down, but there was absolutely no reason for it at all. It became so much fun that we were laughing and cheering and having a great time.

Thunder Mountain was a regular attraction at the Porthole for a few weeks prior to this rally. The Porthole's drink special at the time was $1.00 Long Island Iced Tea pint's. This was the first time I had ever tried an LIT, and boy does that sneak up on you. I was sitting at a table, just finishing my third one and I stood up to hit the restroom. I took one step and realized at that point that my legs weren't going to cooperate too much with my effort. It was rough, but fun. For those who are drink recipe challenged . . .It's made with vodka, gin, rum, triple sec, and sometimes tequila, with a sour mix fill and cola for color. (Some places don't add the Tequila unless you request it). Funny thing is it tastes exactly like an Iced Tea. It's just refreshing in an entirely different kinda way. (See above description)

Another great gig (tongue in cheek) was at the Brighton Bar as I mentioned a second ago. This place was such a dive that we had bumper stickers made up that said, "The Brighton Bar sucks" and we all put them on our cars. I have to say, with pride, that these guys were our house band for the longest time. Then there came a time when they just disappeared. Two of the members from this band would be a part of my life for a long time. (Present day) The drummer, Donny eventually married my friend Patty, whom I met when she was very young, and the Bass player Larry, who has played in several different bands over the years. I've also reconnected with lead guitarist Terry, and rythym guitarist John. When I ran into Terry after not seeing him for almost twenty years, I gave him a CD copy of the only Thunder Mountain show I ever recorded, back in 1980 at the Tropical Pub in Belmar. I also made copies for Larry and John and the end result was a Thunder Mountain Boys Reunion. The boys, now known as Thunder Mountain Band, are now slightly older, but better than ever. (And I am taking full credit for getting these guys back together)

These days we have another band in our midst known to all as Blue Hiways. Chris, Bobby, Kenny, Kevin, Donny, Bunker and numerous guests. They are an class act. They have a repertoire that is matched by no one. Every year on Halloween, They put together a special show. (the first year they dressed as Devo and performed Houses of the Holy) They pick an artist and perform a complete album from their collection. This Halloween gig has become the stuff of legend and has added countless songs to their already incredible repertoire. It has also become as popular, if not more so, than their New Years show. Since their performance of *Houses*, they have also covered Who's Next, Revolver, The Doors, Dark Side of The Moon, The Joshua Tree, Some Girls and Born to Run. A lot of bands, who perform regularly on the Jersey shore, never quite find the time to rehearse much,(I would think that every gig is a rehearsal for most, maybe I'm wrong) but for these special gigs they take the time and literally put on a show. It's a phenomenon that their fans (all of us) look forward to every year. Can I say enough about Blue Hiways? Maybe not.

Shortly after coming off the road from a tour in the Colorado Rockies, (Red Rocks '83) when I was just about 22, my brother and two friends decided to get a place together and split the rent. It was a winter rental so it would be inexpensive. One friend was Billy and the other was Mark. We all got along really well together, so when the idea was brought up to get a place together, we all wanted in. We found a four-bedroom place in West Belmar and became roommates. The house had a brick face with stucco sides and an open front porch with shaky wooden railings and an overhang. Neighbors on both sides made for an interesting situation. It had a large living room just inside the front door and a large bedroom off to the right of that. An extra, full size fridge in the kitchen that we kept stocked with lots of beer.

My brother had a Ping-Pong table that had been stored in our parents garage for a while and he decided it might be a good idea to set it up in our oversized living room. Since we didn't use it for TV or anything like that, it seemed to be a great idea. The first Christmas card we received the first year there was addressed to the Ping-Pong Palace and the name stuck like glue. We had some great fully blown Ping Pong tournaments and some fun friendly games. It's surprising now that we never thought of bouncing a ping pong ball into a plastic cup for a drinking game, huh? Eventually it became warped and cracked from being sat on one too many times by drunkin idiots, so we had to trash it. The Ping Pong Palace was one of the places where I totally lost myself once. I walked into my bedroom during a high point at one of our parties and saw four people randomly perusing through different boxes of my tapes. Oh my God, it was a moment all right. "Everybody needs to leave 'this area right here' like now" I thought I might explode in all directions and somebody was going to feel some pain. Nothing literal mind you. It was just a fleeting moment. The parties that we had at the Ping Pong Palace were somewhat legendary. There are people, whom I don't even remember, that still remind me of those incredible times.

There was yet another group of colorful characters in our shore area town that we met and started hanging around with. It was funny to me how we kept meeting new people, all the time, who were into the Dead. Most everybody in this crowd of new friends was into hanging out and listening this amazing music. These guys had an eight-bedroom house that was four blocks from the beach, and we would hang out there all the time. So much so that we were buying kegs two or three times a week out of shear necessity. This became our flop house so-to-speak, and although there was room available, and we all became friends, none of our crew ever moved in there. This was what I will refer to as the 11th Ave house, and the cast of characters included Z-man, Arney, Leo, California Bob, Jimmy and and one of the most interesting guys I've ever met, Neil.

I will never forget the first time I met Arney. We were hanging out at the 11th avenue house right after the holidays, in January of 1981. When he showed up he had a tape of a Dead show from Pembroke Pines Florida, 11-26-80 where they'd played the Stones' 'Satisfaction' for the first time. I remember this moment because the 26th is my birthday, so I was really jealous that I wasn't there for it. Arney had taken an unauthorized leave from Uncle Sam, and had been 'hiding out in a rock n roll band', (from one of my favorite Dead songs, U.S. Blues) He was literally on the road with the Grateful Dead for over a year and a half. I thought that was the coolest thing I had ever heard.

Then there was Z-man. He was the main drug source in the house, the guy with the money. For the longest time none of us (Ok, maybe just me) really knew anything about any of it. He was never flashy about it. He shared a house with five other guys and his story was vague, which kept us guessing. Throughout the early 80's, as is the case now I suppose, drugs were so available that they were difficult to refuse and the popularity of acid among Deadheads was fueled by the availability and the quality of it. The acid that was around on tour was mostly blotter acid or four-way. There was also the kind that was like molded hard plastic. I first time I saw this on tour was at the Spectrum. It came off a large sheet, roughly the size of a pane of glass and it broke into little square pieces, hence the name, Window Pain. Those two and little barrels that came in a variety of different colors were the most widely available amongst those Heads on tour, but what we had available in our little circle, was liquid.

Liquid was made up of crystalized acid, dissolved in distilled water and it was extremely potent, depending on the dilution. (More about that later) This being said, there were people at shows that would walk around with those personal sized spray bottles filled with water and randomly spray the crowd as they walked through. It was actually very refreshing to get sprayed, but. . . sometimes those water bottles were dosed too, which made for a very interesting evening for some unsuspecting person. Imagine that surprise creeping up on you.

I first met Neil at the 11th ave house in Belmar in the winter of '81. Neil was a taper with tons of cash. (Because he was also a dealer) Neil traveled to Europe with the Dead over the next tour, in Spring '81 and recorded everything, so we had tapes of all those shows as soon as he got back home. Those shows included that incredible acoustic performance at the Melkweg in Amsterdam, (I mentioned earlier) a show that also included rare performances of Gloria, Hully Gully and Lovelight in the electric set. Because of Neil, these shows were floating around our circle almost immediately. He was such an incredibly nice guy. He seemed really smart and was very friendly and generous. He passed away in the Fall of 1981.R.I.P. One of the other guys that I knew pretty well told me that when he was on the road with the Grateful Dead he was the their main connection for acid, for at least a short period of time. So we had the same acid connection as the Grateful Dead. . . . That was a Wow! And this was very easy to believe since the whole Dead community seemed so close to us at that time. We had our own information hiway without the internet back then. We knew people from one end of the country to the other, so everybody played phone tag.

'California Bob' was also a part of the group that lived at the house. Z-man introduced us to him exactly that way, "This is my friend 'California Bob', we grew up together and then he moved out to Cali for about 6 years. He just moved back cause things didn't work out so well for him out there. Now I bust his chops all the time calling him 'California Bob'." He was as nice a guy as you could possibly meet. He's the guy that sits down next to you in your favorite bar and buys you a drink just for the conversation. No pretension. No bullshit about him. Just a real straight shooter and a good friend.

Jimmy is a naturally easy going, insightful, comical guy. Really into the acid scene. A lot like Arney in the sense that he could go to a family function tripping his face off, as long as he knew he could smoke some pot along the way to take the edge off. On occasion, I ran into people that would take acid and go about their day as if they were simply having a cup of coffee. They were both like that, and they were both very friendly with my friend Fredo, who was also exactly like that.

The weirdness in that house made us all take a step back. It was a really great situation though. Any time you wanna stop by and check out the crowd, there was almost always something going on. Sometimes early in the evening during the week it would seem somewhat normal, people just hanging out watching TV or making something to eat, but if you stopped by on a Saturday or Sunday morning there would be unfamiliar bodies, lying asleep, in whatever position they landed in, the smell of stale beer and wet cigarettes filling the air.

Garcia and Hunter

During an interview in years past, Jerry was asked about what priority the Grateful Dead did or did not hold over his own band. Whether he would ever consider leaving the Dead behind to pursue his own interests and his response was simple enough and humorous. Not verbatim. 'It's kinda like being married and having a girlfriend on the side. The Grateful Dead is essentially my wife. The players in the Grateful Dead care a lot about the music and can share a stage like no other group of musicians in the world, which makes the process of making music always fun and interesting. My band, in what ever form it takes, with whatever players are in it at the time, is a wonderful outlet for my other musical styles. I wouldn't want to give either one of them up.' And so it goes with 'the wife and the mistress'. . .

Regrettably, I didn't see the Garcia Band a lot. Considering how often he showed up on the East coast I should've seen him a lot more. I think I saw Jerry Band 28 times compared to over 150 Grateful Dead.

The first time I saw Jerry's Band was at The Barn at Rutgers University, on February 22, 1980. I went with six friends plus one that lived on campus at Rutgers. Myself, my brother Ray, my old faithful Joe, his brother Tom, Mike and Patty, our friend Gregg and Maureen, who was our host and Joe and Tom's sister. We made it to her apartment a little later than we would've liked, but not too late to enjoy the atmosphere and imbibe. The only concern I had was not having a ticket, but this worked out very well for a first timer. We were able to walk the short distance (about five blocks) to the Theatre or Hall or whatever they called it, yes The Barn and thankfully it wasn't a far walk because it was a bit brisk that night. Outside the venue, I was still looking for a ticket when a student stopped, upon hearing my plea and offered me his extra for cost. Face value for a student was $8 dollars. He told me it was an orchestra seat, 2nd row center. In one ear, out the other. Had no clue what he was talking about. I don't think I even heard what he said initially. I was just happy to have a ticket. Well, as I walked in and passed by the ticket takers, I told my friends I was gonna go check out my seat and that I'd see them in a bit. (I really didn't want to sit alone) They were all headed up the stairs to the balcony as I made my way through the crowd and walked down the center aisle of the auditorium. When I made it to my seat I found that it was right in front of the microphone, second row! Center! Guess that's what the guy meant when he said, "Second row, center orchestra!" There was one seat between me and the stage. The stage was literally five feet from my seat! Needless to say I decided to stay right there. Big surprise? Only if you're an idiot. It was so amazing to see Jerry so close up! I really wish I was more familiar with him at the time, but I was definitely familiar enough to realize how freaking lucky I was. Funny thing is, my friend Bob was at this show with another mutual friend, but we hadn't had met yet. That wouldn't happen until three months later in Hampton. By the way, my favorite memory of this, my first Jerry show, was watching Jerry play Sugaree, his fingers moving effortlessly up and down the frets during the very long middle jam. The other tune I remember very well was I'll Take a Melody;

'I've seen the rain coming down, the sky was grey with a speck of blue.
Peek through a whole in the clouds, the sun was screaming, HEY YOU!' Hunter/Garcia
Such cool lyrics.

Opening up for Jerry that night was Robert Hunter. Most people reading this probably already know, but he is the guy behind the lyrics for Jerry's music. When I was just a young Deadhead hanging out with Mike and my brother, we would listen to Hunter's Tiger Rose album a lot, along with any Grateful Dead material that we could get our hands on, so I was familiar with a few of Hunter's own songs and a nice chunk of tunes that were written for Jerry. It always seemed to me though, that an artist never plays the songs that you're prepared to hear, like the material on Tiger Rose for instance, but the combination of material made for a great show experience anyway.

I remember seeing Hunter come out on stage with his guitar wrapped around his shoulders, but I don't recall what he played. More than likely though, he opened with Box of Rain and included Pretty Peggio, Brown Eyed Women, and maybe even one of my personal Hunter favorites, Cruel White Water. But I don't know. I saw Hunter for the first time on the first of this month in New York City, and I have seen him a quite few times over the years opening for Jerry and by himself. At this point I was familiar with the material on Tiger Rose, but not much else, other than those songs that he wrote for Jerry. Even those were all still pretty new to me.

Just to clarify; Hunter has recorded several albums of his own material, tunes that were never recorded by Jerry or the Grateful Dead. Even though Jerry was free to delve into whatever material he wanted, the lyrics that Hunter presented to Jerry were written with Jerry in mind. Hunter had a lot of stuff that was never performed by Jerry. Robert Hunter is a poet, who wrote about life. He didn't write three minute love songs like Lennon and McCartney did. His songs aren't about falling in love, so much, but more about having adventures. The stories Hunter told would touch your heart and speak to your soul. They are filled with imagery and metaphors revealing life's struggles. Check out the lyrics to Ripple and then listen to Built to Last. These two songs were written 19 years apart and you can see that the same person was responsible. Hunter painted a colorful masterpiece with his poetry.

Bob Weir's writing partner over the years was John Barlow. Writer, Rancher and Politician, Barlow met Weir when they were both very young, attending the same boarding school in Colorado. It was these two gentlemen, Hunter and Barlow, whose singular contributions to the Dead's catalog helped to keep their music fresh and almost constantly changing. Bringing them out from the depths of cover band hell to create their own unique style and repertoire. These songs were so unique that they were the inspiration for a poster that I bought in 1979, through Relix Magazine. Relix was primarily devoted to Music for the Head and included current articles on the Grateful Dead and other Bay Area bands. The poster was numbered and signed by the artist, Gary Kroman, an illustrator for Relix Magazine. It has 100 Grateful Dead songs drawn on it in a landscape format. I could have had it framed, but I never did take that step.

The first time I saw Hunter perform was at Town Hall in New York City, on February 1ˢᵗ of this same year. Sonny Terry and Brownie McGhee opened the show for him. Sonny and his partner Brownie were Blues singers from the South, and were really good. I went to this show with Mike and Patty way back then and the three of us made the trip back 25 years later to once again witness the acoustic magic of Robert Hunter.

His stage presence was simple, yet very confident. He reminded me of a troubadour. An older, grey haired gentleman with a soulful heart, whose head was filled with exciting stories from a well traveled life. Mike and I had pretty good seats in the floor/orchestra section, with great visibility and excellent sound. I had been listening to Hunter's music again recently and had actually written down the lyrics for one that I particularly liked, so I decided to request this song for myself, just to see what might happen. After Hunter played the first five songs, there was a very quiet moment, so I yelled out;

Arizona Lightening !

Hunter heard me clear as day and started to talk about the song a little bit. He said, "You know, that's a song that I really miss playing. It's not real easy to pull off by myself though. But I really do miss playing that one, you know? That song was written while I was watching Richard Nixon on the television, resigning his presidency, but I really can't do it with out the full band. Not with the same effect anyway."

Then he played a full verse of it, *Arizona lightening, cut out like a thunder shower, voice heard clear across the USA*, with the chorus, on his acoustic guitar and then stopped, repeating and agreeing with himself that he really couldn't 'pull that one off by myself'. This was definitely a moment in time that I will remember forever. Hunter heard my request, addressed it, appreciated it, explained why he couldn't possibly do it, and then moved on. It was so cool. Go ahead and look it up, it's a fun song.

Hunter speaks quite eloquently, as one might expect of a poet, and he enjoys telling a story or two during his shows. He made mention of the shows he had done back in 1980 with Sonny and Brownie and while doing so another fan from across the audience to our left yelled out, "We love you Hunter."

He then added that, "Jerry wasn't shit" and "Hunter rules".

Hunter then stopped what he was talking about to give this guy some attention. He explained to him that, "I don't know where this is coming from, but I have to tell you that Jerry was a really good person. Jerry was pretty much a genius and just a regular guy all rolled up in one."

As Hunter was managing this guy's anger, the crowd was starting to get a little upset about the way the guy was talking about Jerry (I know I was), but Hunter talked him through the bullshit, calmed him down a bit and then continued with his show. The consummate professional, Mr. Robert Hunter. (Someone went to get an usher, and the guy was escorted out)

Another bummer about the show, and a real shame this was. Hunter was playing a beautiful version of *Rueben and Cherise* from Garcia's Cats under the Stars album and someone yelled, "Wahoo!" during a very quiet guitar part. He was doing such an incredible job, had the audience captured, and then he stopped. He folded his arms and rested them momentarily across the top of his guitar and said, "Have you ever just had one of those moments when it was just. . .right there. . .and then it was gone??? Well that's what just happened to that song."

Though we begged and pleaded, but he wouldn't finish it. He said it was done and he was sorry it had ended that way, but that was it. Anyway, Hunter didn't really enjoy the whole 'touring thing' that much anymore, but since he and Jerry had been friends for a very long time, once in a while he could be coaxed into touring a little with "The MAN".

The story he told went like this;

"They asked me to go out and tour with him again and I just said 'Oh, I don't really want to get involved in all that', and they said, "But, you're the only one who can tolerate his. . . moodiness."

Then the first morning, while getting on the bus, Hunter looked at Jerry and said, "Good morning, your great, white, eminence." Tongue in cheek.

Jerry replied, "Rrrrhh. . ." Walked past him and found a seat.

Just one funny, silly Jerry story, as told by Mr. Hunter.

It was just another show on the Garcia Band tour, but this one turned out to be a very special one. It was also the night after my first show at Rutgers, so this would be my second show in a row on consecutive nights. Using my single stereo mic from Radio Shack, (Honestly I had to use it sometimes, not knowing what I was gonna find once inside the show) I taped from the back wall of the orchestra/floor section and the highlight of this one was Dylan's Positively 4th Street. *'You've got a lot of nerve, to say you are my friend'* I was recording with my friend Rick and Jerry played a really extended jam on Friend of the Devil. As the jam picked up tempo Rick sang into the mic; *ladil, ladil, ladil,* (if that's even how I should spell it). Anyway, upon playback his little commentary fits almost perfectly with the jam, but it can definitely be heard. In fact once you pick it up the first time, it's very distinctive. But also very funny. . .

This recording, February 23, 1980 holds some real significance for me, as I made some mention of before, in that it opened up a new avenue of tape traders for me. At one of my garage parties in the Summer of 1980, just about a year after I had met him, my taper friend Tom saw that I had a copy of this show sitting on the stereo ready to be played.

"Where did you get a copy of this show?" He asked, seeming very surprised. I said, "I taped it myself." I said with some pride.

He said, "This Positively 4th Street was incredible."

I said, "You were there too? How funny is that?"

"Yea I was, and I need a copy of this right away. You can have anything that you want from my tapes. I have of ton of shit, seriously."

I said, "I'm sure you do. It's not a problem"

I went inside and grabbed my second tape deck, set it up with a blank, and proceeded to make him a copy right then. We listened to the whole show. Everybody was still asking me to play DJ and keep changing it up, but I was taking care of a friend. Thats what we do, Right? This was the first time I had listened to the whole tape since right after the show too, so it was great to hear it all the wat through. This moment right here was the start of one of the best tape connections and genuine friendships that I've had over these past last 30 years.

And while I'm on the subject of Dylan covers.

One of my favorite Garcia covers over the years was Tangled up in Blue. It's also a Dylan tune of course, and we all know that Jerry loved Dylan's music and played his tunes often. I have loved this song since 1981, I mean really loved it. I knew the song existed before this, but the story about why I love it so much is pretty cool.

In February, 1981 we had been hanging out at my friends house in the Grove and we were having the usual gathering for the usual reason. (His parents liked to head down to Florida in the winter, which was good for us) The one thing about Shooter that was different than the rest of us was his personal search for new and different music. He turned us on to the likes of David Byrne and the Talking Heads, The Clash, Tom Waites and Elvis Costello. However, one of the most memorable moments happened one seasonably mild evening in February when he decided it was time to play the living shit out of Dylan's Blood on The Tracks album. When I say 'played the shit of it' I mean he played Tangled up in Blue over and over again and we sang along with it every time. By the fourth or fifth, or maybe tenth time there were six of us in the little music room (at his parents house the music room was where the stereo was) and we were all singing at the top of our lungs in a classic moment. It's the one strong reason why I'll never forget the lyrics to that song. We listened to the rest of the album too and Buckets of Rain, Shelter From the Storm, Idiot Wind and Lily, Rosemary and the Jack of Hearts are all amazing songs as well. It's definitely one of my favorite albums and one of Dylan's best.

Later in the Fall, Jerry came back around for a few shows with his band, so we went to the Tower Theatre in Philly for Halloween. You would think that Deadheads would come out of the woodwork, all dressed up for Halloween, but it was a bit sporadic. Those that were dressed up went for it, but most didn't bother. Jerry always played great shows with his own band. The major difference with him was that he would play five songs for one show, but it would still last for an hour and a half. Jerry loved to jam a song way out. He played an early and a late show that night and showed us a great time.

Six days later we took off to the Capital Theatre in Passaic for another pair of shows and then Jerry hit D.C. on the 7th, without us. We caught up again at Rider College in Trenton on the 8th. This show was a full house in the Gymnasium on Campus. He opened with The Way you do the Things You Do, and followed it with They love Each Other. Next song was Love in the Afternoon, which I had never seen performed live, I was so psyched. As I was checking my tape and holding my Mic stand, (right, I was holding my mic stand) I saw a flashlight in my face. The guy from Campus security told me I had to stop taping, "Now! And come with me!" He escorted me from my seat and took me to the security office. They confiscated my tapes and my deck and then allowed me back into the show. I couldn't believe how much trouble I had recording Garcia Band over-all. This is why I don't have very many Garcia Masters at this point. The tapes were always available somewhere and the effort was mostly proven to be futile. That said, two days later, another Jerry show at the Palladium in New York. Two shows again, early and late. I recorded from the balcony with a patch to AKG 1000's. Peter Rowan opened for Jerry, but I didn't tape his performance, possibly because we were late getting there or I wasn't cassette tape prepared, if you get my meaning. All said and done, walking out with a tape of that show was an 'in your face' moment for me, considering the bullshit from Rider College. Granted the tapes didn't sound all that great, but it sounded exactly the way we heard it so that's good enough. The following April we hit the Capital Theatre again, this time for two Garcia, solo acoustic performances. Very interesting watching Jerry play by himself on that stage. Almost two weeks later we caught him again, this time at the Beacon Theatre in Manhatten with John Kahn on bass. Dr. John opened for Jerry a lot through the years and this was the first time I saw him. He was pretty entertaining.

The following June there were two more shows at the Capital Theatre and then a benefit show at the Palladium on the 25th. The concert was billed as Jerry Garcia and Friends. As the night went on into the wee hours of the morning, we all became quite disgruntled about the misleading billing, because there were so many other musicians there that night and Jerry didn't come on until 3 am. On the schedule was Rogue, Bo Diddley, Ronnie Spector, Garcia and Kahn, Robert Gordon, and Moonbeam. (Thanks Deadbase) We were all a bit unenthused, (putting it mildly) exhausted and felt a little taken by the whole situation. Garcia and Friends would lead one to believe that it was mostly about Jerry and that the other artists would be joining him on stage, which give me a break, would have been awesome. That's not the way things turned out. Anyway, we all left right after Jerry did his set and sucked it up and moved on.

At the end of June 1984, they (Grateful Dead Ticket Sales; the powers that be. . .) announced that Garcia would be playing at Caldwell College, in New Jersey. This Caldwell concert was an outdoor event, which was not a normal setting for Garcia Band, at least not for me. The city of Caldwell was definitely not prepared for the crowd that showed up for this. People were parking on lawns and abandoning their cars along the street. This was the first year that Caldwell College sponsored any type of concerts in Caldwell and because of all the problems that popped up, including but not limited to neighborhood complaints, this was also the last. The show was on August 11th, and Hunter was touring with Jerry again. This time I went with Bob and our new friend Andy, that Bob and I met out at Red Rocks in 1983 with Bogie and Tokie. We drove up to West Orange via the Parkway to exit 153. From there the College campus is very close. I brought my deck with me, and Andy and I set up in right in front of the board. Hunter's set was short but sweet. He was introduced by John Scher and he played Blood on the Streets Rosanne, which I can say quite frankly is an incredibly long song that I'm not a big fan of. Promontory Rider was next and I love this tune, followed by Brown Eyed Women and Gypsie Parlor Lights. Another song that sounds like he's still working on it right in front of us. Box of Rain followed and then break time. Jerry opened with an excellent Cats Under the Stars and followed with They love Each Other, a song also played quite frequently by the Grateful Dead, and then Dylan's Simple Twist of Fate. Jerry closed this first set with Rhapsody in Red, a rockin song also from *Cats*.

During the break my friend Andy and I were approached by one of the guys from the soundboard and asked about the tape we made of Hunter's set. I told the guy I recorded it, and asked him what he needed to know. He told us that Hunter wanted to know if he could get an audience copy of his performance from someone, so he could check out the differences for an upcoming live album. He asked if he could borrow my tape. My friend Andy and I looked at each other and said, "What d'ya think?"

I said, "We would love for Hunter to check our copy of his show, but we would really like to give it him ourselves, if possible."

He told us he would talk to Hunter and see what he thought. The guy came back about ten minutes later, after we had given up hope, and escorted us to a partial back stage area. It wasn't quite backstage, but it was beyond where we normally would be able to go. Hunter came walking up to us with another guy, presumably a security guard and spoke to us for a minute. I was a bit nervous and felt a little stupid because when I shook his hand I said, "It's nice to meet you Robert, or do you like to be called Bob?" Honestly calling him Robert sounded too formal to me, but I never heard anyone refer to him as Bob. (And did it really matter?) What do I know?

He said, "It doesn't matter. As I already said, I really want to check out the quality of your audience copy and if I use anything on it I will credit you on the jacket. Ok? Just stay in touch through Relix Magazine and that way, I can get your tape back to you." That was it. It was very quick, and it meant a lot more to me than it did to him, understandably. We went back to our seats feeling pretty good.

Jerry finished up his show on a very high note. Opening up the second set with one of my all time favorite Garcia tunes, Mission in the Rain, and closing the show with the very rare Like a Road into Midnight Moonlight.

During the break that night, Andy and I found out that there was a Folk Festival the next night at the Lone Star Café in Manhatten to Benefit the Hungry. Hunter was Headlining, so we decided we would go and check it out. When we got there, I went to the backstage area to talk to him and he was really nice to me. Andy stayed out of the picture for this, although I kind of begged him to join me. I saw Hunter hanging out. I said hi with a wave of my hand.

He nodded. Politely acknowledging my presence.

I also met and spoke to Matt Kelly.

He shook my hand and said, "I'm Matt Kelly."

I said, "I know who you are, it's a real pleasure to meet you."

Then I said, "I'm a huge fan."

Matt smiled politely. He was in Kingfish, a band that Weir was with back in the 70's between Grateful Dead gigs. When I looked back over toward Hunter, he was softly strumming his guitar, living in his moment. I approached him and 'felt the air' for a second. The vibe was sincerely friendly, so I asked him for a favor. "Hey Bob," I said, "I Saw you last night at Caldwell. Loaned you my copy of the show. Remember me?."

"Oh Yea, How Are ya?" He said, politely engaging my inquiry.

"Very good. Would you mind very much if I patched into the board to record the show tonight?"

He said, "Well, thanks for the tape, but you know what, that's really up to the soundman."

Then I said, "I asked him already and he said it was up to you."

(Now I'm pushing it a bit, but. . . we'll see).

Well, he gave me that look 'yea right' and said, "You know, it's like mom said it's ok if you say it's ok, and dad said it's ok if mom says it's ok. . . I don't really know what to tell you, man"

I said, "Really Bob, he said it was fine with him, but if you don't want me to tape, then I won't tape. It's cool."

Well, he took a long deep breadth and said, "You go right ahead, but on one condition,"

I said, "Sure. What's that?"

He said, "I want you to give it to as many people as you can. Ok?"

I said, "Well, that certainly won't be a problem, everybody's gonna want a copy of this. Thanks again."

I shook his hand and left.

The conversation with him was so extremely casual, not like at Caldwell at all. I felt like I was talking to a friend.

No condescension at all. Very cool.

Downstairs, Andy had struck up a conversation with Wavy Gravy, one of the original Merry Pranksters from the acid filled, acid test days of the 'good old' Grateful Dead era. I actually smoked a joint with them, (right there in the bar) just so I could say that I did, and I had a very abbreviated conversation with Wavy. Dam, I wished at the moment I had something interesting to talk to him about. One good question would have been worth a hundred thousand words. . . ya know?

Now, Hunter comes out to play his set, opening with three of my favorite songs (not including the first one cause I really don't know what it was. Still don't) Dire Wolf, Promontory Rider, and Wild Bill. Then he did an interesting rendition of Oh Babe it Aint no lie into Easy Wind. Then, after a short break he came back out and reminded everybody, "Ok, ladies and gentlemen, this here is a folk festival. . . So I must play some *folk* music."

He opened with his own Blood on the Street and then played Brown Eyed Women. I really like his take on Brown Eyed, especially on acoustic guitar. There's not many that could pull that one off, but this is where the story gets really kinda funny, and very cool, from my standpoint. There was a girl that was standing right up next to the stage for most of the show. She was making her presence very known because she kept begging and pleading for Hunter to play a song called Tiger Rose. (*'Tiger Rose, he got new clothes the ladies, love him so'*). The title track from the aforementioned album. He just finished playing Whiskey in the Jar, another great old folk tune and apparently he hadn't played Tiger Rose in a very long time, because he kept insisting that he couldn't play it because he couldn't remember the words. He said that he was really sorry, but he just wasn't prepared to play that song at the moment. He apologized over and over again, but she kept insisting over and over again so, being the crowd pleasing pro that he is, he finally gave in (or caved in) despite his own insistent protests, and probably just to shut her the hell up. (Although he never said that) He started playing Tiger Rose and he ripped through it at lightening speed, most likely hoping that he'd more easily remember the lyrics that way. The song came off really well, by the way and I was just as happy to hear it as she was and the crowd absolutely loved it. As a matter of fact, as annoying as it was to listen to her badger him about playing it, I was really glad that she kept it up. I had never heard it played live before and actually, have never heard it again since, dammit! Whomever she was, my hat's off to her for her relentless persistence. She did a fine job.

So, to recap. . . I was able to get permission directly from Hunter to record the show. I was able to listen to him play on a small stage, literally five steps away from me, in a bar sitting next to one of the oldest living hippies in the world, Wavy Gravy!. . . And!. . . I walked out with a sound-board recording of the show. . . .How do you like them apples?!

All in all I saw Jerry about 28 times I guess, over a period of only about four years. Well not just four years as you will see. My most frequented venue was the Capital Theatre, with a few Tower Theatre shows (Philly) sprinkled in and around some random College gigs. Jerry was playing a pretty consistent repertoire, comprised mostly of the same 15 to twenty songs in no particular order on any given night. He played the West Coast a lot and some out of the way places, so I didn't make as many travel dates for Jerry as I did for the Dead. Then sometime in October 1987, Jerry came back with a new configuration for some incredible shows at the Lunt-Fontaine Theatre on Broadway, armed with some off the usual grid set lists, that brought the attention back to great music.

And by the way, Andy stayed in touch with Relix Magazine about the tape we loaned to Hunter and he eventually got it back, signed by Hunter. Our tape wasn't used for the live album.

Garcia on Broadway

n the Summer of 1986, in the midst of failing health (brought on by undetected and untreated diabetes) and some addiction issues, and also while suffering from extreme exhaustion, Jerry collapsed into a coma,. I will write more about that later, but as I was reading Blair Jackson's book, *Garcia: An American Life*, I came across an explanation for the Broadway shows. While Jerry was making his way back, relearning the guitar and re-acquainting himself with a normal lifestyle, his old friend Sandy Rothman was back in touch with him. Jerry and Sandy reconnected with David Grisman as well, so when Jerry was invited to do a benefit at The Auditorium in Oakland he invited his two buddy's and John Kahn to join him. When Bill Graham saw what these guys had managed to accomplish together he said, "We need to do something special with these guys." Garcia jokingly said, "Hey, lets do Broadway". And the idea was hatched. Bill set up the shows with this particular ensemble, that also included David Kemper on drums. That's how "Garcia on Broadway" was born. Blair Jackson's book is really awesome and everybody should read it.

In October, a full year later, Bill Graham made it happen. He scheduled fifteen nights on Broadway for Jerry and posse, billed as The Black

Mountain Boys, or The Sleepy Hollow Hog Stompers, or just plain and simply, The Jerry Garcia Band. At the time Jerry, Sandy Rothman, Dave Nelson, Dave Kemper and of course John Kahn, were the whole of the band. They played acoustic and electric sets from 10-15-87 thru 10-31-87, that included five matinee performances on thirteen dates, playing a total of 18 shows altogether.

Wow. . .! I only saw two of these shows. My friend Robin got me a pair of tickets for one night and Brian came with, and the other, I went with Tom. Tickets sold out in record numbers, even for Broadway, so they were really impossible to get. These shows featured tunes that had not been a normal part of Jerry's repertoire in recent years. Forever Young, Get out my Life Woman, I shall be Released, My Sisters and Brothers, Crazy love, Stop That Train, Lucky Old Sun, and a few more that were just incredible. Jerry brought his passion for good time music and old time blues tunes with him to Broadway. These were songs that I honestly don't think he had room to play with the Grateful Dead and really, so be it because this was the perfect avenue for him to let loose.

The taping situation on Broadway was difficult, to say the least. Maybe worst than Radio City back in 1980 because of infringement rights. This *was* Broadway when all was said and done and recording of performances of any kind is never allowed on The Great White Way. That's just the way it is. (and who are we to think that we can just 'waltz' into a theatre on the 'famed boulevard' and set up recording equipment) Well, needless to say, it happened anyway, because where there's a will, there will always be a way. People had to go to real extreme measures in 1980 to get tapes out of Radio City.

My friend Tom, that I had been trading tapes with recently, reconfigured two Nakamichi 300's and put them in the sides of a cowboy hat for Radio City. The tips of those mics were built to come apart at the end, so he figured let's just "lose" the rest of the mic for logistical purposes. Then he tucked them into the brim of the hat, so they were nicely hidden from security. Of course, the other problem would be getting the tape deck past the front door. You've got some very thorough security guards at these front doors, protecting the integrity of these famous theaters. I don't know how he worked that out, but I saw someone use a Deadhead chick once for this purpose, a very willing girl to say the least. She heard this guy ahead of me talking to his friend, wondering how the hell he was gonna get his deck in and she interrupted their conversation. She suggested strapping his tape deck between her legs, under her dress. (He looked at her like she was crazy and asked if she was serious. She said, why not?) Well they worked it out right there in line and she just walked right in. If I hadn't seen it happen, I wouldn't have believed it. So with this in mind, all things are definitely possible if you give it some thought and have some serious cooperation. Seriously!

Back to Broadway. . .When the time came to record the shows on Broadway, part of it got a little simpler. (Believe it or not) Recording equipment had gotten even smaller in recent years and younger Deadheads had grown into sneakier, more innovative tapers. DAT (digital audio tape) decks were turning up everywhere. The DAT was half the size of the D-5M that I was carrying and the sound reproduction was impossible to beat. After just a couple of shows there, someone figured out a way to tap into the hall moniters that were set up right outside by the concessions, so we were now getting soundboard tapes of these shows, with one downside. There was some audible hiss and some dropout involved. Not to take away from the effort though, because the tapes sounded really great aside from that. There were really good tapes of these shows circulating soon after they happened anyway and honestly, after I got a couple of them, which didn't take long, it was enough to satisfy the need to relive the experience.

The advertizing for Jerry on Broadway was a full page in the New York Times. It featured Jerry wearing a tux, waving a magic wand over a top hat like a magician. At the first show everybody in attendance was given a Top Hat upon entry and all were instructed to tip their hats to

Jerry when he came out on stage. That must've been a cool thing to be involved in.

The Shakedown Street flea market didn't appear at the Broadway shows, but it did materialize in smaller groups. The heads that normally spent their time in that capacity or venture, did so right on the street going around the corner, while being very unintrusive. This being New York City, you know that a certain amount of vending is put up with anyway, however they did confiscate anything that said Broadway or Lunt-Fontaine Theatre on it because you know some artists were practicing their art without a license. The Grateful Dead related stuff was around, as were a bunch of Garcia Band shirts. I bought a beautiful Garcia Band tie-dyed t-shirt that was covered with bubbles and drippy liquid with hands that appeared to be grasping for nothing while holding on to something else. Very nice shirt, I must say. I have found over the years that the nicest shirts came from Liquid Blue, although for a short time I found some very nice tie dyes that were done by Ed Donahue. His were the first ones I ever saw that had the 'tie dyed ribs' that went down the sides of the shirt so that it's not just a mish mash of colors, but an actual design.

These Jerry shows held a great deal of interest for me, with all the new and different material that I mentioned before. Jerry's love for 'old timey' blues tunes introduced his loyal fans to some great old music. From the look of things Jerry had a lot of fun playing these shows and I know that he made a lot of people very happy.

In July of 1989, it was announced that Jerry was coming around for an East Coast tour. He was playing all the same venues that the Dead would normally play, and he had Bobby opening with an acoustic set, accompanied on stand-up Bass, by Rob Wassermann. I chose to go only to Merriweather Post Pavilion in Maryland, because I had never been there before and it would be a nice Jerry road trip. I'm always up for a road trip, especially when it's a new adventure. My girlfriend came with me this time, and we actually experimented with some mushrooms together. Well, I think she was experimenting, while I was just searching for rainbows in a clear blue sky. Ha ha! I really didn't think she would indulge but I was wrong, and it was a lot of fun. We were standing on a hilly place on the lawn, just enjoying a very beautiful, sunshiny day when she suggested that we find someplace to sit down.

I said, "Why don't we just sit here?" She looked around and said, "Because this looks like a walking area and I don't want to be in people's way."

I said, "Well. Don't you think that if we sit down, it then becomes a sitting area and the people will just have to walk around us?"

Well. She started laughing so hard which made me start laughing and we just sat down and continued to enjoy the day. After we sat down, one of her first observations was that Bob and Rob were already playing and no one was paying any real attention to them. I explained to her that no one was really here to see them. All anybody really wanted was Jerry Band. That's all anybody ever wanted. To see Jerry play, right? Bobby played some Bobby and the Midnites stuff along with My Masterpiece and an old blues tune called Fever. He also did Me & My Uncle and Cassidy, stuff like that. It was an acoustic set and they came sounded pretty good, considering their limitations. Wasserman played an extended bass solo, I guess we would call it 'space'. These shows were September 1st and 2nd 1989...., and they were both released as part of the Pure Jerry Series just a few years ago.

Bobby and the Midnites also toured a lot when the Grateful Dead took a break. The first time I saw them was at the Palladium in N.Y.C. This was Bassist Alphonso Johnson's birthday show, February 4, 1982. The next night we partied at Jeff's house and listened to the Capital Theatre show live. I remember I had to bring my stereo receiver with me because his didn't have a proper output jack for my deck to patch into. Of course I needed to record the broadcast! There were about 25 people hanging out that night and it was a lot of fun. This actually turned into a bit of a tour for us. The next show we went to was the Livingston Gym at Rutgers University, in Piscataway, N.J., on the ninth. I remember walking into the gym as Weir was starting the show with a song called Poison Ivy, and then being so surprised when I heard Big Iron being played next. I always liked that song from Weir's Kingfish days and always thought he should have brought it to the Dead's repertoire. I remember running into Bob and his girlfriend at this show too. Then four months later on the 12th of June we all went to the Capital Theatre. Bobby had some great material with the Midnites and it was so different from the Dead's usual stuff. Bombs Away (almost a hit), Too Many Losers, This Time Forever, Book of Rules, Wrong Way Feeling, Josephine, Shade of Gray, Heaven Help the Fool, and covers that included Poison Ivy, Youngblood, Satisfaction and Milk Cow Blues. Even Minglewood and Around and round made it into the line up. The music was always rocking because that's just what Weir does. He was a genuine crowd pleaser; a rock 'n roller at heart. He could be accused, very slightly of being cheesy, but I don't care. I loved it.

One of my favorite Bobby shows was in Atlantic City at the Garden Pier the night after the Capital show. The Garden Pier was located down the street from the Showboat Casino on New Jersey Avenue & the Boardwalk. I went with Mike and Patty and Rick and I remember that it rained like crazy for about an hour right before showtime. I mean a torrential downpour kind of rain. Ironically, this show was supposed to be on the 13th but was postponed one night due to heavy rain. It was right on the boardwalk, so everything got soaking wet along with the chairs that we were supposed to sit in. I recorded the show with my single stereo mic, because I had no way of knowing what the situation would be like for patching into mics there. It was a good decision too, because I was pretty much taping the show by myself. Bobby and the band had a lot of fun here, playing two shows, one early, one late, and completely different. After the rain, we had beautiful weather..

In 1983 we made a special trip to Nassau Coliseum for an unusual line up. Bobby and the Midnites opened for Hot Tuna so, we had to be there. We, once again had to deal with the inevitable headache that comes with 'Nausea Colostomy'. . . Yes, I realize what I just spelled. We sometimes referred to Nassau that way. It was a fuckin headache from the time you get out of your car until after the show when you're finally back on the Belt Parkway and traffic continues to move. It was actually my friend Bob Smith who coined the phrase. What made this trip so worth our time though was the encore. Hot Tuna came out for the encore and Bobby shared the stage for a lead vocal on White Rabbit. It almost literally brought the house down. Amazing.

Bobby played closer to us just about two weeks later when he hit Rutgers University again on the 10th of November. This wasn't in Piscataway like last time, this was in New Brunswick, N.J. We went see Bobby and the Midnites at the Capital Theatre in Passaic, on August 1st 1984. This was Jerry's birthday, but there was no mention of it and it wasn't expected. The Greg Kihn Band open for Bobby. *They don't write em' like that anymore. Our Love's in Jeopardy,* Those were his biggest hits. He was huge in the loathsome 80's. I refer to it as the loathsome 80's because it was the age of MTV. Every goddamn band that put out a decent single was contractually obligated to shoot a video to go along with it and for the most part, they sucked. They made good songs corny and bad songs soo much worst. Only two good things came out of it; Michael Jackson's Thriller video, which was a stand alone masterpiece; and for the first time we were able to see some of our favorite artists on the screen, even if 90% were lip synching. There were also some live performances thrown in, along with some very old performances from variety shows back in the day, which made it a little more interesting.

Now Where Was I. . .

When last, we left the Grateful Dead, I was telling of the Raven, by Mr. Phil Lesh at the Baltimore Civic Center. My tour buddies and I didn't go to Baltimore, but we had just witnessed the Earthquake show in Hartford. Now that we're all caught up, we can move on to the Capital Center in Landover, Md. 9-15-82. Road Trip! Opened with an incredible Playing in the Band > Crazy Fingers > Lil' Red Rooster, followed by Dupree's > Beat it on Down the Line. It must've Been the Roses > Let it Grow into Day Job finished off a great first set! Second set started strong with a jammy Shakedown Street into Lost Sailor > Saint > Drums > NFA >Stella Blue >Round and Round >Good Lovin. The reason I bring this show up so vividly is because the Grateful Dead played their future chart buster, Touch of Grey for the first time on this night for the encore. Played faster, and with a slightly different lyrical arrangement, maybe due to not really remembering the words all too well for the first go round. Also possible the words weren't quite the way he wanted them yet. Bob drove us home after the show and the next day we split for Portland ME. Now I'm not lying when I tell you that I don't really remember much about this trip to the Civic Center in Cumberland County, but my Masters prove that I was there, and I'm listening to them right now and they sound so great. I can't believe it's been such a long time since I've pulled them out.

(Audience recording with AKG 421's to my trusty D-5M, from right side of the board) By the way, Bertha >Promised land opener; Twelve song first set closed with Throwing Stones, first time played, into Deal. How's that? I labeled my tape Ashes Ashes for Throwing Stones because that's what we thought the name of the song was. The first Touch of Grey, at the Cap Center was played for the encore. Tonights Touch of Grey opened the second set. I was calling it We Will Survive at this time. Instead of singing 'We will Get by', leading up to the chorus of We Will Survive!' Jerry was mostly singing 'We will Survive' for the lead up lyrics. It was definitley interesting hearing their first version of the song again. This was followed by Women are Smarter and incuded a sweet Spanish jam, (somebody keeps yelling very loudly on my tape, first "Rock n Roll!" then "Dark Star!") then it rolled into a slamming, Phil Bombing, The Other One > Goin Down The Road Feeling Bad > Morning Dew > Suger Magnolia. Before they played the encore, Weir says,"Hey listen, thanks for keeping us alive for all these years." Amen. Encore US Blues.

These two were number five and six on an East Coast tour that started deep in the South in New Orleans, then hitting West Palm Beach and Lakeland, in Florida and Charlottesville, in Virginia. After Maine, we skipped past the Boston Garden and then hit the New York Garden for two shows. That's the classic Madison Square of course. The last show of this tour was most interesting for me and my touring entourage. Another road trip all the way to Syracuse to visit our friend Mr. Belletier and see the boys at the Carrier Dome, September 24, 1982. If I remember correctly there were twelve of us, including his college friends, staying at his off campus housing residence. I'm thinking now that it was his roomates parents house, which would of course mean that he totally lucked out on that one. What stands out? Everything that we wanted to do, including going for cigarettes, beers or a bite to eat, was just a ten minute walk away. Jimmy must've said, "It's just a ten minute walk", ten times within thirty minutes or so. Just too funny, if you get me. Opened the second set with Far From Me into Playin >Crazy >Throwing Stones. . .Drums > Aiko, Truckin, GDTRFB. Black Peter >Around and Round >Sugar Mags closed the set. Amazing times with a bunch of longtime friends and my best touring buddy, Bob Smith.

Spring tour started in April of 1983, so we went to the first show in Hampton, Virginia. Hampton Roads Coliseum. The boys opened with Bertha >Promised Land, played eight more songs including the set closer China/Rider. The second set was the killer; opening with Help/Slip/ Franklins, which was crazy. The one thing that really stands out this time was the lack of tickets. The secret was finally out. Hampton was the place to see the Dead play. Don't miss a show in Hampton Va. From here the boys went to Morgantown W.V. I dont remember why, but we skipped that one and the next two; Binghampton and Burlington, New York and Vermont, respectfully. In Binghampton there was a double encore of Not Fade Away > Baby Blueand in Vermont Brent debuted his Maybe You Know (How I'm feeling). I liked this song. Brent didn't play it much. Five times this year and then only once later in 1986. Not recieved well? Maybe he never quite liked it himself, for whatever reason, it was dropped. We caught up again at the Meadowlands, Brendan Byrne Arena, later the Continental Airlines Arena, now simply The Izod Center. Whatever. Here at Byrne, I had the worst seats I have had since my 3rd show at the Spectrum. I think there were four rows between me and the absolute upper level back of the Arena. They played twenty-one songs and brought with them an apperance by Stephen Stills. people still talk about these shows because of him. The ten song first set included Brent's short lived tune, Maybe You Know, Looks Like Rain> Touch of Grey, which was still finding its place in the line-up. (like there's a place) The second set gave up the China/Rider, Uncle John's> Truckin, then after drums Stills joined in for his own Black Queen, which went into Aiko Aiko all day! This was followed by a new little thing that Weir had been doing called Bob Star. *"Long as we got to be, long as we are. I just want to be, one of those little stars. One of those stars, that'll be just fine. All you got to do, is hang up there and shine. . . . Hang up there and shine. Hang up there and shine. Hang up there and shine. hahhh!"*

He did this three times on this tour and that was all we heard of it. No idea what it was about. Maybe a girlfriend. Probably. The next night I had shitty seats again, but I couldn't reach the back wall with a spitball, so I was a little happier. With seats like these there was no taping, which was disappointing at the time. Stills showed up again tonight. The boys opened the this one with their future chartbuster, Touch of Grey.

Getting used to this one. Very exciting. Dupree's followed > Beat it on Down the Line, Roses, Cassidy, Big RxR Blues. Great set. Played eleven songs including Fennario and a Might as Well closer.

Second set; Help/ Slipknot > Franklin's Tower, Women are Smarter > Playing in the Band > drums, and the band is once again joined by Stills for Love the One You're With > The Wheel >Playing> Throwing Stones, which I am still calling Ashes-Ashes on my tapes. Stephen Stills looked like he was having alot of fun up there with Jerry and the boys. I wish I was closer these two nights. The boys split for Maine, Rhode Island, and New Haven next, and we waited patiently for two shows at the Spectrum in a week. The 25th and 26th in Philly were outstanding and I was taping again patched into old reliable 441's to my D-5. Very happy once again, to be walking out with master copies of these shows. I think the show everybody talks about would be the 26th. The Shakedown opener has achieved legendary status, and the Morning Dew was once again epic. I can't begin to describe how intense this Dew was. Most of my readers will probably go put this tape on right now. If you don't have the tapes, you should most certainly go to Archive.

On June 18th, the Dead played up in Saratoga and followed with two shows at Merriweather - Post Pavilion. I didn't go to either of those, but they were also scheduled to play City Island in Harrisburg Pa., so it was time for another road trip. June 22, we headed out to City Island, Pa. The venue is located in the middle of the Susquehanna River, about 15 miles upstream from Three Mile Island, the nuclear power plant, where the worst commercial nuclear power plant accident in U.S. history happened on March 28th, 1979.

I only bring this up because now I'm thinking, 'How interesting is this gonna be.? The Dead aren't real politically out spoken as yet, but some of us certainly are. Deadheads and politics crossover quite frequently as far as I've seen. I thought it was going to be very strange for the band to be playing so close to an area where there was an environmental disaster, without saying anything about it. Well, Bobby took advantage of the opportunity and right before the start of the second set he said, "On your way out you might want to file out by one of the booths that they have set up out here. The Susquehanna Valley Alliance is trying to keep the Three Mile Island place from being opened up again. . .

I don't know. You might also want a. . . a . . radioactive. . active volcano here, what. . .whatever, . . whatever..."

Aside from that, they were just here to play music, and that was just fine with us.

We parked in a lot about a half a mile away and I remember thinking what a long walk it would be back to the car. The walk in wasn't really so bad, in fact it was very casual. Deadheads everywhere, just taking their time strolling along the river, checking out the scene, shaking hands and sharing hugs. Access to the island was gained by way of a footbridge that looked like it was built from an erector set. With steel girders placed strategically across each other for structural support, and covered overhead with a chain link fence type of material. The entrance to the footbridge was lined with beautiful bushy green trees. Sometimes I wish I could go back to places like this and really take it in. I think alot of the background may have gone unappreciated, or at the very least, under-appreciated. Lost, in the sense of being taken for granted. But I guess that falls under the category of not realizing how very lucky we were at the time. Deadheads in the 80's were very lucky. Never had to wait very long for Jerry and the boys to come around, and once or twice on a tour you get to see them in a setting that'll take your breath.

It was a beautiful day to see an outdoor show. Once inside, blankets were laid out and tapers were set up right in front of the soundboard. I immediately ran into several people that I knew. I always loved outdoor shows, maybe because I was so unaware at Englishtown, my first, I don't know but they were always very exciting for me. You never really know what the outdoors might inspire the band to play or how extensive the jams might become, just because of the inherent vibe. The first set was a bit abbreviated, with only six songs played before the break. They played Stranger, Friend of the Devil, C.C. Rider, Ramble on Rose, Brother Esau > Deal. Very short, but I know that they were having issues with equipment, which could account for the abbreviated first set. Weir kept breaking strings; They were plagued. The set was really great though. It wasn't a hot day, but really sunny, so the atmosphere was very enjoyable. The second set was longer, opening with Hell in a Bucket from the new album, a first for us. (At this point the refrain was 'at least it's one hell of a ride' instead of 'at least I'm enjoying the ride', which is what it became). I was calling it "Elegant Pride" at that point too. Bucket was followed by Chinacat > Rider > Playin > drums > Spanish jam> Miracle > Stella Blue > Goin down the Road Feelin bad > Not Fade Away. The encore was Brokedown Palace.

It was a great show, no doubt. People were having a great time dancin around, with themselves and with others. Some with their eyes closed and arms waving in the air, while others just stood in their own space, taking in their special moment. If you take a moment to look around at the crowd during a show, while any given song is being played, you can see the enjoyment and feel the excitement all around them. The people in the audience at a Grateful Dead show have always respected each others space. The freedom of expression that you can experience is one of the best parts about being there. People will move with the music, however they feel, with no concern of judgement for simply allowing the music to send them in any direction that it happens to be going. It's a most liberating feeling, unlike anything else I've ever experienced.

I have to say that I had a very strange, yet normal, human experience right after Stella Blue started. I was really enjoying Stella, and I found myself crowd watching as usual. Then I looked directly behind me and found myself face to face with a cute young girl. I looked directly into her eyes and smiled. She smiled for a moment and then blinked and tears streamed down her face. I also noticed there was a guy standing right behind her, but I reached toward her anyway and placed my hand around her between her shoulder blades and gently pulled her toward me. It was very natural. I was still aware of the guy, but as I continued the motion she came toward me and allowed me to give her a strong hug and returned it. Then I leaned into her and said, "It's ok, Stella Blue gets me sometimes too." Which was followed by an even stronger hug. Then, as she turned to walk away, I gently grabbed her hand and we held together for a mutual squeeze. Then she was gone and I became one with Stella Blue once more. The set ended with Goin Down the Road Feeling Bad into Not

Fade Away, which was like a dance marathon. They closed the early evening with Brokedown Palace, another welcome addition to the day.

Well, as it turned out, that walk back to the car was a much longer one for everyone after all. We all had to funnel onto that same footbridge (the only way in or out), and now that I'm thinking of it; with the whole crowd essentially leaving at once, there was a whole lot more combined weight going over that bridge now than there was on the way in, don't you think? Though I'm certain that no one gave it much thought at the time.

After the City Island show, the boys took off to the mid-west and California for a few months, but within just a few weeks we got the word that they were hitting Red Rocks again in September, so we made plans to hit the Mountains again. This time we wanted to make a vacation out of the tour so we decided to drive, figuring we would stay for a longer period of time; a full week. This was not the usual group of touring buddies here. Bob and myself were joined by four new friends. Frank, Bruce, Rob, Robin and Gagen. Gagen was another taper, who had his own mics, Sennheiser 421's, so we taped together.

We left on Saturday afternoon taking the Garden State Parkway up to 280 west. We took that to I-80 west and just kept on going. Once we got into Pennsylvania we thought the drive would never end. Pennsylvania is one long ass state. Christ it seemed to take forever. Over three hundred miles worth of forever, but it's absolutely beautiful. All along the highway, aside from the billboards advertising hotels and restaurants, there are clusters of mountains with dense patches of trees and thick forests stretched across them for miles. Then you ride for several miles with nothing but cornfields and cow pastures and silos off in the distance. (This was my first big road trip for a Dead show, so I took a lot of pictures) The next state we hit was Ohio. Another 200 miles of farmland, but compared to Pa., it was a cakewalk. We hit Indiana next, which was filled with more billboards and such. A hundred and sixty miles later we hit Illinois. Anyway, on our way out there we drove through the night, switching drivers only twice. In fact one time we switched without even stopping the van. I stood behind his seat and held the steering wheel while Bob slid out from behind it and then I slid smoothly in behind him. It was a funny moment for us and then we just kept on driving. Eventually, we made it through Iowa and almost five hundred miles later we hit Nebraska. While driving through Nebraska overnight, Bob discovered a kind of natural phenomenon. He figured out that if he could creep up close enough to an 18 wheeler on the highway he could coast for at least a little bit. It wouldn't work behind any other vehicle because the wind rides the outside of the car in front, and then hits the next car in line. So Bob would set the van right behind the trailer and could virtually coast under the power of inertia. The van would slow down and lose the connection, but it would be cool for a little while. He'd put the van in neutral and say, "Look guys, no gas !!"

We stopped in Nebraska very early in the morning and grabbed breakfast. Then we did something that I had never done before nor have I done since. The 'dine and dash'. How did that happen? Well, everyone had gotten up from the table separately to go to the bathroom and freshen up and Bob went outside to start the van. Then as each of us returned to the table, we observed that the waitress was really nowhere to be seen. So one by one we just left and piled into the van and drove away. So we had breakfast on 'Sally' the waitress. We're so sorry. It wasn't meant to be malicious, in fact it was funnier than it was necessary really. It was just one of those things, in the moment.

Once in Nebraska we started heading south. Rt. 76 off of I-80 and twenty minutes later we were in Colorado. We then found Rt.70 and ran right into Genesee Park where Chief Hosa Campground is located. We made one stop at the beer store before going to the Campground, and that would be the local supermarket. We bought five cases of Coors, Cold Mountain, Fresh Brewed, ice cold beer, and then headed off to Chief Hosa. We drank those five cases of beer the first day, but guess what we didn't know? When we arrived on Sunday afternoon the liquor stores were all closed and the only beer that can be sold on Sundays in Colorado is 3.2 beer. It's 3.2% alcohol by volume rather than the typical 5%, we were accustomed to. What did we know? But that's why they went so fast, it was like drinking spring water.

The campground was nicely laid out, very clean and spacious. We were the only people there at the time because we were three days early for the shows. We had the site at the very top of the campground and there was more than enough room for about 12 tents in a large circle. As we prepared the campsite for our tents we pulled all the equipment out of the back of the van and all at once we realized that we had a pretty good fireside seat staring us in the face. We pulled the couch out of the van and carried it over toward the bench that was provided. The couch moved several times before it found a real home, but it was a great idea that we could all take credit for. We spent our first two days in the camp playing frisbee and hackey-sack. We even took a walk through Red Rocks National Park to see the Amphitheater where the band was going to play. It's a pretty amazing sight to see even when it's empty. We spent an hour or so hiking and exploring through the venue and the Park. I went all the way up to the top where the rock formations come to a point and I could see all the way into the downtown area. It was Tuesday afternoon when people finally started arriving and our little campsite was starting to hop. I had called my friend Tom back in N.J., and told him where we were staying. He eventually showed up with Donny and Wayne. This was Wednesday morning and the camp was beginning to fill up.

Another group of Deadheads that we met there who were also from New Jersey, a town called Matawan. Jimmy, Andy, Bogey and Toki. All were instant friends and welcomed into our little communal party. Jimmy was going to college, Andy a taper head, Toki an amazing artist, and Bogey was a fun loving, amazing human being with the ability to turn any given situation into something positive. We all remained friends for a long time, staying in touch after going back home. Bogey joined us for an East Coast tour in 84 as well. Bogey and I became instant friends and developed a catch phrase while we were hanging out together that followed us through all three shows in Colorado. We were both obsessed with the song, Money Money, from Mars Hotel. The lyric is, *'Here she comes finger poppin' clickety click. She say furs or diamonds you can take your pick.'* (Music and Lyrics, Hunter/ Garcia) For a full day before the second Red Rock's show, every time we saw each other we would say that in unison. Eventually we would just say, 'Here she comes finger poppin' and high five each other. It was very funny. I still think of Bogey sometimes. In 1984, after our East Coast jaunt, Bogey went to see the Dead at the Greek Theatre in California. The night of the 'shooting Dark Star' on July 13th, Bogey fell from a ledge outside his hotel room window. He was found early the next morning by some passers by and he was already gone.

Bogey (John Fitzgibbons) was a restless spirit, always looking for a good time, so I believe that it was just a freak accident and nothing more. There was a sadness and an uneasiness at his wake. I wasn't sure how welcome we would feel, considering the circumstances surrounding his death. Since he was on tour when it happened, I really thought that we (Deadheads) would be looked down upon, but it wasn't the case at all. When I went to greet his mom, whom I had never met until that moment, she held my hand and thanked me for being his friend. It was a short conversation, and that was all that was necessary. Rest in peace my friend.

Red Rocks Amphitheater was a very special place to see the Grateful Dead play, with spectacular views and some particularly amazing shows being played there. It was however, one of those places that was known for its frequent casualties. We occasionally heard of someone that was hurt or fatally injured at a show, after a show or while on the road. These things will happen and I guess a lot of times they can't be helped, but I am very thankful at this point in my life that it wasn't a frequent occurrence and that all of the people I was with remained safe.

Second night of the Red Rocks Experience brought me my current favorite song, Jack Straw. As I stood in the crowd next to Bob, I heard something in the air. I felt a familiar tone about the next song. I said to Bob, "If the opener is Jack Straw, I'm running down as close to the stage as I can get, so see ya." I love Jack Straw. Not even sure why. It might be that version from Red Rocks '78 when I first heard it in my car in its entirety. Sitting by myself. The jam at the end of the song is off the charts at that show. Anyway, I heard those familiar notes from Bobby's guitar and I was 'away like the wind'. I was stopped in my tracks at about 10th row and without being intrusive on anybody else's good time, edged my way to a great vantage point. I stood in that spot through the next four songs, Candyman, Lil' Red Rooster, Loser, Brother Esau, and then returned to my seat for the end of the set. It was absolutely a pretty special place to see your favorite songs performed.

The third night (9-8-83) opened with the killer Shakedown Street, followed by Mama Tried and Big River and now I have to pause for the mention of standout. Ramble on Rose. I think Phil was trying out a new bass or a new string or something, because he bounced some rocks out of place with this one. If you have a tape of this show and don't know what I mean, then give it another listen. *"good bye, mama and papa,"* careful now Phil, *"good bye, Jack and Jill,"* Wow! It definitely deserves mentioning, believe me.

So let me recap. Even without a complete set list, looking back over the three nights, there were 52 songs played and only two songs were repeated. Throwing Stones and Hell in a Bucket achieved those honors, but in the defense of the repeats, they were working out a couple of new songs and it was over three nights. Show me another band that would repeat only two songs in a three night stand. I challenge you.

The campsite grew pretty large and the partying that took place over the 3-night run was epic. The only plan that we actually made, was to go out there to see these shows. Everything else just fell into place and the fact that our other friends from New Jersey had planned to come out as well was an unexpected surprise. We had a campfire every night at the site and plenty of cold beer. The weather in Colorado that week was generally mild. The afternoon temperatures peaked around 80-85 degrees and the nighttime temps got down to 55-60. (Some things you just don't forget) We were about 7000 ft above sea level, the skies were clear and bright. The stars we could from that elevation were really spectacular.

As we readied ourselves for our departure we took great care in leaving the site just as we had found it. "Leave nothing behind but footsteps" is how it goes. Leave the camp the way you found it or better. It's always nice to leave a courtesy pile of wood for the next group of campers too. The drive home was sooooo long. It took us 32 hours to drive out there and a little bit longer than that to drive back. We took the north route again and hit Pennsylvania the next day in the afternoon. Once you get to Pa., it still seems to take forever.

After our short trip out to Red Rocks, we only had to wait about one month for the Grateful Dead to show up on the East Coast again. After only five more shows the East Coast tour started again. Instead of the usual start-up in Hampton they played shows in Richmond and Greensboro first. Though it didn't mean much at the time, rumor had it that they sound checked with St. Stephen in Greensboro. They randomly sound checked a lot of different songs on tour that we would never get to hear. In October '83, the band showed up at Madison Square Garden. My friends Rick and Bob and I took the train all the way from Belmar to New York-Penn Station for the show. There have been times when we decided it best to drive up there, but we were pretty psyched to take the booze train. We were allowed to drink beers for the whole ride up with no hassles. The only drawback was 'commuter traffic' in the form of human bodies. Oh, and a stop every eight and a half minutes. That was definitely a pain in the ass.

So, as I made quite clear earlier in my story, our presence was quite acceptable in the City of 'unique personalities'. Madison Square is an excellent place to see the Dead. Not unlike the Spectrum, the venue itself adds an inexplicable energy to an already hyped atmosphere. The first set on opening night had Weir digging in with Wang Dang Doodle > Jack Straw. Then Jerry did Loser, which always captures our attention. The second set started off with a semi-normal opener; Chinacat > I Know you Rider then Playing in the Band > China Doll, which lead to a rather intense drum jam. Out of drums the band went into a very strange, spacey jam. This space jam lead to something unbelievable for us. Garcia started hitting a very familiar note sequence that had Deadheads looking all around at each other, especially in the taper section. We all recognized what was happening, but we still couldn't be sure until that exact moment. Well, the moment came, and the band brought St. Stephen back into the line-up for the first time since January 10th 1979. There were 352 shows played since they last broke out St. Stephen. (Thank you Dead Base) The audience tapes of this show are barely audible because the crowd that night went absolutely crazy. We joked about it later, saying that they were scraping Deadheads off the ceiling of the Garden for weeks after that show. It was one of those moments in time where you just hoped that it didn't end too quickly and you were thankful for recording capabilities. We just had to relive that moment over and over again. It was a very special time on tour for everybody. St. Stephen went into Throwing Stones and then into Touch of Grey. Touch was relatively new at this point, but was gaining some momentum with its *"We will survive"* chorus and all. Since its debut at the Cap Center, this song has continually gotten better over the years. It's really no wonder to me at all that it brought so many more people into our world.

Continuing the experience at the Garden the next night, we saw the rarity of It Must've Been the Roses and the always welcome Cassidy followed by Cumberland Blues in the first set, then and an amazing He's Gone followed by drums into a rocking Truckin'. The highlight of this particular show was the encore, which surprised us all. Jerry played the opening notes and everybody just kind of looked at each other and then started to cheer. The Grateful Dead were covering John Lennon's Revolution. Wow!

Bob, Rick and I continued our trek up North to Hartford for two shows, where we stayed at the Ramada Hotel right downtown and we were able to walk to the show from there. Our seats for the first night were behind the sound board, but the chairs provided a pretty good view of the band. I patched into a nice set of mics called Bouer, that belonged to my new friend A.J.. This was the first time I had used these mics, but not the first time I had heard of them. My friend Bill Nolan told me about these before and he liked them a lot, but aside from all that, I was happy to try something new. The first set this evening started off with Alabama Getaway into Greatest Story Ever Told. This combo was being played pretty quite frequently of late but it was great. Afterward Jerry played a nice They Love Each Other and Bobby hit us with C.C.Rider. The second set opened with Scarlet> Fire -Estimated> Eyes into drums and then Bobby and Jerry, alone on stage, jammed out a nice rendition of Alhambre. This jam was also referred to as Spanish jam, but my tape is labeled with the former. This jam turned into the Other One as Phil, Brent and the drummers returned to the stage. Then Stella Blue and Sugar Magnolia ended the set.

The second night in Hartford was extra special and I'll tell ya why. We were sitting in the 21st row center, and I was patched into my old faithful, yet still not quite favorite, Sennheiser 421 mics. The first set included a few not-to-oft played; Brown Eyed Women, Wang Dang Doodle and Big Railroad Blues and ended with (Keep Your) Day Job, which was the only song repeated from the two nights. It was the encore the night before. The second set is where the real surprises take place. Jerry opened Chinacat and that jammed into I know you Rider, then the seemingly unavoidable Weir standard, Playin in the Band into Jerry's soft ballad, China Doll. At the end of China Doll the band slipped into 'rythym devils', so they rocked the house for about eight minutes. At this point Jerry and Bobby stepped out on stage and began to play off each other, becoming one in their musical interlude. Pretty soon the rest of the band joined them, and then it happened. What happened? This is what happened. Jerry began to play that series of notes that are so familiar to those Deadheads that are looking for it, and then those two notes come flittering off Jerry's guitar; dot--daah. (Phonetically speaking) And here it comes again. For us it's the second time Jerry has played St Stephen in four shows. The first was just three shows ago at the Garden, but the thing here is that we are much closer to the action. Also, it's so much better, even for the crowd the second time because the drama and excitement of the first time is kind of over and now we can all enjoy the song as it's being played rather than just being thrilled that it's being played. I vividly recall being somewhat proud of the fact that we had all been there for the first one, though I'm relatively certain that a lot of these people were right there with us. Bobby followed 'Stephen' with Throwing Stones again and then rocked the house with One More Saturday Night. The encore that night didn't matter much after all that and honestly it doesn't matter that much now either. It was Brokedown Palace and it was becoming quite the staple encore after a series of shows in any given city. . .

Springtime in 1984

The Grateful Dead were making their rounds again in the Springtime 1984. This was part of a thirteen show East Coast tour that we were jumping on the bus for. It started with two shows in Hampton on the 13th & 14th. We stayed at the same campsite at the same KOA, (I think they were really starting to like to us) and set up 'house' for the weekend. We all had tickets this time, a lesson we learned from last time, so we didn't have to worry about that. We got beer and a couple coolers of food and had a blast. We even had some mushrooms for this trip. (That would be the Psilocybin kind, not the stir fry) These are grown in and around cow manure and contained a natural hallucinogenic. It was a much more comfortable high, less edgy and not as trippy as acid, and an easier comedown. I found it much easier to be normal in any given situation, when necessary. Thought processes are more controlled, making it a lot more fun. The shows were typical for this time in Grateful Dead history, still figuring out what song goes in which position, as if there is a reason for any placement. They opened with Day Job, not a typical opener, but we were happy to hear it, not as an encore and then came Dire Wolf, a personal favorite of mine. The set ended with Hell in a Bucket > Don't Ease Me in. Second set included the Wheel > Truckin'> Goin Down the Road Feelin Bad, very sweet.

Going back to the campsite after the show we were all a little restless and expressed it freely. We had a fire going and someone (probably Mike) put an oversized log on an already blazing fire. We thought for sure we were gonna get a visit from the camp master at least, if not the cops, but there was no sign of either. My friend Bruce, who was with Bob and I out at Red Rocks last year found himself in a bit of a situation. He had eaten some mushrooms like the rest of us, but had also indulged in some acid and was exploring the outer edges of his own universe at this point. He now decided to take a stand and express his thoughts via 'soap box' as he stood on the log that had overtaken the fire and proclaimed that the "K.O.A. was AOK...!!!" And that all this could happen, "Only in Virginia. . . Only in Virginia....!!!" Now I'm thinking. . .

"Bruce, you really oughta think about getting down off that log, before it really catches fire." (I'm sure someone must've said something to him about that, but I'm not sure who. . .)

It was a great night, with a clear sky full of bright stars. We couldn't have asked for a more perfect setting for our 'after concert' party. We drank the beers and listened to the show on an acceptable boombox, while we talked and laughed and had an awesome time. The next morning everybody woke up the feeling pretty good, considering and then had to go out and replenish. More food, more beer, and a full day of the parking lot squat. The scene in the lot was always lively and exciting between shows, so that's where we spent the better part of our day, checking out t-shirts and seeing new faces and meeting old friends. Killing time talking about last night's show, wondering who was going where next. It was all part of the larger than life, social gathering. This is what most of the parking lots were becoming, a seemingly unintrusive hang. The problem was that by the mid 80's, people that didn't get in would just hang out all night in the lot sharing stories. It was innocent enough at first, but later on it became a bigger problem between the band and the venues where they staged their magic show. After *Touch of Grey* hit big, the crowds got even bigger because everyone showed up thinking they could always find 'just one ticket'. Then they stopped caring so much about getting in, because the scene outside had become so inviting it didn't matter anymore. I'd say that nearly half of the 'Shakedown Crew' had already planned to stay camped with their wares, so they were very content to keep those ticketless heads company. The more obvious this became, the more trouble it created, even though the problem wasn't so evident as yet.

Anyway, the second night was filled with more great songs, another two shows in a row with no repeats. Our first set started off with a nice long Feel Like a Stranger followed by They love Each Other, then C.C. Rider, Brown Eyed Women, and My Brother Esau, then Tennessee Jed into Let it Grow finished off the first set. Even though it was a short set by some standards it was excellent to hear They Love Each Other, which doesn't get a lot of stage time and Brown Eyed Women is a great sing along song. The second set started slowly with a Touch of Grey opener. Touch usually starts out with a strong bass line, but this one was a gradual jam that led into the song. Then Playin in The Band > Terrapin followed by a new Brent tune called Don't Need love. This guy had a thing for love gone bad, good times gone real bad, all good tunes though. This went into drums and flowed into a beautifully powerful Morning Dew > Throwing Stones > One More Saturday Night. The encore was Baby Blue.

After the shows in Hampton Bob, Rick and a new fellow traveler Dave, drove up to the War Memorial in Rochester, N.Y., for one show and then on to the Niagara Convention Center on the 17th for another one without me. After that, the boys were headed down to the Civic Convention Hall Auditorium (that's a mouth full huh?) in Philadelphia, for two more. The band hadn't played at that venue in Philly since 1973, so there was some hype surrounding it, however over the years, I had heard tapes from those shows in and the sound quality wasn't all it could be. Anyway, Bob called me from Rochester the next night and asked if I might want to meet them in Niagara and that he would drive me home the next day. I told him that I wasn't prepared to commit to something like that, but that I'd definitely see him when he got back and then we'd head down to Philly together. I was telling this same story to two of my co-workers the next day and they thought I was being ridiculous. First; it was a Tuesday and I was only working until noon that day. Second; I was off the next day. My friend Lisa kept telling me that I should just go. She wasn't even a fan of the Dead, but I guess the idea intrigued her just enough to talk me into it.

She said, "I don't know what the problem is.

If it was me, I would just go. Why don't you just go?"

I didn't have an answer to the question, not one that made sense to me anyway. So my internal wheels started spinning. At that time, Peoples Express Airlines flew business flights to key cities on the East Coast with really affordable rates and they had flights to that area everyday. When I got home, I called and made a reservation. I got an early flight and drove like a mad man up to Newark Airport. I parked in long-term parking and ran to the Peoples Express Gate. I boarded the aircraft, which was full of Deadheads, and within minutes had a ticket in my hand. I brought my tape deck with me, which could be considered a little risky because I didn't know exactly what the situation might be up there, but so be it. We all got off the plane at Niagara International Airport, and as I started looking for a cab or something for the next leg of my excursion, I found that there were buses that ran every half hour that went straight to the Convention Center! Holy Shit! I hopped on the first bus that was available and sat very content, waiting for my next stop. After a twenty minute ride, I got off the bus, put my tape deck over my shoulder, my jacket on over that, and proceeded toward the entrance of the Civic Center. I walked through security with no problem at all, and who do you think was the very first person I ran into. . .

My friend Bob. . .!! He took one look at me and said, "Noooo, I'm not coming! I can't commit! What the FUCK man, how did you get here? Did Scotty beam you ? . . !(both of us laughing)

But really, why didn't you tell me you were coming, man? I would've met you at the airport dude."

I said, "I just decided to come up this morning, and the trip was going so smoothly that I just figured I would surprise you. How's that?"

He said, "Nice job Jimbo. Cool surprise." (Big Hug)

The show, by the way, was excellent. (What else?) I was patched into Nakamichi 300's, sounded awesome. They opened with Jack Straw, Direwolf, two of my favorite songs. I remember going for a beer during Jack Straw and as I was headed back to my Deck, Jerry broke out the Dire Wolf. I won't go into the rest of the set list, but as I mentioned before, they played an excellent Eyes of the World in the second set, so needless to say, it was well worth the trip. Sometimes being spontaneous is so much a part of being a Deadhead. The next day we went to the Canadian border and crossed over to check out the Falls from that side. We ate lunch at a restaurant that overlooked the Falls and then went outside and stood along side it, just watching it for what must've been close to an hour. It was really strange and very exciting being so close to the Falls. I thought about what it must've been like to take the barrel. I envisioned barrels going over and splashing down under the weight of all that water thinking, what the fuck are those people thinking. It's not really something you can actually practice, right? What an incredibly crazy thing to do. I also thought about that scene in 'Superman II' when Lois jumped over the railing to try to prove that Clark was really Superman. Ha! That failed miserably.

What was really weird though was the heat that the water generates. I could literally feel the heat coming off it. If you've never experienced Niagara Falls up close and in person then it's a must. We didn't do a tour of the Falls or anything, but just the sight of it up close is awesome and it was fun to be there, if only for an hour or so. We took the whole day to drive home and of course, we had to stop at Newark Airport to pick up my car. This remains the most spontaneous adventure I've ever embarked upon, to go to any show, and it really was worth all the time and effort, if only to see that look on Bob's face.

The next shows that we hit were at the Civic Center in Philadelphia April 19, 20 and 21. The first night we had floor seats, next two nights we had 12th row in the lower balcony. The shows were really exciting of course, but the outside was not as accessible as others where you could actually hang in a lot. There was a parking garage on the corner of Market and South Juniper Streets, right across from Philadelphia's City Hall, but we were not allowed to hang and drink.

From New Jersey we took the Walt Whitman Bridge to the Delaware Expressway North to Market St., and that goes straight into the Civic Center. Leaving this place sucked as I recall, because it's all one big cluster-fuck as everyone tries to leave at the same time. As I said, the shows were really great, packed with Grateful Dead favorites. There were 46 songs played over the three nights and only one song was repeated, but within any given two or three-night stand there were usually very few repeats. I'll have more examples later in the story.

This tour continued on to New Haven Connecticut for two shows, Providence Rhode Island, for two shows and then Nassau Coliseum for two more, but I didn't go to any of those. I don't remember if my good buds went or not, but I'm guessing that work got in my way. The next show that I went to was City Island, Harrisburg Pa., June 23rd . (It was nice that we never really had to wait very long for them to come around again) This time Bob's friend Frank drove his Suburban. So, under the heading 'You can't judge a book by it's cover' we had a cross street neighbor that was mostly silent, but usually cranky when he opened his mouth. As Frank pulled up and we were milling about for a few minutes, getting our proverbial shit together he eventually came walking over toward us with that all too familiar grimace on his face. He was pretty silent as he checked us out, looking at the stickers on the truck and his opening remarks caught us all off guard.

"What is this Grateful Dead? Must be against God to have a name like that. I think you all need to think about what direction you're lives are heading."

"Oh, no. It's not like that at all", we said, "It's just rock n roll. Well it's not really just rock n' roll. It's the Grateful Dead, which is something that's kind of indescribable, unless you have some time."

He walked away muttering to himself and shaking his head. I think he was genuinely concerned for us.

Anyway, there were six of us this time and it was much roomier in Frank's truck. We had a better idea of where to park this time because we'd been there before. The crowd had grown a little, but that was just typical as the years went on. I met a few friends on the inside and one of them had some mushrooms with him. This was Dave who I have, and will speak of again. He had already shared part of his stash with his buddy and when he saw me he asked if I was interested in the rest. The rest wasn't much, only about an inch and a half piece of a stem. It was very dried out looking with faded blue and green colors running through it. (Yes, I remember it that well) That was a good sign, in my limited experience, but I still didn't think that it would be enough for me to get off. I ate it and didn't give it much thought afterward.

This was a sunny afternoon show, and quite crowded in front of the board where we were. I had my D-5, extra batteries and an extra tape just in case. They opened with Alabama Getaway > Promised Land and then played a really sweet Fennario. The set ended with a rockin Music Never Stopped > Don't Ease Me in. Music is a funny song in a way because it's not a really long song, but when the lyrics are done they generally tend to jam it out big. There was that show out in Red Rocks in 1978 that I mentioned before, when they played a version that just might be the best or at least the longest one that they've ever done. Just when you think it's over, someone is just not quite happy with it. . .

The second set offered up a nice, basic selection of songs, but remember those mushrooms that I wasn't really too concerned about? Well, the air slowly became sweeter. Then there was a breeze that seemed to be swirling around me and the band started playing right to me. It was one of those moments that I've experienced countless times before, when it didn't matter what the hell they were playing, just that 'I was there, and the Grateful Dead was on stage'. If you've never been in a situation where you truly believed that you were exactly where you're supposed to be at the moment, then you're really missing out. I've had that feeling a lot of times when seeing the Dead. Every time, I guess.

Oh yea, the second set started with a Touch of Grey, followed closely by Estimated Prophet > Eyes of the World. This was one of my favorite set opening songs and it really is such a great song to see, played outside. Eyes was followed by drums > space > Truckin > Peter > Around and Round > Goin Down the Road > Saturday Night. Encore, Day Job. Excellent show, great time, saw a little rain during the second set, but no big deal.

Saw a little rain, but no big deal? At least, I didn't think so at the time. We packed up our stuff (Yea, I'm the only one with 'stuff' here) and started heading back to the entrance (now the exit) and of course the crowd had thickened. We started up a small hill that lead to the pathway that lead to the footbridge, and my feet were trying to slide out of my flip flops. The hill was slick from that little bit of rain we had during the show, and my feet were sliding to the left and the right as I took each step up the hill. I had to walk up the hill with my toes pointed out to the sides while clenching the little plastic nub between my toes for what little support I could hold on to. What made this even more frustrating was that I was carrying my D-5 by the shoulder strap, and the cassette door (which was broken) kept swinging open and slamming shut, several times along the way. (Given the circumstances I am surprised that I was even aware of that cassette door) The hill also seemed a little steeper going up than when we had come down it earlier. All this time I'm still experiencing a mushroom high that was unexpected and still quite pleasant, considering.

When we finally got to the actual exit something incredibly funny happened. We were moving very, very slowly toward the exit doors, which weren't actually doors because it's outside, so it's like six doorways, sort of like going through customs at the airport. Suddenly someone starts to moo…like a cow moo? We're moving like snails, funneling through these six exit doors and we all joined in for a spontaneous "Moo!". Everyone caught on to the idea at once and we all started to laugh about it and then it was over. It was a very funny moment.

The Full Fall Tour 1984. . .

The Fall tour rolled around and this time we decided to go all out. I mail ordered tickets for the whole thing. We all did. I took a week off from work for the out of area shows. The only show we didn't hit was the last one in Syracuse NY. This tour could be considered one of the greatest run of shows on a tour since the late 70's. I know that's a huge blanket statement to make, but as I go along it will become apparent. For the first two shows we set out in Bob's van with four of us. Me, Bob, Tom, and Donny all piled into the van and went to North Carolina. The first show was in Charlotte on October 5th. We had to pick up another friend in Fayetteville first. He had moved to North Carolina years ago, but had lived in the shore area throughout his younger years. We caught New Jersey Turnpike and followed that all the way down 95 south, through (or rather around) Washington D.C., and down past Richmond, Va., straight to Fayetteville, N.C. We picked up Mr. 'Fayetteville', and then headed out to Charlotte.

The road to Charlotte was all back roads and small towns, such a long ride. We drove for what must've been two and a half to three hours at speeds of up to 45, but not less than 30 miles per hour. Bob made the funniest observation when most of us weren't even paying attention. He noticed a sign as we came around a bend in the road that said 'Limited Sight Distance'. He pointed out to us weary travelers that the first letter of each word read from top to bottom spelled out LSD. "L.S.D.? he he" That kept us laughing silly for a few otherwise boring miles. Once we got to the area we found our hotel and got a few beers. (You know that when I say 'we got a few beers' I mean we bought a couple cases) Then we made our way over to the Coliseum to hang out. We all had tickets to the show so we were good. I was taping every show this tour and I had my taper seats, and my D-5 and I was stoked!

The first show of our tour was pretty special, but the weirdest thing happened. The band was playing Duprees Diamond Blues and I felt something happening behind me. I wasn't exactly sure what it was, but it felt like someone had spilled a soda right behind me and it had splashed up on my pants. I turned around to find that one of our friends (the guy that we had picked up down there, Mr. Fayetteville) was taking a piss on the floor, right behind me, right near my tape deck.

I looked at him and said, "Are fuckin kiddin me, or have you lost your fucking mind?"

He looked at me with a drunkin-ass smile and said, "Well, when ya gotta go." and shrugged his shoulders without another word. I turned away just shaking my head, and moved all my stuff about five feet ahead of where I was. I told my friend Tom about the incident later and he just told me to take it from where it was coming from and really couldn't even begin to explain it. I wrote him off as being a dirt bag and left it at that. I haven't seen him since it happened and I can certainly live without it. God, that was disgusting! We took this guy back to the main hiway after the show and dropped him off, probably twenty miles from where he lived, and he hitched home from there. That just happened to be the plan from the beginning, but thank God it was preplanned that way. I didn't want to spend one more minute in the van with that creepy guy. By the way, this was the furthest South I had traveled to see the Grateful Dead so far. Before this tour, Hampton was our southern trip so since we were so far down south, there was really no one there that we knew except those we were there with.

From here we took off for Richmond on Rocktober 6th 1984. The first set opened with Hell in a Bucket, followed by Dire Wolf. Yeah, I don't know why exactly, but I really love that song. Dire Wolf just really makes me dance and sing, *Pleease don't murder me!..* Followed by Cassidy, They love Each Other, Minglewood, Tennessee Jed. The set closed with Looks Like Rain into Don't Ease Me in. The second set went like this: Scarlet Begonias > Fire on the Mountain > Playin in the Band > China Doll > drums > Throwin Stones > Goin down the Road Feelin Bad > Saturday Night. Encore was Day Job

Next shows were in Worcester, Massachusetts on the 8th of October, 860 miles away. Before we left we picked up our friend Dave again. (The kid I got the mushrooms from in Harrisburg) Dave was much younger than the rest of us, by about 3 or 4 years. That's not really considered much younger, but I was the youngest at 23 and he was 17 or 18, so that's kind of young, I guess. I was honestly a little concerned about the long drive with this younger kid, but it turned out that he was a very smart and extremely funny guy with great timing. We laughed so much on the way to Worcester that the ride went by really quickly. At one point while talking about favorite songs, he started singing a parody of 'Don't Ease me in' that was cracking us up.

Don't eat, don't eat. . .Don't eat green cheese, I've been out all night and I'm really hungry, but don't eat green cheese.

And it went on from there and it was really hilarious. A nice four and a half hour drive (after already having driven up from Richmond for six) straight up 95 North into Worcester. This was a city much like Philadelphia where the Civic Center was, except that we had actual parking lots to hang out in. Some more active partying than others. There were lots of drugs for sale. Sheets of acid, baggies of mushrooms and some weed too. The parking lot scene was really becoming quite the sideshow in the mid 80's. I know that Deadheads didn't invent the idea of tailgating, but for me it was brought to a new level. It was like going to a flea market or a county fair where the theme was 60's memorabilia. You could buy almost anything. Every ten or twenty feet the music would change, fading from one vehicle to the next, neighboring cars kind of respecting one another. In this area you could also stand in one spot to either find or sell a ticket. We would normally go to the outskirts of town to catch cars as they were coming in, but if you had the patience and some luck, you could do it here too. My friends and I had enough experience being ticket less that we didn't go to a lot of shows without them anymore. That was especially true on this tour because we were doing the whole thing.

The first night in Worcester, I found a great rig to patch into. Senhiesser 421's with a 441 blend, also a Senhiesser mic. They opened with a fine Aiko party starter, followed by Beat it on Down the Line. Next, Jerry pulled out a sweet Candyman and Bobby followed with the shuffling, somewhat bluesy, C.C. Rider and then Bird Song, which was followed by Lazy Lightening > Supplication and then Deal. This was almost the last Lazy Lightening they would play, and speaking of 'last time played'. I would really love to know if they drop a song from the repertoire consciously, or does it just not occur to them to play it anymore. Maybe the last time that it was played, it turned out so dam good; I mean they nailed it so well, that it was just done and they had to move on. . . Who the hell knows, right?

The second set highlights included an amazing, extended Terrapin Station opener, which was a rarity. Terrapin was followed by a rocking Samson and Delilah and then Brent played his new cover, I Just Wanna Make Love to you for the last time. The rest of the set was somewhat inconsequential, not so exciting as far as song lists go, ending with a U.S. Blues encore, but everything was great. The band was on fire, at least from our standpoint. As we were hanging out in Worcester, we met a new friend. Ted was his name. He and I shared a birthday, and became instant friends. We all hung together for the two nights in Worcester, and then headed up to Augusta together. In fact, I took a break from the van and took a ride in the 'shotgun' position with Ted, in his brand new Mustang Convertible. It was the first time I had ever witnessed cruise control on any car. It was a four speed on the floor and it was a beautiful Fire Engine Red. Ted was a really nice guy, one of the few people we ever met on tour that we welcomed into our tour circle. We got together again briefly after this tour was over, to trade some tapes, but we didn't stay in touch after that, not even long enough to re-exchange the music.

The second night in Worcester was even more incredible. I was patched into Nakamichi 300's this night. The band was awesome. It was like they listened to the tapes of the first show and said, 'Man, we can do better than that!!' The first set opener was Dancing in the Streets, such a great jamming song, wow! These days when they played this song, it would seem to go on forever, but this was only about seven minutes. Friend of the Devil followed it, which was longer at almost twelve minutes. Uncle > Mexicali was next and then a sweet, sweet Bird Song followed. My Brother Esau, Big RxR Blues > Let it Grow ended the first set nicely.

This show was October 9th, John Lennon's birthday and he had now been gone for four years. (Hard to believe he's been gone now for thirty-five) Though such things are rarely mentioned on stage, they do creep in occasionally during the show, in some obscure ways. The second set opener was Help/Slipknot/Franklin's Tower > Jack Straw, which was amazing enough, but then they went into He's Gone, which we feel is being played for John. He's Gone steamrolls into Smokestack Lightening and then the jam drifts into drums > The Wheel > Throwing stones> Stella Blue > Around and Round into Johnny B. Goode to end the second set. The encore this night was Revolution. . ., and do we have to wonder why?

After the second show in Worcester we headed home to regroup. We were home by 2:30 in the morning, and on the way Bob suggested that we leave by noon the next day for Augusta. We agreed, thinking that it would be nice to spend an extra day in there, and at this point, we were essentially just waiting to leave anyway. Our friend Ted stayed at Bob's house while we were local and then our adventure would in Maine. Bob picked me up at about 11 AM in Wall, New Jersey on October 10. (my Dad's birthday) With Bob at the wheel, he got us there in just about 6 hours. We pulled into the Holiday Inn Civic Center Hotel on Community Drive at almost exactly 5 pm and Oh Boy!, what a surprise was waiting for us.

The first thing we saw when we pulled into the lot was three International Harvester 18 wheelers. The grills of all the trucks were adorned with the iconic Steal your Face, or Skull and Lightening decal. I looked at Bob. He looked at me. Then we all looked at each other in the same moment and realized that we were staying at the same hotel that the Grateful Dead were staying in! Bob pulled the Van into a convenient parking spot and wandered inside real quick to check in without us, and he ran right into the Dead's soundman Dan Healy. The thing about our situation was, as I said before, we were a full day early for our reservations. Bob figured that this wouldn't be a problem, but when then found out that the hotel was booked, booked, booked, so he appealed to the desk clerk's sense of adventure and worked out a deal that, at this moment, would have seemed impossible to most anybody else. The clerk mentioned to Bob that there were some efficiency apartments out back, behind the hotel that weren't being used. He said that we could make ourselves at home in one of those rooms for the night and then move to our regular room in the morning. We walked up two flights of stairs to a comfortable looking room with one double bed and a large, sort of living room that would accommodate the rest of us. Now we were set. We had a comfortable room to spend the night in (as opposed to the back of Bob's van) and plenty of beer for the night. The beer, at this juncture was of no consequence though, as we were all exhausted from the drive and needed to sleep.

The Hotel was set up like a big horseshoe, all open, with no hallways to hide the other rooms except within each section. We were situated on the furthest end of the building and we could see the whole other side just by looking out our window. We didn't even have to appear nosey. At some point somebody said they saw Jerry jumping from one room to another, so we set aside a block of time, watching to see if it would happen again. It was a nice feeling to be staying at the same place they were. We eventually made the decision that it would be best to ignore the situation and just be. . . right where we were. We headed up to the office to see what there was to do here. Was there a pool?, A game room? Anything else? On our way up to the office, Billy and Mickey happened to hanging out on their second floor balcony, (only two floors here) so I said, "Hey, guys, Worcester was a great show!" Mickey chimed, "Yea it was Ok." and went back inside his room. Billy as well. Neither were very uninterested in conversing in any manner. They were cordial enough, but also abrupt. We continued our walk, heading into the lobby. While we were inside of course, I had to call my Mom and Dad to let them know we got there safely. I always did that, out of respect. They didn't know what was going on at these places, but I wanted them to know that I was always safe. We were always safe. We made sure that everyone that we were with was in good shape and made it back to wherever we were headed or wherever we were from no matter what. So I get on the phone and talk to my Mom and tell her about our good fortune.

"Guess what mom? We are staying at the same hotel that the band is staying at."

She says, "Same hotel huh? Well that's nice."

I said, "What are you talking about? Don't you think this is amazing."

She said, "Yea, I know it's amazing, but I'm really surprised that this is the first time that it's happened. You guys are out there all the time and this is the first this has happened to you?"

I said, "Yea, there was no plan for this though. It couldn't have been planned actually, but it's really great." We talked a little while longer and then she said, "Well, you guys have fun and be safe."

Mom was happy that we got there safely and asked me to stay in touch, to call again when I had time. I told her I may not call again for a while so not to worry, and she understood. Thinking back, I'm just as surprised as she was that we didn't run into them more often.

Continuing our stroll, through the passageways of the hotel to see just exactly who else we might run into, accidentally on purpose. The next casual 'bump' was Brent Mydland. The new guy. That moniker was so unfair to him. He replaced Keith Godchaux in 1979, but was still referred to as the new guy by the press and by many Deadheads. He was, in fact, very accomplished and had found his place in the band very quickly. Not only that, but he brought with him originality, and placed several songs in the repertoire that were fun to hear and lasted in full rotation for a good long time. Detroit Medley, (Devil with a Blue Dress/Good Golly Miss Molly/Devil with a Blue Dress) Louie Louie, Hey Jude (refrain) and Dear Mr. Fantasy, come to mind immediately. Anyway he was very nice, we shook hands and thanked him for playing and being there and yada yada yada, what else do you say when you have nothing to say, and a million things you'd like to say all at the same time. We wanted to see who else was hanging out anyway.

On our way back around the other way we ran into, not quite literally, but saw Bobby Weir. He was coming back from a run, down the hillside that rose up above the southern side of the Hotel by the main hiway. The highways in that part of Augusta were winding and full of hills. They were pretty perfect for a distance runner like Weir. As he was coming down the side of that hill, I yelled to him and he stopped for a second. He looked up just long enough to hear me say, "Hey Bobby, we probably won't get the chance in Hartford, so I want to wish you a happy birthday."

He replied with a smile, "Oh, thanks.", and that was that.(we were standing on the upper level of the hotel at this point so we couldn't shake hands or anything else) His birthday is October 16th and they were playing the 14th and 15th in Hartford, so I figured what the hell, Happy Birthday Bobby....Right?

We headed back downstairs where we were just hanging out drinking a few and listening to a boom box that Gagen brought with him. I think Box of Rain was playing (I know Box of Rain was playing) and the funny thing was, I was wearing a tie-dye T-shirt with a Phil Lesh silhouette print on it. It was dyed with a mix of blue and yellow, which gave it an additional tint of green. Made it really sweet looking. I still have that shirt and will never part with it. (The next part of the story should explain why) As we were standing there listening to Box of Rain and enjoying one of the most beautiful October days in Maine, probably ever (it was 75 degrees in the middle of October) here comes Phil Lesh walking down that same hillside that Weir had jogged down not a half-hour before. I realized right at that moment that I was wearing the shirt I just mentioned and as he came toward us, I stepped out to greet him with a handshake.

He looked at my shirt and said, "Wooaohoah!! Where did you get that shirt.?"

I just said, "Yea, ain't it cool. I don't remember, but I'm glad I happen to be wearing right now.

It is so cool to shake your hand Phil. I think you're amazing."

He said thanks and was very friendly. That was the coolest thing that had ever happened to me on tour. I shook Phil's hand while wearing a Phil tie-dye shirt and he commented on it. I had, at the time, maybe ten real nice Grateful Dead shirts and the fact that I was wearing that one on that particular day was just dumb Irish luck. (Now if I had a sharpie with me and had him sign it that would've been the topper. I don't think sharpies existed then??) As I went to shake his hand, I instinctively wiped my hand against my pants so I wouldn't be all sweaty and at that same moment my friend Ted was taking a picture, so that's the picture he ended up with. It was me walking toward Phil just after wiping my hand and just before shaking Phil's hand. I was a little bummed that he didn't get me actually shaking his hand, but I didn't even realize that a picture existed until later the next day. Still.....The coolest thing ever!

Now we wait. We still haven't seen Jerry up close and who knows when, or if this opportunity will ever present itself again. So we wait, patiently. When we saw the limousines pull up, we figured we were in the right place. Weir came out first with one suitcase and a coat draped over his shoulder. A couple of girls were with him, hiding their faces slightly because of the cameras. He was very friendly again, but in more of a hurry now. A little more time passed and then we thought maybe that not all the band members would be coming out this way. Their rooms were spread out a little, so they were probably being picked up at different locations. We didn't see Billy, Mickey or Brent come out on this side, but Jerry's room was right above us so we were pretty certain we were in the right spot. As we stood there reassuring each other that we were where we were supposed to be, Jerry came out of the hallway from under his room and walked somewhat briskly toward his limo. He didn't say anything, had a cigarette in his mouth, but he gave us a nod as he got into the car. He was carrying a briefcase in his hand, which seemed a bit peculiar. What was in there? Jerry was not a corporate kind of guy and it would be too weird to be carrying drugs around in that thing. Wouldn't that just be too conspicuous?

We heard the rumors of heavy drug use by the band in the 80's. I didn't want to believe it, but we had friends who had some pretty close connections to them and the word was that Jerry was not doing well. Thinking back now, he didn't look good either. They said he was shooting up speedballs like Belushi did. The part I found hard to believe was that Jerry could decide that drugs were more important to him than the music. I didn't want to believe that. I heard Jerry was turned on something like hash oil by some Deadhead in Egypt in 78. The hash oil turned out to be something called Persian; smokable heroine, highly addictive. Supposedly the whole band was into it and it had become a very bad situation. These are just a few examples of how the information about the Grateful Dead world circulated amongst our friends. I also read something about this in Blair Jackson's book, **Garcia: An American Life**. Read it, it's an excellent read for anyone that loved Jerry.

October 11, 1984. Opening night

After a full day of interacting with members of the band, even as little as we did, the show was that much more exciting. The first set opened with Shakedown > Greatest Story. Next came Fenario, Mama Tried, Big River, Ramble on Rose, Looks like Rain, Might as well. They'd played Looks Like Rain so many times, I started labeling my tapes, Looks Like Bobby or It's Raining Again or Here it Comes Again. They hadn't played it yet on this tour, but it was a relative certainty. Bucket > Touch opened the second set followed by Women are Smarter, Ship of Fools and Playing in the Band all before drums. That was nice. Fantasy > Black Peter followed drums and then the grand master set closer of them all, Sugar Magnolia, ended the second set. Good God!, Bobby could rock the shit out of that song. The whole crowd is just a dancing sweaty mess by then, including Bobby, sweating like crazy. The encore was *Day Job*, which was still new then. I think Day Job could've been a great song if it was given a better arrangement, but it was too quick and not very understandable lyrically. My opinion.

The ride back to the hotel was simple, especially since I wasn't driving, ha!...Sorry, but I rarely drove when we went to shows back then. It was always Bob doing the driving. But he loved driving and he knew where he was going all the time, and somehow he was always awake. He didn't even really need a co-pilot, but I held that distinction most of the time. The hotel was very close to the venue and once we were there, I set up the boom box to play the tape. I was always a little nervous about playing an audience master in any deck other than my own, but my D-5 only had a little 1 inch speaker in its face and we really wanted to hear that tape.

The next day the local newspaper, the KENNEBEC JOURNAL, which according the front page is Maine's oldest newspaper, led the day with a local story of a man acquitted of murder and kidnaping. Then a second story about George Bush and Geraldine Ferraro defending their running mates. Tucked below these two stories, but still on the front page was this story:

Dead Heads; Truly A Special Breed of People

The paper did a typical story of people arriving the day before with license plates from all over the country, with camping gear and supplies for the two days of shows in Augusta. Several Heads were interviewed about their passion for the band and talked about how friendly the Deadheads are and about the community that is shared, and the love of the music that brings that community together, "It's a group feeling. More than 90% of the audience at a Dead concert are cool people, a good audience." was the comment from one Head. The motels in town were packed. One such motel, the Howard Johnson's Motor Lodge on Community Drive, was packed about halfway with Deadheads and the other half, with nurses that were in town for a Convention that week. What a party that must've been! The desk manager from that motel said, "They're real friendly people. They talk nicely. I mean no rough language or anything. And I'd say they range in age from 17 to their 30's."
I'd have to say that guy pretty much nailed it.

The fact of the matter is that the touring Grateful Dead brought with them tens of thousands of money spending Deadheads, and every cities' economy that we hit benefitted from that. Add to that, for the most part that we didn't wreak havoc or leave a trail of carnage in our path. Now it's showtime. . .

October 12, 1984. The Civic Center in Augusta Maine.
Ain't no place I'd rather be. Damn, what a night that was. Just a real solid show with great song selections. Stranger, Must've Been The Roses, On the Road Again, Jack-a-Roe, All Over Now, Cumberland, Music Never Stopped. Stranger, great opening tune; Roses being the rarity that it is, got a huge crowd response and On the Road Again being an acoustic

song gone electric! Not to mention the Garcia classics Jack–a-Roe and Cumberland with All Over Now sandwiched in between. What a great first set even though there were only seven songs played. Quality, not quantity, kicks in right here ! ! Also, I was patched into the nicest mics ever on these two nights. Nakamichi 700's without shotgun extensions, in front of the board to the left. The sound in that place was really nice, everything sounded so good. I've transferred these shows to CD for myself just recently, so I know for sure that they sound great. The second set was simple in the beginning. Cold Rain > Lost Sailor > Saint, followed by a new Brent tune called Don't Need Love (anymore). When he started out playing this, there was a small crowd response because it was Brent and it was relatively new, but you could hear a pin drop while he was playing and my tape reflects that perfectly. It's like a soundboard. It was clean and pure and crystal clear. Next was Uncle John's Band into drums into Playing reprise, which finished Playing in The Band from the night before. (Only time they've ever done that?) That rolled back into Uncle John's and then slid sweetly into an amazing Morning Dew. This Morning Dew goes down in the books with all the classic versions, and even better than that, I was there to see it. After this show we were soaked through our clothes with sweat from dancing all night long, so it just didn't matter at all what they played for an encore. In fact, if they didn't do an encore we would've understood. It was just that powerful. Instead of heading home early they came back out and Weir treated us to a very welcome, souped-up, stand alone encore of Good Lovin, which deserves singular mention in this story. The encore on this particular night could've been anything because the show was so outstanding, but when Bobby pulled this one out, everybody went through the roof. As I think about this I realize that because it was 'stand alone', rather than being jammed into, it definitely made it more exciting. It was excellent to hear something so familiar after such a great, great show. We spent the day in Maine with beautiful weather and the night with the greatest touring rock n' roll band in the world. . . .

We continue our East Coast jaunt in Hartford. The best tour of the East Coast I was ever involved in. We drove straight down I-95 to 495 south, to 90 south to I-84 into Connecticut. We stayed at the Hartford Ramada Hotel, in Hartford. (Yes, it was called a Hotel then.) We tried to check in as soon as we got there, but this was a middle of the night arrival, so we were turned away and had to sleep in the van for about 5 ½ hours before being able to get our room. The Hotels we stayed in on tour were usually pretty nice because Bob used a credit card that gave him discounts on hotels across the country. Most times we would check in with only two of us, get 2 keys and then the other two or three people would just crash on the floor or in the easy chair that was usually provided. I remember a couple of times where we had ten or fifteen people hanging out with us and more than half of them ended up crashing on the floor. Things like that were never planned, they would just happen. Most of the time there was no more than five of us in a room on any given night. There was a certain level of comfort that we liked to maintain, but when you're partying late, whatever happens. . . happens!

We made reservations pretty far in advance for these shows, so we had some priorities in line. For instance, we liked to have a pool whenever possible, although as I write this I'm not sure why. We hardly ever used a pool during the daytime hours and they were almost always closed by the time we got back from the show. Sometimes the door to the pool would be unlocked (Glens Falls 1982?) and we would just 'have at it' like we owned the place. I don't recall ever getting into trouble for doing that either. Because we were really casual about it.

Once we made it to the Hotel, we went out for food. We didn't like to eat at the hotel unless there was no other convenient food source, which most times there was, and the reason for this is the most obvious... Expensive.! You can, however, bet your last dollar that we would take advantage of the alcohol available at any given hotel. Why? That would be just to feel welcome and to say hi to the strangers among us. The people that we ran into in these cities were just doing their jobs and living their lives and it was fun to chat them up; Tell them where we were from; See their reaction when they find out what we were doing, where we've been, and where we are heading next. They were usually quite surprised because we never came off like dirty smelly Deadheads trying to find money so we could get a bite to eat. We took care of ourselves and looked the part of tourists having fun, not just Deadheads.

So later on, after some food and a shower and a change of clothes (now looking every bit like Deadheads) we would head out to "the scene". Our hotel was located on the Connecticut River and was only about a half a mile away, across the bridge. So this time we were able to walk to the show and back, leaving traffic problems behind. By 1984 the crowds hadn't risen up and taken over just yet. Yes, there were mile long lines out the doors of every fast food restaurant in the town, (again, good for local economy, yes!) and the streets were blanketed with tie-dyes and people looking for tickets, which I'm so sure is not an everyday occurrence (duh). But this was all very controlled, and to this I should add self-controlled. There was no real need for a police presence, no need for undercover-cops yet (there was never a need for that) and I don't believe there was really a lot of disorderly conduct either, by this band of gypsy-like road warrior concert goers who liked being called Deadheads; A peace loving, basically sane group of people who would give you the shirt off their backs if they thought you needed it more that they did, or if they thought it would get them a floor seat or a back stage pass, ha ha.

So now we are off to the first of two shows. Everything is all set, we have our tickets, I have taper seats so I'm psyched. I get in, get set up and patch into the same mics that I had in Augusta. Nakamichi700's. Sweet, sweet, sweet..! The boys opened with Alabama Getaway > Greatest Story, then played Dire Wolf, Lil' Red Rooster and Duprees Diamond Blues. Bobby played Brother Esau, Jerry followed with Loser. Then Minglewood Blues, Row Jimmy, I Need a Miracle straight into

Might as well, which ended the first set. This was quite a long set compared to what we've been hearing lately. After a while you start counting in your head and realize that it's going to be over soon, then they throw Might as Well at you in the end. The second set was just as long and sweet. A China > Rider opener followed by Samson and Delilah, High Time, Estimated Prophet > Eyes > drums. A nice spacey jam flowed into China Doll, then Throwing Stones > Not Fade Away, then WHAM!!! right into Turn on Your lovelight. . . Bobby loved to play the shit out of that song too.

After the show we went back to the hotel and partied for a while. The pool was open for Deadheads only and we were certainly cordial enough to accept that invitation. We hung out there until probably 3a.m., but honestly you can't expect me to remember that can you?...It always seemed like we were up half the night, especially after the first show of any run, and that made getting up and continuing the adventure just a little bit exhausting. If you even consider enjoying a Continental Breakfast, then you really have to get up early. I wasn't really into bagels and cream cheese much at the time (now I love 'em), that I do remember. But give me some OJ and a little cereal and a cup of tea and I'm just fine. A short nap in the afternoon (always nice, but sometimes just not possible!) before heading back out to the masses, and we're all set. There is a beautiful park directly across from the Civic Center and we took full advantage of that too. We played some frisbee and some hackey-sack, and enjoyed a nice sunny afternoon with friends. We also managed to drink a few beers, nice and casual, no hassles necessary. We made our way into the Civic Center about an hour before the show so I was able to get my stuff set up.

Second night's musical adventure went pretty well with a Bucket > Sugaree opener and a nice El Paso, followed by Bird Song, C.C. Rider, Tennessee Jed and Jack Straw. Relatively short, but sweet enough. Scarlet > Fire > Playing > drums > space> Wheel > Wharf Rat back into Playing > Sugar Magnolia. The encore was Baby Blue.

Oh, my, God!....What a great northern run! These shows were so incredible, each in their own way, that I had to share these set lists completely. They were really uniquely amazing and individually fantastic. You get the idea. Now we head back home to our own back yard for the last couple. October 17 and 18 at the Meadowlands in New Jersey brought about some pretty interesting set lists. The first night was especially long, 19 songs plus an encore, opening with Aiko-Aiko > Promised Land and closing with Looks Like Rain, into Might as Well. The latter had become a more frequent set closer lately. Second set opened with Help >Slipknot > Franklin's > Women are Smarter > Terrapin Station. Terrapin, to this day, is still one of my favorite songs, despite its length. By that, I only mean that a really long song takes up a lot of time where other songs could be played. That's all. In fact, I would even say that really I love the studio version. Anyway, Bobby picked up the action after Terrapin with The Other One> Truckin> and Jerry ended the set by Goin Down the Road Feeling Bad. (That would be 'bad' as in 'good') The encore was Brokedown Palace. Brokedown was another one of those songs that was truly beautiful and great to hear, but became very overplayed. I really think that it could've been moved to the first set pretty easily, in the position of, oh say, Candyman?. . .but that's just me. Right?

The second night was more of the same amazing stuff with the highlights being the second set opener, Dancing in the Streets > Touch of Grey > Playing in the Band >Uncle John's Band > China Doll. They hit the drums and jammed right back into Playing and then Throwing Stones into Not Fade Away. The encore was It's All Over Now Baby Blue. As I've said before, doing the whole tour this way is so amazing. Going to any other concert you can imagine is always great for the moment, but when you know that the next day there's another and on the other side of that yet another, the excitement grows and intensifies. Not having anything to do with any drug intake at all. Despite what people assume, it's definitely not always about drugs. The last show of the tour was at the Carrier Dome at Syracuse University, and it was the only show on tour that we didn't go to. (That's quite the distinction huh?)

I have recently revisited the show in Syracuse and I have to say that it was quite the standout. Highlights for me start with the opener Bertha, Greatest Story, C.C. Rider, and a show stopping Jack Straw. Also an incredible Shakedown second set opener, into a strong Samson and Delilah. I think Samson came across a lot stronger in the 80's than it did in '77 when it first came around. My opinion. Maybe others would disagree. Either way it's always a treat. Then He's gone followed by Weir belting out Smokestack Lightening. I mean moaning and growling. This show might be considered a sleeper. Sweet!

So *what did we do?*, while the rest of the touring Deadheads went up to Syracuse. We headed on over to Rutgers University to see Tom Constanten, better known to those familiar with Grateful History as TC. He took over on keyboards when Pig Pen became ill. Eventually he moved on with his music career and was replaced by Keith Goddchuax. TC's tour was called "From Ragtime to Dark Star", and it was very interesting to say the least. When we arrived the first thing we did was ask at the board if I could get a patch to record. The guy told us we had to ask TC and when we asked where we might find him, we were told he was hanging in the hall just passing time. We went over to him and introduced ourselves and asked him a bunch of questions. He was just as friendly as he could be. We told him what we were doing and he thought that was a really neat thing to do. He told us it was fine with him if we taped the show and to have fun with the tapes. We listened with much anticipation to everything that he played. His repertoire included songs that anyone would know, but you wouldn't be able to name. Theme from Sting comes to mind, along with Dark Star of course. It was a fun change up from what we had been doing for the last week and a half, so it was worth not going all the way to Syracuse this time. TC set up every song that he played. He told us a little about the origins of the song and then how he came to play it and enjoy it. Then he played it through, making it that much more entertaining to everyone in attendance.

The very next show the Grateful Dead played was at the Berkeley Community Theatre on October 27. It was here that Dan Healy allowed the first ever Taper's Section. It was set up right behind the board and the only restriction on taping from then on was no "front of board" taping. This of course lead to several Deadheads now trying for the ultimate 'FOB' tapes.

Notable; At the Halloween show when Bobby sang One More Saturday Night he sang 'Halloween Night' instead. This six night run at BCT also included the last Lazy Lightening and also featured the debut of some Weir cover tunes, including Ain't Superstitious and Down in the Bottom, which were most often paired together and a new cover for Brent called Gimme Some Lovin. This song was originally done by Spencer Davis Group, and in the Grateful Dead it was sung by the whole band

Back on the Road with the Grateful Dead Spring Tour 1985

One of the most surprising shows of 1985 came on the 27th of March this year, but to get there we first have to head back to Hampton real quick. March 21st 1985, found the Grateful Dead back in Va., again and this would be the first casualty of my new job. (I took a night crew job to go full-time) The boys played these shows on Thursday and Friday of that week and then headed up North to Springfield Mass., for two shows. Next, they hit Nassau Coliseum for three nights. I had to pick just one of the shows at Nassau and although it was really tough to pick just one, I think I picked the right one.

This was my 80th Grateful Dead show on the 27th of March. As we stood roughly halfway between the soundboard and the stage at this general admission show, there was something very noticeable and peculiar on stage. A mic stand was set up at Phil's position on the stage. This was the first time in a very long time. In fact before this, I had never seen a mic in front of Phil. I was taping about forty feet from the stage and the floor was completely chair free, leaving plenty of room for dancing. The perfect scenario really, for a Dead show. As we watched our favorite band perform from our excellent vantage point, it brought an instant smile to our faces. Jerry opened the first set with Mississippi ½ Step, followed by Bobby's Hell in a Bucket. This was the first ½ Step since late 82. West L.A., Mama Tried > Big River followed and then Phil stepped up to his mic and sang Dylan's *Tom Thumb's Blues* all by himself. Needless to say the crowd went nuts. Tom Thumbs is another Dylan tune that never mentions the name of the song, in the song. (You have to love that). Phil has performed this song many times since then and has definitely made it his own over the years. Of course, everybody has been anxiously awaiting Phil's return to the mic. Now we had only to wait for the return of the Box of Rain!! They hadn't played the 'Box' since 1973.

Following these Nassau shows, I started a vacation week and picked up the action in Portland Maine on the 31st with the rest of my touring buds. I didn't take a vacation soon enough to make the shows in Hampton because logistically, it didn't make sense. The show grouping for the rest of the tour was much more convenient. (Had to make the best of the time I had available to me)

The Civic Center in Cumberland County is a nice enough venue and definitely had that special spark to it. First of all, the show opener was The Music Never Stopped, which is not typical by any means, but mostly it leaves open the possibilities for a set closer. Jerry played a heartfelt Loser next and Weir followed that with Beat it on Down the Line. The first set also included Duprees Diamond Blues. I always loved hearing that song. I remember hanging out with my friend Joe at the beach in 1979 and hearing him recite random lyrics;

Papa said son you'll never get far.
I'll tell you the reason,
if you wanna know,
cause child of mine. . .
there isn't really very far to go.'
(Words by Robert Hunter)

I said, "What was that?" He said, "That's Duprees Diamond Blues Jimbo". I'd heard of the song, but I wasn't familiar with all the lyrics. After that, I was hooked. Every time I heard Duprees, I paid close attention and learned the rest of the words eventually, kind of.

The second set was rockin, opening with a nicely placed Aiko Aiko > Samson, but the best part of the evening happened toward the end of the set when Bobby broke loose with Day Tripper. . . .Unreal. Bobby loves to rock a great song and he was currently having himself a blast with that one. It's great to see the best 'cover band' in the world try their hand at Beatles tunes. This was a fun one too. (Would have loved to have heard 'Drive my Car' one day)

They ended the night with It's All Over Now Baby Blue, and I really have to say that I was kinda getting tired of this song too, as an encore anyway. Sorry, but sometimes you just want a little more effort put forth for an encore and Baby Blue to me, just seemed more like a first set song. Just because the lyric says 'it's all over now' doesn't mean it has to end the show. I would love to hear it instead of Bird Song some time. Same with Black Peter, it would a great first set song, (was a great first set song in the acoustic sets back at the Filmore right?) but it absolutely became for Jerry, a second set 'close to the end' kinda song.

The next show we hit was at the Civic Center in Providence Rhode Island; April 3th 1985. The song selection was definitely getting more interesting on this leg of the tour. Weir was playing around with the two blues tunes I mentioned earlier that he'd recently introduced to the lineup; Down in The Bottom and Ain't Superstitious. Weir had a style for playing tunes like that, along with Lil' Red Rooster and C.C.Rider, but he was still an absolute rocker at heart. Sugar Magnolia certainly took on a life of it's own in the mid 80's. Listen to Sugar Mags back in '72 or '73 and then fast forward to 86. It became something bigger. Give Bobby a song like that and he could rock to death. I remember it being around this time when Weir would actually amp up the end of Sugar Mags by running from one end of the stage to the other, having himself a great time. He would hop up on the different levels of the stage and play right to the fans at the sides and toward the back stage area. That Bobby Weir was usually a sweaty mess by the end of the second set. (God love him!) Guess that would explain why sometimes the encore would be something simple rather than something special, just to get them the hell out of there. We can forgive them for that...We were a sweaty mess after a show like that too!

It was during the second night in Providence that Jerry treated us to a new tune from the Dylan collection called She Belongs to Me. Another one of those Dylan tunes where he never says the title of the song, in the song. You would think that the title of this tune would be She's an Artist, but you'd be wrong.

Second set in Providence opened with a crazy jammed out I need a Miracle. This song was truly the battle cry of every ticketless Deadhead in every parking lot from the East Coast to the West by now. They jammed the Miracle into the sweet and very underplayed Crazy Fingers and followed that with Samson and Delilah. The rest of the set was one big beautiful non-stop dancing jam, ending with Lovelight and an encore of U.S. Blues, and that was just fine.

The next night we were back in familiar territory again. We had three shows at the Philly Spectrum on the 6th, 7th, and 8th of April (85) and there were definitely some treats in store for us there. The first night though, was all about the parking lot. The flea market outside had grown to a somewhat spectacular level. The Deadheads labeled it "Shakedown Street". It was a huge tailgating party with tents and tables set up everywhere. Reminiscent of a county fair with a Grateful Dead theme. (Is that not the greatest idea?) They had everything for sale, except drugs. Yea, well, there were drugs available too, but not openly for sale. If you wanted something for your head, all you had to do was keep walking and keep your ears open for offers. "Weed, LSD, shrooms, acid, hits, liquid, loose joints", people would just repeat over and over again what they were selling or looking for and eventually there would be a connection made. Back in the mid 80's no one really had to worry about getting snagged by an undercover cop unless you were at Nassau Coliseum, (Man what a reputation that place garnered for itself) which is where all the narcs hung out. You couldn't trust your own mother in that crowd. 'Shakedown' was a great flea market, slash food festival. The vendors sold water and cold beer, plus a wide variety of food, along with jewelry, tie-dyes, dresses and skirts, large tapestries, blankets, posters, pictures and almost anything else you might be looking for to commemorate your Grateful Dead adventure.

Shakedown Street was a great place to run into old friends. This is where I would usually run into a dozen or so Heads that I would never see outside the scene. There was one particular guy, whose name was Bob (I think) that I saw at every Garcia show, and Bobby show that I went to for two and a half to three years on the East Coast. This became very funny for both of us because it was never planned, but somehow always happened. One time when Bob and Rick and I went to see Bobby and The Midnites in Piscataway, a show that I mentioned earlier, I had to run back to the car for something real quick. On my way back to catch up with my friends I ran right into him. This guy Bob. You see what I mean right? If I hadn't had to run back to the car at that exact moment, I probably wouldn't have seen him that time, but there we were again.

A couple of years later while turning the pages of The Golden Road, Blair Jackson's incredible Dead Fanzine (as they call it) I ran across a story about Grateful Dead cover bands and how they feel about the music that they play. The story was about several different bands, but there was only one that was pictured and it was of a band called 'Living Earth' whom I had heard of, and I knew they were really good because I had a tape of one of their shows in my personal archives. The peculiar part, or more to the point, the amazing thing was that one of the members of Living Earth was this same guy Bob (Yes, his name was Bob!) that I had met on tour and had run into all over the place for all those years!

Now getting back to the show at the Spectrum, where the music was always inspired and energized. There was some talk that the band had so much love for the atmosphere there, that it brought out the best in them. I am a believer. The first night, there was no real magic as far as songs were concerned (and what did I just get done saying) except for a first set Duprees and the seldom played Big RxR Blues. The latter happens to be on my Desert Island disc; The Grateful Dead's 'Skull n Roses' album. The songs on that album captures the Dead's live magic really well.

The second night opened with a Lennon/ McCartney classic, sung by Mr. Phil Lesh, who asks the musical question, "Why da-don't we da-do it in the Road", or on the drums or in the street, or whatever makes you happy, into another one of my favorites, Mississippi ½ Step (uptown toodeloo). The second set was adventurous enough, winding down with another great combo including Gimme Some Lovin >Truckin > Smokestack Lightening into an incredible Morning Dew. This one rocked the house and the tapes that went around from the board feed were like a gift from God. (Or Dan Healy) We thought the Dew sounded great just being there, but when those tapes were circulated it was realized as a certified mind blower. The first two shows there were phenomenal, but what was coming for the third night couldn't have been planned or expected. . .

The third night was, off the charts amazing. They opened the show with Midnight Hour, which was a Pigpen standard (by Wilson Picket) going back to the mid 60's. There was a very early unofficial release called Vintage Dead that had a version of Midnight Hour that covered one whole side of the album. Pig Pen would jam it out for 45 minutes sometimes because that was just how Pig operated. When I say jam it, I mean Rap it. When I say rap it. I mean he ripped through a monologue like he knew exactly what he was trying to say. Pig was rapping way before anybody was rapping. *'And that's your fault cause it's none o' mine'*

Well anyway, they jammed Midnite Hour right into Walking the Dog and that went into Big Boss Man.... WOW! This was one of my favorite opening sequences ever. The second set started off with Revolution into 'Bucket > Touch of Grey and ended with the amazingly jam-tasticle, undeniably danceable, 'Goin Down the Road Feelin Bad'. They finished off the set with Stella Blue, Round and Round into Lovelight.

Obviously this whole tour meant a lot to me, as the memories from each show would remain with me forever, and these Spectrum shows rank pretty high for this part of the tour. I really have to say that these three shows at the Spectrum solidified the experience for me. They were absolutely magical. Sometimes I find myself complaining about set lists and too much repetition, songs being too often in rotation or what have you, but these shows restored my faith. Good things *do* come to those who wait. Accepting the expected, only makes the unexpected that much more exciting and these were some of the hottest shows that I had seen, in succession up to this point.

In the Spring of 1985, the boys were on the West Coast again for two shows at Irvine Meadows Amphitheater in Irvine Ca. After which they went into The Marin County Veterans Auditorium for some practice sessions. Practicing was not something that the band was able to do very often, in fact I think a lot of the shows we saw could've been considered practice as well. Ha, ha. These performances at the Vet were filmed and eventually released as a video project called "So Far" as in, "This is the Grateful Dead so far, how do you like us now?" (At least that's my take on it) But it was during these sessions, performing live in an empty hall with no audience, that they came up with a great new idea. Performing live was always the best way to go for the band, so they revisited this idea when they went back to record the album that would become 'In The Dark'. The album that included the single 'Touch of Grey' and put the band on track to amazing commercial success and unimaginable problematic touring. Personally, I think the album should have been called 'We Will Survive'. It's way more catchy!

Next there were two shows at the Frost Amphitheater at Stanford Un. in Palo Alto (in their backyard) and then three shows at the Greek

Theatre in Berkeley. These shows saw the debut of Keep on Growing, with Phil on vocals and a revival of Comes a Time, Stagger Lee and Cryptical Envelopment. The latter hadn't been performed since September 23rd 1972. Some 791 shows in that time. That's the kind of thing you find out right away from the taper network. (It's also listed in Deadbase)

The boys were now making their way back east with shows played in the Midwest; Alpine Valley in Wisconsin; River Bend Music Center in Ohio; and Blossom Music Center in Cuyahoga Falls, Ohio. These venues were famous for amazing music, in the strangest conditions. Very wet and rainy. . .Very hot, dry and dusty. Definitely some great shows, but I never saw any shows out there.

The East Coast tour started in Saratoga Springs, NY, and then scooted on down to Hershey Park Pa. where we caught up again. Hershey Park Stadium is inside the park. It's a Theme Park like Six Flags, but surrounded by Chocolate. (Did I really need to explain that?) It's an outdoor stadium, with bleachers set up in horseshoe fashion (like a football stadium) linked at one end by the stage.

For this show Bob drove and I rode shotgun as always. We also had with us Bruce,(only in Virginia) and his girlfriend. On the road with Bob and I were Jeff and his wife Cook driving their Volari and Brian and his girlfriend Donna in his prized Chevelle. Bob made reservations at a Motel called the Rising Sun on the main strip, about five miles from the park and once we arrived on the scene we took the place over. The Motel was situated on a back lot, directly behind a bar (to the left) and a large liquor store. The morning after we arrived a very funny thing happened as we entered the bar for a refresher. There was a young couple having breakfast that had ordered Spam for part of their meal. As the four of us left the bar area and walked outside, we spontaneously broke into a chorus of Monty Python's Spam song, "Spam, Spammm. Wonderful Spam. Spam, Spammm, Wonderful Spam!. . . Spam, Spam, Spam, Spam." Ok, either you get the joke here or you don't.

Anyway, I remember we were sitting on the right side of the stage, where we had a very comfortable view, whether sitting or standing. This was another 'acid drenched' Grateful Dead show for us. The bleachers were unassigned and each step up those hard aluminum seats toward our final, carefully chosen resting place, was like climbing toward a wickedly dismal, cloud filled sky that looked as though it was about to unload a flood on our heads.

The first set opener was Cold Rain and Snow, right into Promised Land, which was a great way to rock into the moment. The next real highlight was the set closer; Bird Song > Comes a Time > Deal. (Three Jerry tunes in a row, really not so common) Comes a Time is from Jerry's solo effort Reflections, which is full of excellent tunes that the Grateful Dead didn't cover regularly and this was a song that definitely didn't get a lot stage time either so we were all real happy to hear it. The second set was yet another mind blower, and a wet down at the same time. I said before that the sky was dark and dismal. Well, there was an ever so slight chill in the air that had indications that a cloud burst was in our future. The set started with the Music Never Stopped and while they were jamming, it started to rain. And the rain just kept on coming. We were all tripping solid by show time, but it was all good. The rain was steady, but not hard and you know what? Sometimes rain is just rain, you know what I mean? It's not necessarily always a bad thing, or necessarily annoying. Sometimes it's a welcome relief. It was not cold at all. Actually, all in all, it was quite comfortable. I found myself looking up into it and letting the raindrops fall all over my face. It was refreshing and kinda fun.

Music never Stopped was followed by Tom Thumbs Blues, then Estimated Prophet > Terrapin Station, which I love. That went into drums > Miracle and then one of the sweetest and most powerful Morning Dews I'd heard in a long time, during which. . . the rain stopped! That went into Throwing Stones > Not Fade Away. The encore was. . . .Day Job.. Uhgggg!! But sometimes the encore just doesn't matter. Especially after the show they just played, it just didn't matter.

Spring/Summer 1986
Jerry's health problems

The boys played Hampton again in March of 1986 and the first night there, Jerry debuted Vision's of Johanna, from the Dylan collection. I eventually heard this one at the Spectrum this year and I'm sure I had never heard Jerry sing a song with so many lyrics before. I couldn't believe how long it was. The second night Phil played Box of Rain for the first time since July 28th 1973. (Thank you Dead Base) The third night Bobby played Road Runner, a song he used to perform with Kingfish, back in the day. I was unable to go to Hampton because of my work schedule, so that kinda sucked. The Spectrum shows that followed were on the 23rd 24th and 25th of March and I was able to hit the bookends. The first night brought about some pretty interesting news though. Word had spread quickly that 'the boys' had sound checked Heard it Through the Grapevine before the show. The band always played something for Dan Healy so that he make sound adjustments before the show. Most of the time the first song of the night ended up being the 'test song' anyway, but they liked to run through something just to see what was going on. Personally, I always thought Heard it Through the Grapevine would be a great song for the Grateful Dead to cover. First, because it's a great song, no doubt and second because it fits the motif so well. The Grateful Dead's grapevine was very long and fruitful and the information received via this grapevine was mostly reliable and seemingly instantaneous, as we heard about Grateful rumors, true and false, very quickly from the West to the East Coast.

The first show at the Spectrum opened with Gimme Some Lovin > Deal, and then Hand Jive. Willie and The Hand Jive, is a very old song, but Eric Clapton's version is surely the best known. Weir sang Spoonful in the second set (also a Clapton standard) and second night featured a first set Box of Rain, so guess who missed it again??. . . Fucker. . !

The third night in Philly opened with Feel like a Stranger, Tennessee Jed, C.C. Rider and Tons of Steel. Tons is a Brent tune off the new, as yet unreleased album. The elusive and very underplayed It Must've Been the Roses was next and then Bobby broke out another Dylan tune called Desolation Row. I had never heard this one before, and like Visions it was one freaking long ass song. It's a great song from a classic Dylan album, Hiway 61 Revisited. The second set opened with Scarlet > Touch, then Phil did Tom Thumbs Blues. They followed that with Black Peter and Throwing Stones and the set ended with Lovelight. The encore was Brokedown Palace.

Due to the steadily growing popularity of the band through 1986, they were set to play a stadium tour for the summer. I really don't like the stadium shows much because the intimacy factor is lost, but this tour would be great. It would include Bob Dylan, backed by Tom Petty and the Heartbreakers. Their first stop was the Hubert Humphery Metronome, in Bob Dylan's hometown of Minneapolis, Minnesota. The show I chose, out of these very special line-ups was July 6, 1986 at RFK Stadium in Washington D.C. Dylan backed by the Heartbreakers opened the show and I really wanted to see them play, but we didn't get inside early enough to catch their set. The problem here was that no one else that I was with was motivated, so it just didn't happen.

A mutual friend of ours at the time, went to college down there and she lived in a place called The Crystal City Apartments. She invited us all to stay over during these DC shows and we had a great time. This building was really amazing because it included all of life's essentials under the first floor apartments. I've never seen anything like it, before or since. It was literally a city, in and of itself. It had a post office; it had restaurants; strip malls, movie theaters, even a bowling alley. Plenty of bars and a huge supermarket. I don't recall anything else, but I'm sure you get the idea. I had to leave the next day for work, so I missed the second show. I hate my job. . .

So, the one that I missed was accompanied by an incredibly hot day in D.C. Though it was hot the first day, everybody I talked to said the next day was worse and Jerry was not fairing well at all. I think the word sweltering might have been invented to describe this weekend weather in DC. There were only five songs played in the first set. It opened with Ramble on Rose, which is an absolutely pure, middle of a first set song, and had no business being an opener. Minglewood Blues came up next and then It Must've Been the Roses. After this, Dylan came out and lent a hand on Baby Blue and Desolation row. According to the Heads that I know who were there, Jerry was noticeably ill during the show. He looked horrible and he kept missing lyric cues and really not playing well at all. At the first show when I *was* there, it didn't seem as evident to me that there might be, or was a problem. There was a complete first set and a great second set. We had a pretty good vantage point on the field too, so it was very enjoyable. On the second night, the second set opened with Mr. Phil Lesh on lead vocals. Once again, I missed my fucking *Box of Rain*. I couldn't fuckin believe it! They were literally playing the Box of Rain in every city on this tour right now and I just keep on missing it. (Almost funny) The rest of the set wasn't even that impressive song-wise, but it was still really good. Playin > Terrapin > drums> Other One > Wharf Rat > Around and round > Good Lovin. The encore was Satisfaction, with a twist. During the middle break of the song Weir decided to pull a 'Springsteen maneuver' by introducing the band. The band never introduces each other during a show and they are almost never introduced before the show, except in a festival situation. (We already know who they are) Of course, when they played in San Francisco under the guise of

Bill Graham, he enjoyed introducing them and sometimes, but not every time, when their show was being broadcast locally or nationally they were introduced as well.

With all that being said. . .

Bobby starts off with;

"Like to say goodnight to the people of Washington DC, . . .You've been very kind to us, . . .just as kind, as people could be. . . Like to get off with these few words of advise. . .I'll to try to knock off... (laughs). . .Awe fuck! (somewhat off mic). . .We'd also like to fuck . . . or thank....Mr. Phil Lesh on the Bass here...Ya know he kinda defines the meaning of. . .'space'. . .Over on the left we have Mr. Mydland.....He's a man of much action...and very few words....Then we got Billy and Mick, the boys on the drums....When I try to describe their work...It just makes me feel, kinda dumb...Then of course over here we got ol' Jer, (which was followed by a huge crowd response and an off the charts guitar riff and something that sounded like someone tripped over an amp or something) Jerry then introduces Bobby as "One of my favorite people in the whole wide world...Mr. Bob Weir."

Ya know, considering what they've meant to us for all these years, that intro brought a tear to my eye. Satisfaction ended in a huge climax and everyone in that crowd went home with a huge grin on their faces. Even though I wasn't there, I know how they felt after that incredible ending. No doubt!

Jerry by the way, is definitely not doing well at all at this point. The two shows in D.C. took a toll on everyone and Jerry, being in poor health already, wasn't handling it very well. Those that were there were more aware of the situation, but he really hadn't been looking very healthy of late anyway. Two days after they returned to San Francisco for break, Jerry collapsed at home and slipped into a diabetic coma. We heard about the coma rather quickly because of his status in the world of rock n roll. All the news, TV and radio, picked up the report. (Before the internet or Cell phone explosion) The advantage we had as Deadheads, was knowing what the circumstances were right away, so we could ignore the rumors.

Upon his awakening we found out his progress rather quickly. When he did wake, several days later the first words out of his mouth were, "I'm not Beethoven." Strange enough, huh?

Because of the coma Jerry's strength was depleted and his musical ability was stunted. The way he explained it was that he lost the connection that he had between wanting to play music, loving the music that he played and actually being able to play the music that he loved. His good friend and former musical collaborator Merl Saunders would stop by to see him frequently and go for walks with him and talk about his musical projects. Then Merl would hand Jerry a guitar to see what he could do. The first few times were frustrating for Jerry, but eventually his hard work paid off and he was able to reconnect the music with the guitar, so to speak. As Merl continued his 'musical therapy', John Kahn had begun making some appearances as well. The reason I know about this at all is from reading Blair Jackson's book, *Garcia; An American Life*

Even though Jerry had once again become comfortable with a guitar in his hands, he was very nervous about playing in front of people again. He even wondered if anyone would even want to see him play again since, in his opinion, he was not quite up to the level he had been. To this end, he had John Kahn schedule a few Jerry Band shows for 'The Stone' in Berkeley Ca., in October just to see what might happen. The 1600 seats sold out in an hour. They added several shows within the same week and on opening night when Jerry hit the stage the crowd went nuts. They say he was a little overwhelmed by the outpouring of love that he received from his fans, even in the wake of his admitted bad decisions regarding his own health. Jerry claimed that the love and positive vibes he received during his hospital stay was in large part responsible for his recovery. Even the Doctor's were surprised at how quickly Jerry seemed to bounce back.

Jerry's Comeback Shows

At this point the Grateful Dead have been off the road for the longest time since their self imposed retirement in 1975. When they announced their comeback shows, it was decided they would play three nights in Oakland, at the Alameda County Coliseum. This would be the first time Jerry would be back on stage with the Grateful Dead since his coma, so I really wanted to be there. I had to be there. I certainly wouldn't go to California for any other rock band in the world and I don't think I would go for four days just to see a friend, with the exception of a wedding for a family member. I don't have any family in California, except for my bro Joe Hackett. Even then, I would definitely have to extend it to include a few more days. An actual vacation. For the Grateful Dead, the travel was always worth it because of the community that we shared and the experiences and the music that we all craved. For me, it was always the music that was the most important thing.

I ordered three tickets for each show and asked my friend Tom (not my taper friend, but a friend none the less) if he wanted to go out there with me. I asked Tom rather than my usual gang of touring buddies because a trip to California is not something that just anybody can afford to do at the drop of a hat, at a moments notice, spur of the moment, you get the idea. Tom was self employed and had the resources available to take a quick vacation to California if he wanted to. Besides, even though we've been friends for years, Tom and I had never done a tour together, so this 'Grateful' excursion, though not really a tour per se, would be a first for us. Anyway, as I suspected, he was totally psyched about the whole idea and that meant it was on. We hopped a flight a day early and stayed with one of his buddies that lived out there. Tom's girlfriend would join us the following day. She wasn't able to make the first show so I gave the extra ticket to Tom's friend Dennis. He was hosting our stay after-all. Going to California to see a show was something that I had always wanted to do and what better reason (aside from New Years) than for Jerry's come-back. I've heard it said, the feeling out there is so different because the Dead is 'their band' and because they get to see them a lot out there, that it might be less of a special event for them. We actually get to see them a lot on the East Coast too, so I don't see it that way at all. I know that there is a more laid back feeling out there maybe because the Grateful Dead is from there, but those of us on the East Coast know that we're a bit of a livelier crowd (so they say, so we say, so who knows). I think that the number of fans on the East Coast (for that matter even New Jersey) outnumbers those on the West. Just saying!

The first night we were out there we were hanging out at his friend Dennis' house and Tom pulled out a bag of cocaine. I'm pretty sure that I've never seen that much coke in one place before. I mean sitting in front of me. Tony Montana style. (Maybe not quite) He brought it with him on the plane, which I was totally unaware of. (Better that I didn't know, for sure). We had a few cocktails, relaxed a bit and then started doing lines. Tom was putting out lines that could choke a fuckin horse. I couldn't believe it. . . This went on for a while, but it wasn't exactly all for free. It was great to have it sitting right in front of us though, so who was I to argue about a little contribution. We must've done a gram each in a half an hour, and it didn't stop there. It was amazing shit. We were talking, sharing war stories and listening to some tunes on a boom box in the living room while enjoying the first night of our vacation with the Grateful Dead just a few miles up the road the next night. We were up until at least 4:30 in the morning, probably closer to 6, and the next thing I knew I was waking up in my clothes in another part of the house. I remember it being about 6:30 pm. I rubbed the dust out of my eyes and shook the clouds from my head and realized that it was the night of the first show and that we needed to get rolling. I woke Tom up with, "Hey....We gotta get going. . . It's almost 7 o'clock and showtime is 8." I scrambled for the bathroom and showered real quick, put the same clothes back on.(whatever) His friend Dennis threw his keys in Tom's direction and told us he'd meet us there later.

When we walked in to the Oakland-Alameda Coliseum, there was an amazing ambience, an electric feeling in the air. As we waded through the crowd and headed toward the closest gateway to the floor, I could see that there was a volley ball game going on. I've never seen a volley ball game being played pre-show, but I have heard of it happening. This was between Bill Graham Production's and a team made up of Deadheads and crew members. I watched the action very closely, really took it in. This is definitely the kind of thing that does not happen on the East Coast. I was also checking out the crowd and my surroundings during the game because, that's what I do. I am a people watcher for sure, especially out there because it's so far from home. I love running into old friends at shows, and seeing someone that I know way out there would be a real special surprise.

Toward the end of the game people started walking up to Bill Graham to say hi and thanks and shake his hand and as I was watching all of this, taking it all in, I had this thought; 'When will I ever get a chance like this again. Never right?'. . So I walked toward Bill Graham and as I extended my hand I was about to say, "Hey Bill, how you doing? Thanks for all the great music over the years. Very nice to meet you."

But it didn't come out of my mouth that way. What did come out of my mouth?? . . .

"Uncle Bobo. . .!!."

I don't know what possessed me, but I reached out to shake Bill's hand and called him "Uncle Bobo". Very enthusiastically I might add; big smile on my face. It wasn't much appreciated. It didn't come off well at all. In fact the moment I said it, I knew I shouldn't have. The Nickname Uncle Bobo was given to him by the Grateful Dead (More specifically Bob Weir) one year for his birthday because as Weir put it, "We didn't have any money to go out and buy him anything and 7-Eleven was closed."

He explained this scenario during the closing of Winterland show in 1978.

To say that I got an angry response would be putting it mildly.

He said, "Why would you call me that name? Would you like to go through life with a name like that? It's a rude name and I don't appreciate it".

I said, "I'm really sorry, I didn't realize it was a bad thing."

"Well, maybe in the future you should consider other peoples feelings before using such derogatory language."

I *wanted* to tell him that if Bob Weir wanted to call me "Uncle Bobo", then it would probably be pretty funny to me. Of course, I didn't say any of that. I really thought I was lucky enough, he didn't have me thrown out of the place.

On the plus side? Well, if there is a plus to this story it's gonna be that number one; It's a great story I can tell. I love the reaction I get every time I tell it. Second; my friends that were there at the moment will never forget that I called Bill Graham "Uncle Bobo" to his face and got yelled at for it! My friend Darren, a close friend of the family from the East Coast was standing with me when this conversation took place and he says that it's one of his favorite Grateful Dead moments of all time. It's one of mine too.

I started out saying that the Grateful Dead experience in California is really different, especially if you're used to the East Coast frenzy. The atmosphere is one of laid back enjoyment rather than crazy excitement, and the weather is almost always beautiful out there, as opposed to our most frequent touring season, that being March and October back East.

The comeback shows were very exciting for me. It had a lot to do with Jerry's recent brush with mortality I suppose, but the fact that I was seeing the Grateful Dead in their back yard definitely added to the already magical atmosphere, and being a part of this comeback experience was awesome. Everyone was so engaged in the musically charged atmosphere and so happy to see Jerry back on stage again. It was mesmerizing. It really never mattered what they played anywhere, at any time, but here in Oakland on this night, at this time it mattered even less. These shows were extra special for those of us lucky enough to be there. Set lists were so unimportant at this point that they could've stood on stage and tuned up for ½ an hour and no one would have complained. It was truly a special happening.

The opening song of their triumphant return was Touch of Grey, naturally, and the crowd was extremely enthusiastic during the "We will survive" chorus, as was Jerry. He was pumping his fist into the air and he was very noticeably mobile and energetic, more so than I had seen in recent years. As for the rest of the set lists, they were filled with the same kinda song selection that we had become used to, but the second set on the second night opened with the one song that's been eluding me for several shows in a row now. Phil stepped up and sang me my Box of Rain. I think I might have been only person in the whole crowd that hadn't heard it yet. This was my own personal Box of Rain. I accepted it and I loved it. I was crazy excited about it. I was also taping these shows and used the same mics for each night; Sennheiser 441's. I was set up in the first row right behind the soundboard and was able to hang out with all the friends that I met up with there.

The Neville Brothers showed up and joined the band during the drums portion of the show and stayed on for New Orleans style renditions of Hand Jive and Aiko Aiko all day! The Aiko settled nicely into a sweet, soulful Stella Blue and then they rocketed into Sugar Magnolia. Always a fun set closer no matter what. The boys came back at us with an encore of Midnight Hour, with the Neville Brothers in tow. At the time, the Neville's were enjoying some huge commercial popularity, due in no small part to Aaron Neville's amazing Grammy Award winning vocal performance, joining Linda Ronstadt on the hits 'Don't know Much' and 'Tell it Like it is'.

During the last of this three night stand something very unusual happened. It was probably the strangest thing I've ever experienced at a Grateful Dead show, or any other concert I've been to.

Anyway, on the third night in the middle of the first set. Weir apologized for repeating a song! Weir stepped up to his mic and said, "We're gonna beg your indulgence, and do this tune again, because we need to work on it."

I've seen some strange goings on at multiple shows, but in ten years of seeing the Dead play, I never heard an apology for anything. Funny thing is though, it wasn't one of his tunes. Jerry debuted When Push Comes to Shove at the first show. This was a new Hunter/Jerry tune that was just being worked out. At the second show they played 'Push to Shove' again toward the end of the first set. Then the third night, after his apology, Weir followed 'Push' with a sweet Music Never Stopped. I don't ever remember hearing Bobby apologize for playing Lost Sailor or Saint of Circumstance every fuckin night for two fuckin years in 1981 or 82, or whatever year that was. . .Just Kidding.

Getting back to the first night. After doing coke all night long the night before, we were both a little brain fried and needed something different for this first show of shows. We decided to check out the alternatives. Eventually we stumbled upon some mushrooms. "Hey Jim, guess what I just came across." (Awesome!) We gobbled them up and socialized for the rest of the night. I was taping all three shows out there, but that really can be on auto pilot if you just let it, you know? These shows were very high energy. There was no Dark Star or St. Stephen those nights, but the set lists were lively and long and the crowd enthusiasm couldn't have been better. Jerry said in an interview later that year, "There wasn't a dry eye in the house man."

After the show on the first night, Tom and I were headed out the back exit doors with everyone else and I thought I saw a girl that my friend Rick used to go out with. I told Tom that I thought I saw someone I knew and I took off running, not to *catch her* necessarily, but just to see if it *was* her. I didn't want to catch her or to even talk to her for that matter, but I hadn't seen her in such a long time I wanted to see if *time* had been good to her. She was always a cute girl, though exceptionally weird, and I was curious. I don't know what happened, but suddenly I realized I was just running for no apparent reason. (Ahh, mushrooms) It was a very strange feeling. Lost her as quickly as I had found her. . . And it didn't matter to me in the least. I turned around to see if Tom was still behind me and I saw him off in the distance, so I waited.

We found the car. . . right where we left it—always nice when it's still there—opened the doors and sat down to figure out where the hell we were going. Both still high on shrooms, we were in such a rush to get there earlier, that we really didn't pay much attention to how to get back. His friend had driven us to his place from the airport and neither of us really knew right away where that was either. Tom pulled out the map to take a futile look, but wound up having it upside down on his steering wheel so it may as well have been a map of China at that point. We both saw an immense amount of humor in this and God we laughed so hard. I have to say now that at times like these (or at a time like this) if you're not with somebody that has a really good sense of humor, you are so fucked! . . .Tom and I wound up laughing so hard that we had to get out of the car and rest our heads on the roof while we laughed. I think we walked around the car once or twice too. . . . God only knows how long that lasted. We finally stopped laughing long enough to realize that we weren't really laughing anymore—remember those shrooms, right??— so we decided it was time to try again. . . Tom says to me, "You wanna try this again. . . ?" I said, "Sure, I'll try this again."

And by the way it was a beautiful balmy night in Oakland, California. If I had to check my memory banks and hazard a guess, I'd have to say it was 65 degrees and dark, though the parking lot was lit up quite well and there were still Deadheads wandering out of the Coliseum at this point, so we had an interested yet non intrusive audience. We got back in the car and picked up the map. (again, not sure. . .Why the map?) You understand that in order for the map to be helpful we would have to know where we wanted to wind up, not just where the coliseum was. I was still unsure whether Tom actually knew where his friend lived. Yet the map was still upside down, and we started laughing again and got right back out of the car and laughed for another ten minutes. . . After a few, we got our heads back together and this time we were prepared to get going. The moment had passed and it was all good. Mushrooms are so much fun. Can I just say that? We made it back to his buddy's house by 3 AM, or so and all was good. We woke up at a reasonable hour and had a great day before showtime. This is still one of my favorite stories from the road and Tom and I still talk about it every once in a while.

The next day we went to the airport to pick up Tom's wife, who wasn't able to join us for our original flight. We did a lot of driving that day, all around San Francisco and eventually came across Lombard Street, so of course we had to drive down it. Lombard actually runs for 12 blocks between Broderick Street and Van Ness avenue (it's actually part of Route 101), but it's best known for the one block section between Hyde and Leavenworth Streets, which consists of eight sharp turns or what they like to call switchbacks. It is known as the crookedest street in the world. It was originally designed this way to alleviate the natural 27 % grade of the road, and because most motorists weren't able to make the climb straight up, it was eventually made a one way street reserved only for East bound (downhill) traffic at a speed of only 5 mph. (After having driven down this road, I challenge you to go faster than 5 mph.)

As we were rolling along, we were enjoying the view and checking out all the people who were checking us out, it was too funny. When we got to the bottom of Lombard Street and found Van Ness, we made a right and headed over to Geary Blvd., and then made another right. Then we made a left at Masonic Avenue and a right on Waller Street. (Yes, I am getting to my point) Guess where we are now? We are on Ashbury Street where the Grateful Dead shared a house at 710 with a bunch of other hippies from June of 1966 thru October of 1967. These old Victorian homes were allowed to run down by their landlords at the time, hoping for some redevelopment plan that they had been promised by the city, which apparently never happened. At the same time the hippy movement was happening, so they were all able to move into these beautiful Victorian houses and split the rent ten or fifteen different ways, which made for very affordable living quarters in San Francisco. After a good, strong, full year of this, the media caught up with it and the Grateful Dead decided not to be part of the documentary and split for Marin County. Jerry said, "As soon as we saw the first tour bus come through, we said 'we're outta here'." My friend Tom, and his wife and I took pictures of each other on these famous steps at 710 Ashbury. After enjoying an afternoon of Grateful Dead history and nostalgia, we headed back toward the scene of the present day Tie-dyed party.

The following January, the band went back to Marin County's Veterans Auditorium to record their first album in seven years. They set up as if they were playing to a live audience (just like they did to rehearse) with a remote truck outside where their sound engineers put down the music. While they were there, Bob Dylan started hanging out and the idea was brought up again for a tour together, which was eventually worked out.

At the end of January the boys once again scheduled shows commemorating the Chinese New Year. Three full shows included 57 songs with no repeats and a couple of special treats. The first night they opened with Shakedown into Lennon/ McCartney's *Get Back*. That was the only time that song was ever played. Apparently the band was having some type of equipment problem after Shakedown Street, and while they were trying to mastermind the situation, Weir was sharing random thoughts; "Technical difficulties, one, two, three...bravata, bravata...uno, dos, tres". . . then some chords were being played with and suddenly there it was, they were playing Get Back. The crowd went nuts of course. It actually came across sounding pretty good considering it was most likely unplanned. The only downside to the attempt was that Healy kept fucking with the vocal mix, making Weir's voice sound a lot like Mickey Mouse. The second night, the Chinese Symphony Orchestra opened the show, which I'm sure was really special. The third night, first set closer was a four song combination that was really amazing; Beat it on Down the Line > Promised Land > Chinacat Sunflower > I Know You Rider. There was a lot of great music to be enjoyed, and excitement filled the air. I was not at these shows, and neither were any of my friends, but the tapes came my way very quickly. Even though I never made it out to any New Years shows, I did make it to a few very special shows on the West Coast.

At this point, I am still working the overnight shift, so as with any extensive touring situation, I had to take a week off. Taking a vacation week to see the boys in California is a no brainer, but going back to being up all night working again afterward was not an easy situation to deal with at all. In fact, I don't mind saying that it sucked! I hate, hate, hate my job. Now three months later I'm planning another excursion down South to Virginia. That's right, Hampton again!! This time for three shows. It would be a weekend of great music and good times with a bunch of friends. The first night in Hampton, on March 22, 1987 was my 100th show. That's usually some kind of milestone isn't it? It's the 100th time that I've been lucky enough to witness the magic of the Grateful Dead. I felt privileged. I felt special. When a network television show broadcasts it's 100th episode, there are all sorts of celebrations and commercial time leading up to the big episode, but not in Grateful Dead land. Here it was special mostly to me and to some close friends. I told people about it during the course of the night, but I didn't make a real big deal about it. There are so many Heads that have shared this and many more milestones like it on tour, so it wasn't such an unusual accomplishment in these circles, just in my own head. Even my main touring buddy Bob had surpassed my number because my work schedule had stifled my touring availability so drastically. There were, however thoughts and memories flashing through my head all evening. After all, there was a lot of effort put into going to all those shows. A lot of time spent getting tickets and making hotel reservations. A lot of miles put on our cars and trucks (and sneakers) and a lot of money spent on beers and ice. (Can't leave out beers and ice now can I?) What we got in return was plenty of great, great music, plenty of new friends and lots of travel to beautiful and interesting places.

The show itself was fairly spectacular, and I'm just gonna go ahead and list the whole thing. Hell in a Bucket > Sugaree, All over Now, West La Fadeaway, El Paso, When Push Comes to Shove (4th show in a row hearing that one) then Cassidy > Deal to finish it off. The second set started off with Sugar Magnolia (nice touch Bobby)> Scarlet Begonias > Fire on the Mountain > Estimated Prophet >Drums >The Wheel > Black Peter > Sunshine Daydream. Sunshine Daydream and Sugar Magnolia are rarely split up, and when it happens it's a lot of fun. So they gave ME a big Sugar Mags sandwich for my 100th show, even though they were unaware.

The next two nights were special in their own way, but I'm not gonna list the songs. They were just great. We stayed at the KOA again, this time for three nights and then headed home to re-group before going to Hartford for two more shows. The Marriott in downtown Hartford served as our home away from home, our preferred hotel for a few years because it was really nice and somewhat inexpensive, which suited us just fine. The first night at the Veteran's Memorial Stadium gave us the always pleasing Midnite Hour first set opener followed very closely by old faithful Cold Rain and Snow. C.C Rider and Row Jimmy were followed by My Brother Esau > When Push Comes to Shove. Esau, we have just recently learned, was written by Bobby and Barlow years ago but was never quite ready for the stage until recently. Bobby did Desolation Row next, one of my favorite Dylan covers. I am really thankful that Bobby kept that one in rotation. That flowed nicely into Bird Song and then Promised land ended the set. Great music and an excellent Master recording; D-5M with Sennheiser 421's. Second set featured our China/

Rider sequence and a crowd loving He's Gone. The post space Miracle, Peter, Round and Round, Good Lovin kept us dancing all night and the Mighty Quinn encore was welcome after a an amazing set. One more night in Hartford, then we head home for the much more local Spectrum shows.

When I was relieved of the Night crew shift and took my position on days, I wound up in Ocean, New Jersey and met some really great people. One in particular relates to my story. Her name is Chris. Tina. Christina. I called her Chris. She was friendly with everybody, a bubbly adorable Italian girl. One day while working, I asked her if she ever saw the Grateful Dead play. I knew the answer to the question because of the music that I knew she liked so I simply added, "If I got you a ticket, would you come with me to see a Dead show at the Spectrum when the time comes." She kind of reluctantly agreed. We were just friends at work, nothing more. Maybe she was concerned it could be construed as a date. Maybe. Not sure. Anyway, when the time came I made the call and she agreed. Cool. We made it to the Spectrum in plenty of time and I ran into 30 people that I knew. Oh what fun it is to turn somebody on to this music, or try to. So I was taping and she's cool about it, but has never seen anything like this before. The tricky part here was I did not have floor seats. I handled this the same way I always do, but I'm usually alone for the process. I found a gate that was quite crowded, I turned to Chris', held her hand and said, "Just follow me and keep moving." When I saw my chance I slid past the guard and she was right with me like she had done this a million times before. We kept moving over seats and down through many aisles of people until we reached the floor wall. Then we hopped over it! Done it a thousand times before, what's one more, right? I patched into some nice Neuman mics and found two seats that were open and we took them over. "So How's this?" I asked, proudly. "Ha ha, this is great so far." I taped the show and it was awesome. I was concerned, as I would be with any other first timer, that she would have a good time. I really hoped that she would enjoy it and not break it down too much, as could be the case. Take in the crowd. Enjoy it. Get to see Jerry have some moments. The man had some excellent moments here, including Half-step, Playing jam into China Doll. Then Goin Down the Road Feeling Bad, post drums. It was a great night and she was taken in by the vibe and the crowd and enjoyed the music, but was not quite drawn in like I had been 8 years prior at Red Rocks. We drove straight to a diner I'd seen after the show the night before, which was right off the main hiway and talked until 4 am. The traffic had dispersed by then, and although that was not really my plan, it worked out nicely. Nice girl. Real person. Good friend. Thanks Chris. Glad you had fun and got to see Jerry play.

The crowds outside were amazing by now and Touch of Grey, which was really catching on even before the album came out, probably did as much damage as it did good. The scene outside had become very newsworthy at this point and there was even more curiosity about this phenomenon than usual. People were drawn to the excitement by the excitement, if you'll forgive the redundancy. Jerry's health problems made big news a year ago and the mere fact that he was back and the Grateful Dead was touring so strongly again after that crisis, was enough to garner some strong positive publicity. As a group of Deadheads that had been around for a few more years than some of the rest, we were all a little awe-struck by the attention being shown to our band of merry music makers.

I was speaking a moment ago about the crowds outside. The problem we were having stemmed from one small demographic. Some of the younger fans seemed to be a little misguided. These kids thought the whole idea was to get really drunk and see Jerry play. Some of these new-bies, or Touch Heads as some were labeled, were carried out on stretchers by the end of the night. Overdoses on unfamiliar drugs were becoming more frequent. Everybody has found themselves in that situation at least once in their younger lives. Trying to get drunk in too short a period of time and making themselves sick. I've done it. Usually once you' ve done that once or twice you wise up. After a few years of going all out, I decided that I really didn't want to drink a lot prior to shows anymore. I figured this out quite accidentally one night. Not intending to go sober, we were running late for a show somewhere and because we had little time to suck down any beers, I spent the whole night sipping the ocassional beer, without having going to the bathroom. I decided then that not drinking was not such bad idea. I would have a beer or two before hand, but not enough to generate bladder interest. Then after the show I'd have a few more and keep my head. I could stay up late with the buds and I still get up feeling pretty ok. That's definition of a good plan. As a taper, going to the bathroom during the show was such a huge hassle and I really didn't want to have to leave my seat for anything. (Not even for a "bathroom song") I did figure out a pretty neat trick to get back to my seat faster though. Being a taper I had a flash light with me most of the time, so one night at the Spectrum, on my way back to my seat I started shining my flash light on the people in front of me, lighting my trail (trail blazing, if you will) everybody in front of me assumed it was security coming through, so it parted the crowd very conveniently thank you very much! That was great! Anyway, the only way to not have to go to the bathroom during the show was to not drink so much before the show. Worked like a charm.

The Betty Boards

The taping network had grown quite a bit by the late 80's and then something extraordinary happened as a result of that. Let me explain; The Grateful Dead, thanks in part to Stan Owsley a.k.a. 'Bear', has about 15,000 audio tapes, about 3,000 video tapes, and more than 250,000 feet of 16mm film, in their vault. The formats include just about everything that has been around since the mid 60's. That would include 1/4 inch reels, ½ inch reels, 1" reels (8 track tape, from which some albums were produced), 2" reels, (16 track and 24 track, where most of the live and studio albums came from after 1969) Digital Audio Tape (DAT) and CD's and cassettes. The list continues, but here's the point. Betty Cantor-Jackson was the main recording engineer for the Dead for several years, and had since left the band. (Money disputes?) When she left, she had hundreds of hours of audio tapes that she had recorded directly from the soundboard. Eventually personal finance problems built up and she lost her home. Her personal belongings, including these tapes, wound up in a storage facility in Marin. When payments fell short, the contents were auctioned off. Even though they were aware of what was taking place, the band refused to bid out. A few hundred people showed up for the auction. Two or three Deadheads caught wind of the sale of this particular stash from some incredibly reliable source – know one really knew what the contents of the storage container was, until after the sale – and they put some money together to purchase this small chunk of Grateful Dead Legacy. They digitized them and started distributing some amazing music to the vast taper network. I was lucky enough to be a part of that network at the time.

News of the purchase spread quickly, like a fire in the dry mountainous regions of California. In-fucking-credible. The first tapes to surface for us were from the Capital Theatre in Portchester and the Manhattan Center in Manhattan, N.Y. These shows in Manhattan just happen to be the same shows where the 'Skull and Roses' Album (My desert island disc) was recorded and what made that much more interesting was the following. On the album, on side two, the album starts off with The Other One and goes into a 3 or 4 minute drum solo and then goes into an unforgettable version of Not Fade Away into Goin Down the Road Feeling Bad . It's a classic version and when it's played on the radio you can immediately tell it's the one. After which, it slides into a bit of We bid you Goodnight instrumental, then fades out. Well, at the show, that jam continues on into a blast your mind Lovelight, with an ever so slight, but noticeable cut toward the end of it. This was one of the problems with the older shows that were recorded on reel to reel tapes. There were cuts in the music that happened at some very inopportune times. These happened for a variety of reasons, not the least of which was the fact that not a lot of attention was being paid to the recording process all the time. In later years the taping process became more important to them, but it wasn't the 'be all end all' in those earlier years. (My opinion, but it seems likely)

A tell tale story about the above musical sequence; When we were hanging out at Chubb's Pub in Long branch and I requested they put this tape on, those in charge wanted to take it off almost immediately because it was so obvious that it was the Skull and Roses Not Fade Away. We only played tapes with live music that had not been officially released, so I had to beg them to trust me and listen to the whole thing. When it came to the end of GDTRFB and Pig started to sing Lovelight, they were shocked and very excited. That's just one example of the stuff we were getting thanks to the Betty Boards. When they first surfaced we were having some huge taping parties. We would get five or six decks together at a time so we could get them all as quickly as possible.

Cornell University, Barton Hall 5-7 and 8-1977. These classic shows had never been heard this clear and perfect. *St. Stephen, Scarlet Begonias, Morning Dew, Fire on the Mountain.* It was all there to feast on. Shows from 1973 -74 -77- 78 - 79, that nobody had good copies of were came to us sounding better than anything we had been hearing. The clarity was incredible.

It's funny now, that all this actually happened because in 1986, shortly after the return from his health crisis, Jerry was asked, during an interview about the possibility of releasing some material from the vaults for those that might be interested in buying it.

Jerry said, "Well, if left to me it would never get done, but it's a great idea for sure."

Jerry also said that looking back at what he had done was always a little embarrassing for him. Who knows, maybe all musicians feel that way. He said that he'd like to go back and just rerecord everything that he had ever played, but in the same breadth he also said that you don't go back. You just don't do it and that there's really no need to revisit that stuff. When asked about the sea of microphones in the audience he always said that, "Once we're done with it's their's to do with what they want. . . If they have the smarts to get it in, past all those people in charge of keeping it out, then have at it."

Regarding the high tech aspect; "If the equipment is unintrusive and you're not spoiling anyone else's good time, then why not go for it."

Jerry said that it always impressed him that the tapers respected each others space as much as they did. We were all there for the same purpose and I'll say that from my standpoint that there was always a mutual respect amongst most Deadheads.

Well, regarding the possible release of vault material for the fans, an old friend of Phil's by the name of Dick Latvala was given that 'dream job'. He was talking to Phil one day about going in and checking out some shit and Phil gave him the go ahead after a short discussion with the band. How did they get so lucky as to have someone take so much time, and give it so much thought? I know that if I was given that job I would've found it incredibly overwhelming. I would have a lot of ideas because of the experiences I've had behind me, but where to start would be a huge issue. 'Dick's Picks' they call 'em, and my favorite will always be number 15, Englishtown New Jersey. September 3rd 1977, my first show.

Dylan with The Dead...

So here we go again. When the Grateful Dead shared the stage with Bob Dylan and Tom Petty, the shows were really inspirational and exciting. The camaraderie that the Dead shared with Dylan spilled over into a new idea, a new concept if you will. Dylan and Jerry put their heads together and cooked up a plan to do a tour. Well, to be honest here, first of all, I don't really know how they did it, just that it happened and I was there. Second, I'm real sure that Jerry had as little to do with the planning as he possibly could. That being said, both wanted it to happen for sure. Jerry, because he loved Dylan's tunes and played them frequently, and Dylan, who recently finished a tour backed by Tom Petty, was probably excited to play with a guitar legend like Jerry. (My thoughts, my opinion.) They called Dylan 'Spike' because he spells his name the same way Weir does. . .They planned a stadium tour for the summer of 1987, which is where we are now.

The first show of the summer tour was at Schaefer Stadium in Foxboro Mass. At this time in my life, I was feeling great. My Grateful Dead touring had been incredibly stunted for two and a half years by the night crew shift, but that was over now. I can't begin to describe how normal I was feeling. I'm not even going to try. It was a freedom that I hadn't felt in long time. My friends and I were still going to Chubb's Pub every Tuesday night and that was still a lot of fun. The owner/manager of Chubb's took good care of us. He ran several bus trips during our tenure there. The bus always had a keg on-board and everybody always had a great time. We were all planning on going to Foxboro anyway, and while he had tickets for a lot of the seats, there was also room for those of us who had Dead Office Tickets. It's a really good thing that he ran the bus trips for a show like this one, because the traffic was atrocious. There was one long stretch of road leading into Schaefer Stadium, and once we could no longer move forward, we just made a space and stopped.

The walk forward from that point was typical of the outdoor Dead show experience. There were so many people that had to walk from there and further that the parking lot seemed to have no end. Luckily, we didn't have that far a walk before we could see the stadium and the main parking lot. Oh, did I happen to mention that this was the fourth of July and the band was introduced this day by John Scher;

"Whoa!!. . On keyboards, Mr. Brent Mydland. On drums, Mickey Hart and Bill Kreutzman, on Bass Phil Lesh, on guitar Jerry Garcia and on guitar Bob Weir. Ladies and Gentlemen, The Grateful Dead!"

The boys played one really long opening set with elements of the first and second sets combined. Starting with the always emotional of late, Touch of Grey. Bobby followed with Hell in A Bucket, after a 30 second necessary break. Bobby, "We gotta take a minute here, while the roadies nail Billy's other foot down." After which, the dancing was seamless. The crowd was filled with dancing rainbows of color and every Deadhead in attendance was very aware of the magic that was to happen that afternoon at Sullivan Stadium. We nearly lost Jerry less than a year ago and now we are about to be treated to a concert that includes what could easily be considered the most classic pairing of two musicians ever, who've only recently been sharing a stage together. This would be the first time in public. After the Dead's extended first set, which included West La Fadeaway, Tons of Steel, Lil' Red Rooster, Box of Rain, Althea, (2nd set nudging its way in) Uncle John's Band, Playin in the Band, drums, space, Truckin,

The Other One, Wharf Rat, and Throwing Stones, Dylan came out and played for us with the Dead backing him. I've only seen Dylan play twice in my life. Once way back in 1981 at the Meadowlands Arena, when it was still called Brendan Byrne Arena, and then again in the summer of 1989, sandwiched between two sets of Dead shows in different cities. Pardon me a moment while I state the obvious. It was a real treat to see Bob Dylan play his songs with Jerry Garcia and the Grateful Dead playing behind him. They played fourteen songs including drums and then 'Spike' came out and played thirteen songs including the encore. Coincidently, no wait. Ironically, they finished with Knockin on Heaven's Door, which is one of the Dead's favorite sendoffs. Times They are a Changing, Man of Piece, and I'll be your Baby Tonight were the first three songs of Dylan's set. I mention this because for 'Baby Tonight', Jerry sat down at a Pedal Steel Guitar, which he hadn't played since around 1973. Rehearsal tapes had been circulated and everyone heard that Jerry was playing the Pedal Steel on one song, so I was kind of prepared for it, but when I saw him sit down to play, it brought real tears to my eyes. Jerry said years ago that he gave up the Pedal Steel because he didn't have the time to devote to it. He felt he would need another lifetime to learn the instrument well enough for his own comfort. I'll tell you what. He played it very well that day in Foxboro.

Their album, In The Dark came out on the 6th of July to rave reviews. The public was ready for a good Grateful Dead album, (This happened to be a great-ful Dead album, pardon the pun) but I don't think the Grateful Dead was quite ready for it. The scene exploded. Touch of Grey went to number six on the Billboard Charts and the album went Platinum in the first week. It was huge for the boys, but it sucked too. There were barely any tickets available before this happened, and now there were even less than that, if that's even mathematically possible!

The scene outside became unruly and at times uncontrolled. Nothing that we had experienced in the past could have prepared us for this shit. I have often wished that more people understood the depth of this music and maybe understood us a little more you know. Maybe learn to reserve judgment for a group of people who go to such lengths to follow a band around the country. Come and check out the music. Enjoy what we've been witnessing for years. But I'd go back to mis understood freaks in a heartbeat after witnessing this turmoil. Everything that I've described about the tour up to now is hardly even relevant anymore. Thousands upon hundreds, (strike that, reverse it), showing up hoping to find tickets that have been sold out for months and no one listens when you tell them to, "Stay home if you haven't got a ticket." Even when the band goes out and issues an official statement, no one listens because everyone thinks they're going to find that one miracle ticket. The miracle ticket doesn't even refer to a free one anymore, it refers to any ticket that you can find. And yes, I could go on, but I think my point has been made!

The next show we hit was four shows later on their itinerary, but it was the next time Dylan played with the band again. JFK Stadium in Philadelphia was the show, July 10th . They played seventeen songs in the first set including drums. . . .Wow! Great show. I was standing at about 25th row, if there had been seats, and I had a tremendous view of the whole stage. Dylan opened his part of the show with Tangled up in Blue, another Garcia Band standard, then I'll Be your Baby Tonight, with Jerry at the Pedal Steel again. The encore for this show was Touch of grey, which Spike sat in for. Spike played thirteen songs that day including Simple Twist, Memphis Blues, Judas Priest, Ballad of a Thin Man, and You Gotta Serve Somebody. I should also mention Slow Train Coming, because Jerry pulled off some amazing leads that even had Dylan's ears perking up. GD Productions released a live CD of these shows entitled 'Dylan and The Dead Live'.

These shows with Bob Dylan were nostalgic, if nothing else. Dylan's voice didn't lend itself to live performing much. (My opinion) He's not much of a singer at all anymore,(my opinion) but it was a sight to see him jamming with Jerry Garcia on songs that we knew Jerry loved to play. That was the relative extent of these shows for me, and maybe for most. The other thing that was really great about this pairing was that a lot of Dylan fans that never got around to seeing Jerry, finally had a reason and that had to be cool for them. We went to Giants Stadium for the final East Coast appearance of the Dylan Dead tour. This time there were two electric sets by the boys and one final set with Spike. Slow Train, Memphis Blues, Tomorrow is a Long Time, which was only played once the whole tour. Then Hiway 61, Baby Blue, Ballad of a Thin Man, John Brown, Wicked Messenger and Queen Jane Approximately. Bobby sucked up Queen Jane and Memphis Blues for his personal repertoire for the rest of their tours. Chimes of Freedom, Joey, All along the Watchtower and Times They are Changing ended the set and when they all came out for the encore, they played Touch of Grey into Knocking on Heaven's Door. Everybody in the Stadium seemed to be having a rockin' good time. Myself included.

Jerry said in a in interview later on that the strangest thing about performing with Dylan was "Teaching him how to play his own songs. Learning 'Desolation Row' was most challenging because it had so damn many words in it"

Asked by Weir if he still knew them, Dylan just said, "I know the most important ones."

Rocky Mountains Revisited
Red Rocks & Telluride

Now that we've gotten through the Dylan /Dead Shows with all the publicity and the large video screens and the out of control crowds, we can get back to our norm. The crowds were not literally out of control mind you, but seriously, unless you have a field seat, the intimacy is gone and although you don't have to be lucky to get a ticket for these stadium shows, you might consider bringing binoculars for a better view. That being said, in less than a month we would be planning the trip that will always standout in my mind as the most exciting, most memorable road trip of my life, that I wouldn't trade for anything. (Except for my son's health and well being, but do I really have to say that?) The Grateful Dead had three more shows to play on the West Coast with 'Spike' and then they were going back to the mountains once more and we were planning to catch up with them right there.

I mentioned earlier that we were last out in the Great Rocky Mountains in 1983, when we stayed at Chief Hosa Campground for a week to catch three shows at Red Rocks. This time I took a week off and added a personal holiday or two and a couple of days off or something, but I didn't have to be back to work for almost two weeks. I always tried to make sure I had some time off when I came off the road to "detox" in a way, because I hated coming off a long road trip and going right back to work. We got tickets through Ticketmaster and then we heard about a ticket scam that was spreading through the crowd. Apparently dozens of counterfeit tickets were being sold for these shows. They said that if you got your tickets from a source other than Ticketmaster, they were probably counterfeit. Well, the next thing you know people are getting turned away with real tickets too! This was crazy. They had a verification system, a type of laser gun, all new technology then, so they would scan your ticket for authenticity and give a Yay or a nay. All this being said, how do you really know until you're inside, whether you're actually gonna *make it* inside. I heard at least one story of a someone being turned away holding a ticket that was genuine and that really sucks! By the way we wound up having no problems with our tickets.

This time out, Bob and I brought one of the girls with us. Kathy was a new friend in our circle and a rare special guest. Everybody knew her as Zombie, I don't know why. No one else in our usual posse was able to make it this time so it was just the three of us. We flew out to Denver and rented a 1987 Buick Century. It was a beautiful little car and it was definitely less taxing on the brain than having to drive all the way and still have a mode of transportation once we were out there. We drove down to Chief Hosa — like the old pros that we were, not old as in 'we're old' but seasoned veterans, you get the idea — and set up camp early. This time we had tickets yeah!!. During our stay at Chief Hosa we ran into Andy again. He was one of the guys we met in 1983 with Bogey and Tokey, but now he was with different friends. Andy really wanted to go to Telluride, but he was riding with "a bunch of losers", his words not mine, so he asked us in the most unassuming way if we wouldn't mind making room for him in our little luxury vehicle. Of course we gave him a ride, why wouldn't we?

So here we are at Red Rocks Amphitheater in Morrison, Colorado. Unlike any other concert venue. Some may say, the perfect venue to see Jerry and the boys play. When the night skies are perfect, as they were that first night, you take the walk to the top of the theater to enjoy the incredible view of Golden, Colorado. Even without perfection, the view is breathtaking and the night skies present atmospheric conditions rarely enjoyed by the average concert audience. At times you can see a storm off in the distance. This of course includes flashes of lightening and wispy clouds, seemingly reaching across the sky, then stretching down to the ground. One can only imagine what it's like for them to play there, even though they have so many more experiences to compare it to, not the least of which would be the Great Pyramid in Egypt; Enough said.

First night August 11th 1987.

They gave us a Cold Rain and Snow opener in Colorado that first night, and thankfully that was the only sign of bad weather. The set included the first High Time since May of '86 and there after we were treated to a little fancy tuning exercise known to seasoned Deadheads as fenniculi fennicula. The second set opened with Crazy Fingers > Samson and Delilah, a great combo on any night, followed by Ship of Fools. When I first heard Crazy Fingers on the Blues for Allah album, it was among the list of songs that I thought I would never hear played live. I need to search my memory banks to find the first version of the song I heard, but I know it was a song that I didn't hear a lot. (Dead Base VII tells me it was Landover Maryland 9-15-82, the same night the band debuted Touch of Grey, as an encore)

Second night August 12th

The second night featured a Hell in a Bucket opener into Sugaree, the first in a long line of this combination. The good thing is that we love Sugaree. It's a tune that Jerry kept on his short list for both of his musical outlets or inspirations. He must have some special love for that song, maybe he loved it more than we did! Next, Brent gave us his Good Time Blues, but right before that came another fun tuning exercise, which became Camptown Races.

As I refer to tuning exercises, I should take a moment to explain. Anytime there was an issue; hassles with equipment, maybe a broken string, or a blown speaker; it didn't matter much what it was, a little Jam might start that would either turn into something they weren't expecting, or go off into its own oblivion and disappear. Over the years they've played *Camptown races* several times and back in 1974 they used the Beer Barrel Polka theme quite a bit. They've also picked up The Adam's Family theme and even the *Close Encounters theme*. Once in Dayton Ohio a little tune up ditty turned into *Mack the Knife*, and was followed by Bird Song. At Giants Stadium in 1989 they played the *Mexican Hat Dance* ditty into Feel Like a Stranger. It turns what could be awkward silence, or in their case actual Dead air, into a slight musical distraction with possible amusing results for all.

After Brent's tune, Jerry took us back to Workingman's Dead with Cumberland Blues straight into Weir's Mexicali Blues, a pretty rare, but very welcome combo. The second set gave us an incredible Chinacat Sunflower > I Know you Rider, followed by Women are Smarter, and a nice long Terrapin Station, which was sweet and amazing. Jerry was all over it with sweet leads and crystal clear vocals. Other One> Fantasy> Wharf Rat> Lovelight closed the second set. The encore was The Mighty Quinn.

After the shows we headed back to the Campground to relax by the fire, drink the beers we had left on ice and talk about the show. We were all pretty spent after the second night because of the excitement of the first show, coupled with no sleep the first night. By the third day we were already talking about how we were getting to Telluride and who all was going. The ticket for Telluride was a weekend package deal, just one ticket for the two days and we had those already. Someone in our camping circle had told us about a Town Pass that was in the local Newspaper, so that was the first thing we looked for when we got into town. The Town Pass allowed the holder to drive into the Town on the day of the show and set up a camp inside the Park.

Third Night August 13th

Well, getting back to the 3rd and last show at Red Rocks; the boys opened the final night with Big Boss Man > Jack Straw, and then Row Jimmy, All Over Now, Loser, and Cassidy, then Brent's tune Far From Me was next, and Box of Rain ended the set. The second set provided the perfect ending to a three night stand, opening with Uncle John's Band > Estimated Prophet > He's Gone > drums. . .Followed by an exceptionally spacey jam into The Wheel > Gimme Some Lovin, (another gem that Brent brought to the repertoire via Stevie Winwood) and that slid nicely into Stella Blue > Throwing Stones > Not Fade Away. I have to talk for a moment about the chant that developed in the late 80's, whereby the entire crowd would sing very loudly, "Ya know our love will not fade away." Let me take you inside the experience for a moment.

The house lights come on for a few minutes and the crowd does its usual milling around. While this is going on the chant starts. "You know our love will not Fade away!. . . Ya know our love will not fade away." Clap, clap, clap, clap, clap and so it goes, on and on for a few more minutes until we have recognition and the house lights go out again. Then the crowd really goes wild. The chant gets louder. "Know our love will not fade away!" The clapping becomes more consistent. The Grateful Dead, over the years, has rarely taken a request from any audience, but this particular time I think it was difficult to ignore. The boys are completely aware of the chant and respond in kind by joining us for a few, 'mmbop, bop, bop, bops'... I would say this was done purposely to "gain control of the room" again, but what do I know? However, once they had control again, they slipped into Touch of Grey very sweetly and tore it up. The crowd really loves this song because of the *"I will Survive"* refrain. Of course, everyone wants their opportunity to tell Jerry personally how glad they are that he's alive and well. After Touch, they finished off with Knockin on Heaven's Door, which is also still very poignant at this time. This was a great ending to a wonderful three night stand at a beautiful venue.(A rock concert on the rocks) Although I didn't know it would be at the time, this was my last show at Red Rocks. I'm hoping that one day when I have some disposable income, I'll make the trip again to see another band command that stage and maybe compare the energy. (As if!)

So now we are heading down to Telluride for two shows in the park. (You know how I love the park) These shows were one of a kind and once in a lifetime as far as I'm concerned. Bill Graham made a special point of holding back a number of tickets and announced that "Anybody that showed up without tickets for the concerts in Telluride would not be allowed within City limits" The day before the shows he released those tickets he held and those Deadheads that took the chance were pleasantly surprised. Bill owned a home in Telluride and made promises to the Mayor regarding the fans of the Grateful Dead, so he had special permission to promote these shows. It was, by any standards, a most incredible place to see the band play. An old friend recently approached me and said, "I want to ask you a question and I want you to answer it quickly. Don't even think. Where was your favorite Grateful Dead show?" Having gone through this writing process, I didn't have to think very long or very hard. I said, "Telluride Colorado, 1987." Surprised by my quick response he asked, "Really, why?" I explained my answer like this; There were two shows in Telluride, never to be repeated. (Honestly, even at the time I didn't think this would ever happen again) The weather was beautiful; crisp and sunny. The shows had an intimacy factor that was hard to explain, but very comfortable and easy. However, the best or the most surprising thing about this place was the welcome wagon treatment we received while we were there.

There was a trust level and a kindness shown to us in Telluride that was quite surprising at a time when the new album, In The Dark, had just been released and the new single, Touch of Grey had caused such a frenzy. We really didn't know what to expect, and honestly, I don't think we would've seen this type of kindness anywhere else. Maybe it was just small town hospitality that we were witnessing, who knows. Every merchant in town kept their shops open and allowed us to venture in and out at our leisure, and they had a huge banner hung up at the entrance to the town that said "Welcome Deadheads" The Dead had never played there before, and it was generally known to most people (me anyway) as a Ski Resort and a celebrity hang-out. What were they thinking, inviting a bunch of Deadheads to a place like this? The truth is, not only were they ready for us, but they treated us with respect. Who knows why it happened, it was just wonderful to be treated like human beings amidst the chaos, rather than being the reason for the chaos. And by the way, there was no sign of chaos. The best part was our apparent payback to them. Everybody cleaned up after themselves, so there was no real cleanup necessary.

These shows took place on the soccer field in Town Park, at the end of Main Street. Main Street is a two lane road separated by a walkway. Heading south into town, two snow-capped mountain peaks could be seen, which were separated by a shallow valley. Aside from that, there was nothing but clear blue skies and sunshine for miles. On the left side of Main there were a dozen little stores selling everything from books and clothing to your basic souvenirs and then there were Bars and Restaurants. The store fronts were each painted a different bland color ranging from pale yellow to lime green, sky blue to brick red and each one had an almost matching color canopy hanging off the front window. Across the street were taller, more majestic looking commercial buildings. These were all the color of Red Brick with a beige trim and green rooftops. One could guess that these structures were all built during the same time period, while those across the way were built up over a much longer period.

When standing in Town Park during the show, the mountains that I mentioned previously were right behind me and to my left, but because of the way Town Park sat in the middle of Telluride, there were also mountains off in the distance in front of me and to my right. I could actually stand in any one spot in the Park and see nothing but snow capped mountains all around me. But facing straight ahead, I could see the Grateful Dead playing in yet another beautiful outdoor setting. Seeing them in a place like this was incredible. This was my favorite place to see them play. Red Rocks was my introduction to 'amazing' way back in 1979, but Town Park in Telluride, Colorado took that amazing feeling to another level that was different and special in its own way. At this point, we were all relaxed and ready for another great afternoon with Jerry and the boys. Whenever I'm in a situation like this I have to wonder if it was like this at Woodstock. (There's no way it was like *this* at Woodstock. . . .)

The show opened with a powerful Stranger > Franklins. Then Bobby did his Minglewood thing, "Couple more shots 'o whiskey, these Rocky Mountain Phillies start looking good...."
Then later, "Tee for Texas, and it's Tee for Timbuktu. Then it's Tee right here in, wherever we are....where the little girls know what to do." Yea, its Telluride Bobby.
Jerry followed with a soulful Candyman, like I've never heard before. Maybe it was the perfect spot on a perfect day and I heard the lyrics just a little differently. Sometimes it just happens that way. The second set was interesting enough, opening with Scarlet > Fire. Then they hit the Eyes of The World that should have followed Estimated Prophet at Red Rocks. The Eyes sank into drums and space followed by Miracle > Bertha and then Morning Dew > One More Saturday Night. The encore was It's all Over Now Baby Blue. Not quite over yet guys. . .

The ambiance at a show like this is hard to describe to someone who has never experienced it. The show is over and people are wandering about, taking in the scenery and enjoying a beautiful afternoon. Not the typical mass exit happening because for the most part, everybody is camping in the park.
So what goes on between the encore from the first show and the first song on the second day? We catch up with friends and make a few new ones in the process. We had our tents set up toward the back edge of the park, but in the mix. Bob had a friend (Dave) that rented a condo up the street, so we were headed that way for the moment. The condo was beautiful. The entrance was in the back, that opened to a kitchen off to the right. The living room was large for a condo, and there was a hallway that

led to a bathroom and a large bedroom on the left with a smaller room to the right and a large hallway closet. The condos were all the same size, mirror images of each other and they were all quite roomy and beautiful.

Another thing about this trip that sticks out in my mind was not having a shower since we left Colorado. That sounds gross doesn't it?? Yea well, them's the facts. No shower for a day and a half will drive a person to extreme measures, and I'll tell you what I mean. The next morning after trying to figure out what would satisfy my hunger (we had nothing with us in that regard at all) I stood in line for the coldest shower I have ever taken, and hopefully will ever have to take in my life. The showers were set up in a long line, much like port-a-potties and we just waited in line. The person ahead of the person in front of me came out and said, "Be prepared for the cold. There's no hot water for miles." (With a semi-grin on his face) I looked up at the mountains and realized that the water couldn't possibly be warm. It was, in fact so cold that I thought the water was coming straight down off the snow capped peaks. It was like ice, crashing down on my head, which gave me an instant headache. If I could have gotten away with just washing my hands believe me I would have, but I figured that this might be the last time I would have this opportunity for maybe another day and a half. . . Whatever. Some people don't mind going for days without showering, but I ain't one of *them*, that's for sure. Anyway, the shower has been taken and will never be forgotten, but for now it's done.

Later in the day, we gathered together (earlier than the day before), so we could catch Baba Olatunji and his Drums of Passion. They opened for the Dead on both days, but we really didn't pay much attention to them the first day. They are really good, don't get me wrong about that, but having been to a ton of shows over the years with a drum solo at every one, save one or two, you have to realize that it's been played. I don't mean to take anything away from our percussionists of course because they are amazing. I have seen the look of intensity on Mickey Hart's face while he's pounding away on those skins of his and it's some serious shit, and Billy is a human drumming machine for sure, but I can count on one hand the amount of times that I actually continued to dance through a drum solo. It's rare. Baba Olatunji and his Passion drummers are a very spiritual group that the boys met while in Egypt in 1978. They built a strong relationship with Mickey and the rest of the Band. I'm going to spare the set list here, except to say that they did pull out an Aiko Aiko and a Big RxR Blues > Promised land to close out the first set. Second set they played a Push to Shove > Samson and Delilah, which is always powerful and then He's Gone > The Other one > Truckin, which is also always a welcome tune to hear. It definitley gets the most air play of any Grateful Dead song on the radio, except maybe for Sugar Magnolia and most Deadheads really still enjoy hearing it. What a long strange trip it's been. . . Indeed!

The end of the show they played Touch of Grey for the encore and went into Brokedown Palace out of it. Brokedown started off sounding a little off for some unknown reason. I mean these things do happen at the beginning of songs sometimes so I thought nothing of it really. *"Gonna leave this brokedown palace on my hands and my knees, I will row row row. Make myself a bed, by the waterside, in my time in my time. . ."* and Jerry's looking at his guitar like some else is playing it. (. . trails off, fades down)

Jerry stops and says, "Wait a minute, this is all Fucked Up, man!",

Then Bobby, "Oxygen deprivation"

Jerry, "We're in the wrong key! . . .(laughing)

You people are used to this, the altitude and all. . . You know"

Everybody got a good chuckle out of this one.

Then they started it over again, and just about made it. It was very funny to watch. They were scratchin their heads as if they didn't know what had gone wrong, but we loved it anyway. We are, after all, a very forgiving audience.

Directly after the show Bill Graham took the stage; "We wanna thank, for making all this possible, obviously first the Grateful Dead and Baba Olatunji. We'd also like to extend a very special thank you for a group of people who, through the years, have put on the greatest sound that rock n roll has ever heard. Ultra Sound, people from Marin County who put up the sound all through these years and made the radio broadcast possible here in Telluride. We wanna mention the next few gigs. The group will be in Tempe, Arizona on Tuesday. They'll be at Park West on Thursday in Utah, in Calaveras County Ca. this coming weekend, or two weeks from now. We wanna thank you all

for treating this town the way you would your own. It's been extraordinary. And last we 'd like to bring out a representative of this community who does represent all of the people in Telluride that made this possible. Mayor Chip Lennahand, Mayor of Telluride."

"Far out! I just have a couple of things I'd like to say. Bill has thanked the bands, but what I'd like to do is. I'd like to thank the entire Bill Graham organization. You people are part of one of the most incredible events in this town's history. And it was made possible by a three way partnership. The Bill Graham Presents group. The town of Telluride, your hosts, the people that live here. . . and lastly, you guys. Thanks to you, it's working. God Bless."

You know, it's really nice when the promoter says 'thanks for everything that you've done', rather than 'let's help clean up the mess, so we will be invited back here next year'. Honestly, I don't think there was ever a chance that we might be back the following year, for whatever reason, but it wouldn't be because of anything that we did while we were there. We certainly can all be very proud of that. Yeahh, Deadheads!

As we left the area that afternoon something really special happened. Mickey Hart had started a drum procession up Main Street with all of Olatunji's drummers. Before we were aware of that, it had already progressed up the street and dispersed, but people were still talking about it, so I ran up the street a little to see just exactly what was happening. What I could see. As I kept up pace with the crowd someone said that Garcia was in the white van that had just passed us. Well I had to see this for myself, so once again I started running, but a little faster now. As I got closer to the van, I saw a shadowy figure getting up from the back seat and moving toward the front passenger side of the van. The crowd had gathered thick around the front of the vehicle, so it had come to a complete stop. Jerry was now sitting in the front seat and had rolled down the window to say hi to a couple of loyal fans. As smoothly as I could, I made my way to the side of the van where Jerry was now casually greeting the crowd. As I reached in to shake his hand the crowd suddenly opened up for me, just enough. I was now face to face with The MAN. I reached in toward Jerry and he happily shook my hand as I said, "Hey Jerry, thanks for coming to Telluride."

He said, "Well, thanks for having me, man." Then I said, "It's great to see you looking so healthy again, keep it up. . .we love you."

As I turned away to give others the same courtesy I had been shown, I heard someone ask Jerry when we'd hear St. Stephen again. He answered, "I don't know, in and out of the Garden he goes." I remember they played it at the Garden shows in 1983 and then again in Hartford the same week. It's times like these when I truly realize that the best things in life are absolutely free. Seeing Jerry up close and personal like that was the perfect way to top off an amazing week of shows.

A note on the side; In his book, Blair Jackson mentions in a passage that "The driver asked Jerry if he wanted him to get outta there, but Jerry said, "No man. I haven't said hi to them in a while so let's do that."

I'm certain that he was talking about this moment, because it seemed like exactly what could've taken place at that moment. As much as Jerry didn't like his guru status in the media, he really did appreciate the fans. The Deadheads. He knew that we genuinely cared for him, especially in these last few years.

The whole town of Telluride continued to treat us like family for the remainder of our stay there. We wandered in and out of shops like we were in our own home town just killing some time. I for one, would have totally understood if they shunned us after the shows were over, you know like "Please go home now", or "You don't have to go home, but we'd appreciate it if you'd just go away." There was none of that. We did split soon after the shows, but not before indulging a little bit more at the condo. I didn't spend much time there, but Bob did. I don't think I saw him all day the after the first show, but no biggie of course. We all got together for a final 'see ya later' and then we were off. Now, remember my friend Andy hooked up with us at Red Rocks for the ride down here to Telluride, right? (He was also with me at Caldwell College for Garcia) Well, he was now hooking up with another ride to go to Tempe and Park West, the next two shows on the grid for the boys. I mentioned to him that I didn't have to be back to work until Thursday, which was four days from then so he said, "Come on Jimbo, let's go to Tempe. It'll be great!" I had no tickets, but I did have some money. I really considered the idea for a few, but I really didn't want to suck up my down time at home before going back to work, so I decided to stay with Bob and drive home. It was the best thing for me at the time.

The Oldest Deadhead I know

Gonna rock on back to Telluride for a moment. During the break, between sets, I had a Fredo encounter. He was another friend I was introduced to through our mutual friend Tom F., from outside my core group of friends. (Fredo is the guy that borrowed my Sony D-5M in May of 1982, to record that Spectrum show). Well, anyway he came stumbling out of the crowd. Not drunk mind you, he was just stumbling around looking for people and ran right past me. I got his attention just long enough for him to say, 'I gotta see somebody real quick.', while holding up one finger to say, 'be right back', and then he was gone. . . in a blurr. . .and that was it. . . I didn't see him again for months after that. In fact, it was such a long time that I didn't even remember to ask him what the hell happened to him out there. Not that he would've remembered anyway. I heard just a few months later that he had been involved in a near fatal car crash. His car hit a phone pole at the corner of his block in Bay Head and he was thrown through the windshield of the vehicle. He was DOA at the hospital, but was revived and while the Doctors were examining him they were perplexed by the amount of drugs in his system at the time. Several of his friends told the doctors what his deal was so they assumed he was a drug addict as well and held him for psych evaluation. After the consult the Doctor told him that they were not fully prepared to deal with a person with his hallucinogenic background and experiences, and relinquished their ties to him, simply allowing him to heal. Now that's a story.

His name is Alfred, but he picked up the name Michael through his childhood like most other people pick up any nickname. Almost everybody that knew him, called him Fredo. Those that were only aware of him referred to him as Fredo. He got that moniker when, upon his return from Vietnam, his close friends were calling him Major Commandant Alfredo Sir. (With the obligatory salute, very 'tongue in cheek') The Alfredo came out of the Lord of The Rings 'Frodo' character, which turned into Fredo from there and then the name stuck.

Fredo was and is an iconic figurehead of the Grateful Dead world in our close circle of Deadheads. His closer friends may not have felt that way, but I always have. As the title states, he was the oldest Deadhead that any of us knew. Certainly the oldest that I knew, and people that know him also know that when you get him talking, the stories that spill from his brain are at once amazing and unbelievable. And if you were dropping liquid acid in the 80's, it's more than likely it had a 3rd or 4th degree connection to him, and if you're listening to a live tape of a show from before 1977 and not necessarily a soundboard, but sounds amazing, it was probably recorded by him, or his friend Jerry Moore (R.I.P., Relix Magazine) or his other friend Barry Glassberg, all of whom were close friends of his and original tapers.

Born in 1947, Mike had the misfortune of being drafted for a short time and serving in Vietnam for a year before finding himself back in California, enjoying all that the Bay Area had to offer. At the time, two friends that he was hanging with were playing around with LSD. At first glance, his friends were off hiding in the bushes, afraid of their own shadows so he's thinking 'I don't think that shit's gonna be for me' and for a brief time, he wrote it off. Within a very short time though, realizing that the dosage could be better controlled, he did partake and enjoyed the experience to its fullest extent. Mike told me that he saw the Grateful Dead, not quite on purpose for the first time at The Filmore East in New York City in 1967 and it was quite scary. The music was 'out of hand' and there were these chicks dancin completely naked up toward the stage which only added to the strangeness of the evening. He remembered that the girls got chased out of the theater, but after getting dressed again were allowed back in only to strip naked again....Ha!

This being said, Fredo wasn't so much a Deadhead at the time, but much more into the LSD experience. Some people that I've met over the years were so much into doing acid that it would seem strange to them to exist in a world without it. Fredo said that LSD, the drug, Lysergic diethylamide was such an amazing mind melder, mind expander and colorful rainbow of feelings and thoughts and dreams and pictures and experiences, that it was just exactly the perfect fit for this band. . .The Grateful Dead. He was also a huge Beatles fan and loved Pink Floyd, but these bands didn't stack up to the acid high as completely, as did the Grateful Dead. Even the Allman Brothers didn't exactly make the cut. His first show was at the Filmore in December 1967. He recalled that it was, "Fuckin freezing cold outside." Still, only there by accident and not high enough to take it in. His next show was at The Filmore again two nights later with the LSD enhancement and he was highly impressed by the sounds he was surrounded by. His third show was at the Filmore again the following January and at that point he was hooked.

The acid that was available then was mostly, but not exclusively being manufactured by Owsley. Two other gentlemen were in on the festivities as well. When Fredo discovered Crystal LSD the whole scene kind of exploded for him and the others involved. (That's not to say that he actually discovered Crystal. I mean that he discovered it for himself. He tried it for the first time.) His mind blowing example of this consisted a few granules of salt randomly dropped from a salt shaker onto the bar we were seated at. He moved most of it out of the immediate area and left about 10 countable granules of salt before me.

He said, "One tenth of this small amount would be enough for myself and three of my good friends to get high for a lot longer than you'd want to be high."

I said, "One tenth of this amount right here?"

"Yea," he said, "and then you and my other two friends take a granule each and I scoop up the rest. (a quick wipe of the finger across the bar for effect and the salt is now gone) So now, I'm gonna crawl under a table over there against the wall and curl up into the fetal position and not be *ABLE* to form a sentence for about 6 hours. I mean this shit they were dealing was mind bending to an extreme, and it would put 95% of the people on their asses while the other 5% would come back for more. What fun is that right? I had to figure then, that since the Crystal had to be diluted with distilled water anyway, then why not water it down a little more and at least be able to enjoy the high, rather than getting totally lost in it."

So somewhere in that scenario there became the greatest connection for liquid acid ever, in our lifetime, or time line might be a better word. Of course, one of the funniest stories related to this incredible phenomenon was the fact that he, in those days, rarely worked so when someone in his circle of friends was dosed to 'the edge' on any particular evening Fredo's first response was always, 'so go home for a couple of days and sleep it off, what's the big deal!' The big deal was that everybody else had a job and didn't have the option of taking an acid 'sick week' as it were. . ha!

Fredo told me another pretty funny story about a trip to the Beacon Theatre to see Jerry Garcia. He and his friend had seats in the 5th row center, and he dosed his friend, knowingly, but soon after the initial dose his friend realized what he was in for and got pretty upset. He started to walk toward the lobby of the theatre to get his bearings and Fredo followed his friend toward the door. As his friend explained to him that he needed to leave the theatre to get some air, Fredo explained to him what he might find outside the door as opposed to what he was presently experiencing inside the theatre. "Out there, you're gonna find 'bright lights, big city' flashing marques and streaks of yellow speeding taxi cabs and honking horns from frustrated drivers, not to mention 'Mr. Policeman', who might wonder why you keep staring at the traffic lights as if you're keeping track of the minutes between them changing colors, *or . . .*you could give yourself a minute or two inside this place with a bunch of other freaks, most of whom might be right where you are at this very moment and so it won't matter to any of them how high you are. Now, how does that sound?" . . . He stayed.

Some years later, my friend Tom, whom I had met at Rick's house in the summer of 1979, told me of a close encounter he had with Fredo before even knowing who he was. He had been on tour with a couple of his buddies when he was still in school, and they picked up two 15 year old Deadhead chicks who were hitch hiking in Connecticut. The show was in Burlington Vermont on May 6, 1978. After the show the girls ran over to one of the limo's to say hi and wound up getting into the limo with the band. As they were getting into the car they yelled back to Tom that their stuff was still in his car, but that they would be at the Sheraton downtown and asked if they would be so kind as to drop their stuff off to them there later. Tom and his friends took this as a very good sign of great things to come, and headed off to the hotel to deliver their back packs and possibly meet Jerry and the rest of the band. When they arrived at the hotel they knocked on the door and as they peaked in, they told part of their story until one of the girls recognized them and they gained admittance to the room. Jerry was sitting at a small table to the left doing coke with Keith, and to the far right Steve Parish and others were gathered for a little smoke-a-thon. As all this was happening around them the girls acknowledged that Tom and his friends were those people that had helped them find their way to the show that night. Jerry thought that was cool and as they kept talking a very tall (at least from their perspective at the time) afro headed man walked into the room, wearing an embroidered Ice Cream Kid shirt, stepping over people who were sitting all over the room listening to the story Jerry was telling and he said, "I heard Macintosh is bringing extra amps to the next show." Jerry looked at him somewhat perplexed and asked, "What color is your stash, man?"

Tom met Fredo by way of introduction a few months later through a mutual friend. He recognized him as the guy that was in and out of the room climbing over people and sharing a brief conversation with Jerry. This remains one of Tom's favorite stories. What a small, small, small, small world. . . Isn't it though?

Fredo told me that in 1975 he and some close friends had decided to take a bus trip to the Tower Theatre for a Halloween show. This was during the Dead's self imposed retirement years between October '74 and June of 1976. There was an early and a late show that day and they loaded up the bus and took off for the Upper Darby section of Philadelphia. Fredo happened to take a bunch of pictures at these shows.

He told me that when he entered the hotel room that night he asked, "Where are those pictures Jerry?" To which he responded, "Not now!". And that's how Fredo remembers it.

Through a series of encounters with Keith Godchaux in local bars on tour, (they both loved their bourbon) Fredo ingratiated himself to the rest of the band with a little help from his amazing acid. The band just loved his stuff, which was what put Fredo in the room where Tom sorta met him that night. Fredo told me that he remembered the encounter because Tom has told the story so often, but he recalled asking Garcia about the pictures that he had sent him a few months prior with the expectation of getting them back. I told Fredo that he probably should have made copies of the pictures himself and sent Jerry them, instead of the originals. . No shit!

1987 Really Was a Great Year

After our excursion out to Red Rocks and Telluride in August of 1987, we made it home in one piece and got our lives back on track. Having that much fun in that short a time can wreck you. No kidding. I always needed a vacation from my vacation, you know?. In September the boys came back East again, (God love 'em) so we made some plans to join them for a few shows. Great Country, America!

I was off midweek at the time, so whenever possible, I would try to make some magic happen. This time it was a one night stand in Providence for me, a solo excursion at that. It was September 7, 1987. I left that Monday at 4 pm, and drove myself to the Civic Center in Rhode Island, making it in plenty of time. I brought my deck with me and hoped that I could get a taper seat to avoid the avoidable. It's never really been much of a problem over the years, but when the Dead implemented the Taper Section, some security guards took themselves real seriously. Anyway, no problem there, and the show was awesome. I was standing at the back of the taper section patched into a pair of Nakamichi 300's w/ shotguns. The first set opened with Stranger, Franklins. Walking Blues > Push to Shove, then Brother Esau. Then a nice performance of It Must've Been the Roses, Far From Me and Let it Grow. Not to shabby for a drive to

Rhode Island. I don't recall how many times I saw the Grateful Dead play The Roses, but I don't think it was many and I love this tune. After that there was a lengthy tuning session and a crowd chant, "We want Phil. We want Phil. We want Phil." etc.

The second set rocked a bit more. Aiko into Saint without a Sailor, but there was a Ship of Fools in the program. Then Uncle John's Band > Playing jam > drums > Truckin. It's such a Grateful Dead thing to hear bits of a another song inside a jam. Playing Jam got thrown around quite a bit through the years. Next was Spoonful, Peter into Around and Round, and they topped the whole thing off with an excellent Good Lovin. As they were jamming through Good Lovin, Weir stepped up to his mic and as clear as day he said, "Wait for it" and then Jerry strummed the opening notes for 'La Bamba', the current hit by Los Lobos` from East L.A. in California. They played La Bamba out to its end and then went back into Good Lovin. This marked the first time the Dead ever covered a song while it was on top of the charts. (The useless trivia is just endless)

The movie La Bamba had come out recently and was almost a hit, but the soundtrack did very well featuring the music of Los Lobos. La Bamba is the story of Richie Valens' rise to fame after being signed to Del-Fi Records at the very young age of 16, only to be killed at the age of 17 in the same plane crash that took the lives of Buddy Holly and J.P.'The Big Bopper' Richardson. February 2, 1959 is still considered, historically to be "The Day the Music Died". The Rock n' Roll genre was up and coming and becoming more and more popular all the time. The music tour that included these three musicians as Headliners was huge and filled with many very popular acts, but when Buddy Holly's plane crashed, it left many people wondering whether rock n 'roll could survive a tragedy like this. On the side; the third night in Providence, September 9, Brent broke out a new cover of Devil With a Blue Dress> Good Golly Miss Molly> Devil With a Blue Dress, also known as Detroit Medley. Another fine rocking tune brought to life in the Grateful Dead by Brent.

My next excursion was to head down south again, this time to the Capital Center again sans my buddy Bob, insert my old buddy J. Bones. I ran into him one night at Kelly's in Neptune N.J. and we started talking about the upcoming tour. We figured it would be nice to hit The Cap Center shows on the weekend of September 12, and 13. There was also a show on the 11th but we weren't gonna make that one. We hit the road a little late for this one and ran into a rain storm (ha ha Jerry creeping into the story sideways) along the way, so when we got there we had very little time to do anything. This sucked for me because I needed a ticket for both nights, whereas Joe had tickets for both nights. During the drive we had agreed, because it was only right, that he would go in on time for the show whether I had a ticket by show time or not . This turned out to be a bad idea for me because we got there very late. No matter. I wound up outside with the crowd, my ear up against the security door straining to hear Jerry and boys play their hearts out. The only good thing about my situation was that I had plenty of time to get a ticket for the second night. This was my first show from the outside. . .

When we got home everyone was preparing for the five night Dead stand at Madison Square Garden. September 15, 16, 18, 19 and 20. Say what you want about the Grateful Dead in the late 80's but if you weren't there to witness it, shut up. The band played an amazing amount of inspired shows in 1987 and these Garden shows are a direct testament to that notion. Jerry and his compadres set the Garden ablaze with their magical, musically interactive dance-fest over five nights. Every time I go back to listen to a show from this year, I am always enlightened by the memories they invoke and never disappointed, to be sure. I was at a lot of those shows myself, so I can bare witness. Over the five night span they played 88 songs, of which only 13 were repeats. No repeats over the first three nights, but six during the fourth night and seven during the final show. The boys are well equipped to play a dozen or more shows without repeating anything. I've been witness to several in a row myself, but as musicians who don't repeat much, these stats are more than acceptable. On the first night Brent opened with his new cover Hey Pockey Way, which I missed in

Providence four nights earlier. Minglewood and Push to Shove followed and then techie problems created some interesting moments.

Bobby, "We've had some Communist sabotage. Some of Brent's communist friends sabotaged my speakers. All American Hero Steve is gonnna fix it for us and Justice will prevail. So we gotta have a big hand for truth, justice and the American way." Beer Barrel Polka. . . "So now that Brent and his buddies have had their laugh, we can get on with the show."

Me and My Uncle >Mexicali Blues followed and then Queen Jane. This was a great tune for Weir. I don't get why people put it down, and I know they do. Placed "just exactly perfect" in the Cassidy or Looks Like Rain slot, it makes perfect Grateful sense. Don't you think?

On the 17th, which was their night off, Bobby and Jerry made an appearance on the Letterman show and had some fun. "Let's levitate Garcia". Check it out on Utube. At the show on Saturday the 19th, the boys dedicated a portion of their second set to a Farm Aid benefit that had been going on most of the day elsewhere. During the first set though, which was smoking by the way, Bobby played a Mexicali Blues > Big River which was a weird placement of sorts. Usually Uncle is followed by either Mexicali or River so the beginning of Mexi was interesting. Then Jerry followed the Polka segment of the show with Push to Shove. Next the crowd started the "Let Phil sing" chant and Phil responded in kind, "You people have contained yourselves remarkably well over the last three nights, so You Got It!" Phil played Box of Rain, with attitude!

Within these past two years on tour, '86 and '87, a phenomenon had crept up on us. Bob, Brian, Dave, Bruce and Frank and I all noticed it; Nitrous-Oxide. People would bring a tank or two of nitrous with them to sell balloon hits at the show. Sometimes they would have two sizes of balloons (for different prices) and they would fill them much like a party store fills Helium balloons, except they wouldn't tie them off at the top. They just hand it to you and then you go along your merry way. One for two bucks, three for five was the going rate, and if you've ever experienced this feeling at the dentist then maybe you can imagine how much fun it could be in small controlled doses. As if this is controlled? Bob and I and the few regulars that went to shows with us, called these parking lot guys balloonatics. We thought that was pretty funny. Of course that was before we discovered the fun that they were having. This became so popular that I went to the city once, with a friend and bought a couple of boxes of the individual canisters. These were actually intended for whipped cream canisters for use in restaurants, then they became known as whippets. There were sold twenty-four to a case. Then they sell a little plastic cylinder that was designed to release the nitrous into a balloon that was attached to the cylinder. Well, this went one step further with my friend that I went to the first Spectrum show with. Sally and I drove into Camden on our way to the show and picked up our own canister of nitrous. I mean to say that she picked it up and I drove her there to get it.

These Spectrum shows were always a constant party. The crowds were still so enthusiastic about seeing the Grateful Dead in this amazing place and about seeing their friends and having a great time. The scene inside at a Dead show is unlike any other, in that there is no real order, but there is no real chaos either. Every single person inside is after the same thing. Simply put, to be in the room where the Grateful Dead are playing. There's that line in the Hunter/Garcia tune 'Tennessee Jed' that says, *"Aint no place I'd rather be,"* and that says it all. Over the course of the four night stand they played 72 songs without a repeat in the bunch. These shows were spread over the weekend; Thursday, Friday, Sunday and Monday.

First show opened with Let the Good Times Roll > Shakedown Street, Walking Blues, and then Jerry played a sweet To Lay Me Down. It still amazes me that this band can rock out crazy with a song so that you can barely hear yourself think, and then play a beautiful ballad like To Lay me Down and have the crowd mesmerized and so attentive and quiet. It's a great show of respect for the band and for one another that everyone can be in the moment together, and let me add to that. If you look around at a moment like this, and I have, you can see the crowd participation is strong. Especially during a song like He's Gone, when everyone is singing the chorus along with Jerry. It's so apparent that the community vibe is present.

Other notable songs during the evening were Bertha > Greatest Story > Crazy Fingers, second set opener and then the crowd pleasing Truckin. The set ended with a Fantasy > Hey Jude > Turn on Your Lovelight. When Brent brought 'Hey Jude' into the repertoire, he only sang the refrain, "naah,......, naah.....naah, nah, nah, nah, naah.....nah, nah, nah naaaah.....Hey Jude." And he goes a little nuts like McCartney did way back when. Actually he goes a lot nuts, like McCartney would have done later in his career. I never understood why Brent only sang the end of it. It's just baffling. Sunday September 11th was Mickey Hart's birthday, so at the end of the drums segment that night, Billy gave him a pie in his face...Happy Birthday Mickey. Ha..ha !!

After the show that Sally and I went to was over, I made my way toward the exits with my deck in hand, and ran into a few people that I knew (you think?). I told them what I had waiting for me back at my car and they lit up like Christmas trees! I had them follow me out to the car and for the first time in a long time the car wasn't where I thought it was. Fuck...!!! It's so much worse than it sounds. . . Oh, I was so screwed.

I walked around the spectrum with these people (in great anticipation) probably three times before I put my head on straight, (not tripping by the way) and realized where the heck I was. When I got to the car there was one very pissed off Sally waiting for my lost sorry ass. She had a line of people waiting for (ahhemm) me and as I approached I handed over the keys to the trunk and we whipped out the tank and started to party. The crowds had kinda diminished by the time I got there so Sally decided that we were going to the park. The park around the corner from the Spectrum was open for the first time to camping Deadheads and "Shakedown Street" was in full swing. Ahh, Shakedown Street. The ever growing flea market where Deadheads gathered pre and post-show to hang out. . . and then hang out some more. The problem here was the hang out during the show. This had become a huge problem everywhere.

Anyway, we stayed in the park, (you know how I love the park. Famous movie quotes for 500.00 Alex), until about 3 in the morning and at that point I couldn't possibly inhale anymore nitrous. I have never done that much nitrous before and I haven't done it since. Not for recreational purposes anyway. It was just ridiculous to do that much in that short a time, but it was free so who was I to argue? We went back to her hotel, because she had one and I didn't, and got a few hours sleep. In the morning she informed me that she needed a ride to the airport. I said 'where the fuck did that come from???' She said she was really sorry, but I was her only source of transportation, and after all, what are friends for? Yea, so I took her to the freaking airport with a good heart, no guilt beyond the first 50 or 60 miles (just kidding). It was an easy ride. That's not to say that I enjoyed the ride by any means, but I did enjoy the company by all means. Sally was and still is a great girl. Nice Deadhead chick, with no attitude and a great personality. Shout out to you! (Jody)

1988; Almost Just Exactly Perfect?

9 would have to say, in my humble and somewhat-experienced opinion, that the Grateful Dead played some of their most interesting and maybe, can I say inspired, music of my touring experience in 1987 and 88. (In a recent interview, Bob Weir agreed with this exact sentiment) Although the adventure from '81 through '86 was also amazing, and I must concede that it's also *really* difficult to pinpoint any particular year of greatness for these guys, because during any given year, with the possible exceptions being '93-95, there was some type of grandeur involved. My touring experience began in 1980-81, when Brent first started with the band and because he had to spend a fair amount of time learning material and becoming comfortable in the jams and what-not, there was a lot of repeated material early on. But by 1987-88, Brent's contribution was most certainly evident as he was throwing new stuff at as us every chance he got, challenging the rest of the band in the process and that really made for sets that were longer and more exploratory. A great scenario for us. I didn't really appreciate how much Brent's playing brought to the band until I started going through all those set lists again. His ability as a performer was absolutely amazing. My only problem with Brent was that he didn't play piano very much. He liked the organ and the synthesizer, with the midi and all it's tricks. I really thought that the piano deserved it's rightful place on that stage with Jerry and the boys. Later in Dead history when Bruce Hornsby joined the band for a few shows, it was much more apparent to me how much I missed the piano.

Also contributing to the bands resurgence was Jerry's newly discovered health regime. Trying to stay on the healthy side of life by eating better and exercising, all while partaking more of life outside of the Grateful Dead. These lifestyle changes inspired the band even further, bringing on a certain energy level that wasn't there before. (this is what we were hearing) All this being said, Jerry had taken up scuba diving recently while vacationing in Hawaii and was enjoying it immensely. When I heard about this new adventure I was caught solid between amusement and disbelief! I really couldn't picture Jerry scuba diving, but I eventually saw a video of Jerry on his Hawiian vacation, under water in his gear, so that removed all doubt. Jerry described scuba diving as the closest thing to doing drugs that he had ever experienced.

So here we go again, it's 1988 and the Dead are back on our side of the country again. There were three shows in Hampton starting on the 26th of March and the tour continued through the 9th of April in Worcester, Mass. I missed the first Hampton show, where the highlight was Hell in a Bucket > Sugaree into a quicky version of Stir it Up. I think it happened because Jerry broke a string, who knows. It ended quickly and was followed by Minglewood Blues. The second night featured Bobby's first time tackling Dylan's Ballad of a Thin Man, which I have come to love. I think he should have done this song a lot more, but he only played it one more time. *"Something is happening here, but you don't know what it is. . .Do you ? . . Mr. Jones".*

So the second night, when I was *in the house*, they opened the second set with a jam that we'll call space, into an extended jam called So What. This is a tune that Jerry recorded with his old friend David Grisman on acoustic guitars, and released on The Pizza Tapes. Ironically, (or coincidently) I've been aware of this song for all these years and when my son played in the Jazz

Orchestra in High School, I heard it included within a medley. I saw it in his music sheets and asked him about it. I hummed it for him and he said, "Yea, how do you know that. Did Jerry do it or something?" (Well, actually).

He was impressed that I was familiar with it. However, it didn't surprise him how I knew about it. . . Whatever Denis!

After So What, they slid into Sugar Magnolia > Scarlet Begonias > Fire on the Mountain > Estimated Prophet > Eyes of the World > drums > space, > GDTRFB > I Need a Miracle > Dear Mr. Fantasy > Sunshine Daydream. Then U.S. Blues was the encore. It was an excellent show. Great music. Two nice long sets and lots of energy all around. The third night was more of the same, with a Mighty Quinn encore. The weather on this particular trip was wet. Not real conducive to camping. So we didn't hang out much. We left after the show and headed up north to hang home. The next shows on tour were at the Meadowlands again. We would be close to home, so we were good for a bit.

During these shows in 1988, Healy was trying out something new. He began transmitting a very low frequency FM signal to feed speakers that were set up at certain places in the venue, so the music could be heard a little better. I asked Dan about this idea and why he did it and he told me that he thought it would keep the peace in an uncontrolled environment.

"I discovered that if I did a broadcast, there would be much less trouble and much more peace outside the gigs from those who did not get in. It was about sharing the music and it also allowed folks to have a board quality tape from off the air which was very high quality. It was for fun! Nothin' deeper than that." End quote.

As tapers caught wind of this, some brought boom boxes into the shows, so they could get the soundboard feed and walk out with a much better sounding tape. Now you could say that this would encourage people to come to the shows without tickets knowing that they could hear the broadcast for free, but it didn't work out that way. It was a very cool thing for Dan to do for those outside the show though, I must say. Eventually, Healy had to stop using it altogether because even though the signal was very low frequency, it was still in violation of FCC regulations.

On the third night at the Meadowlands, we were treated to Weir's second and final performance of Ballad of a Thin Man. Such a pitty. This was April Fool's Day, but there was no mention of it. Brent played a little children's ditty called Little Bunny Froo-Froo right before the opener, which was Mississippi ½ step > Jack Straw> To Lay Me Down. The latter was so beautifully written and yet not over played. Jerry played To Lay Me Down during the acoustic sets at the Warfield and the Radio City shows in 1980. It lent itself very nicely to the acoustic vibe.

Two more shows for me in Hartford and then I'm done. Gotta head back to work. These shows in Hartford were Easter Sunday, Monday and Tuesday, but I had to miss the Tuesday show. Listening back to these shows I have to mention Easter Sunday when Weir sang an incredible version of Memphis Blues. At times he was actually screaming the lyrics, and it was really very funny. So entertaining, in fact that it compelled Jerry to join in with more enthusiasm than usual. They also played a nice mid-set Cold Rain and Snow. The second set opened with a Playing in The Band > Crazy Fingers, and ended with an amazing Lovelight. In my experience, shows in Hartford were always high energy and so much fun. The parking lot scene was filled with smiling Deadheads clothed in their personally selected tie-dyed attire. Lots of Heads are still showing up without tickets. The more experienced came with tickets in hand. The good thing about scalping a ticket in our world though, was that it was most often face value. So if you had the money for a ticket (in my experience a lot of people were looking for the true miracle ticket. That would be free) and you could find one, it would at least be reasonably priced.

My next full tour was coming up in a couple of months, so I needed to pay some bills, save some cash and get my head back together. Honestly, by now the touring was wearing on me just a little bit. I was spending money and the bills weren't going away. Every time we would go to a few shows in a row, either a car or a hotel room would end up on a credit card of mine and the cash in hand would wind up being spent along the way. Everybody knows how that works. I needed to be more choosey about the shows that I was going to. (At least the thought was there, you know?) Although I wasn't feeling the need to go to every show on tour anymore, it could still inevitably happen, if that was what everybody was doing. I mean, it was still fun going to shows and going to new and different places made it more appealing. Plus there were the local shows that I just couldn't blow off. So Hartford was going to be my last stop on this tour and then I'd check out the next tour and decide what to do then.

The boys played several outdoor arenas in June of '88, but they were in the Midwest, so I didn't make it. There were four shows at the Alpine Valley Music Center in Wisconsin, where they were breaking out songs from 'Built To Last'. They also played The Beatles' *Blackbird* as part of a double encore on the final night. They tell me that seeing the Dead at Alpine was really amazing, but without having been there myself I can only imagine. On second thought, the Dead released a DVD called Downhill From Here, which documents this very special venue and it looks like a great place to see them play. (That DVD, by the way, has the best sound of any other DVD release that I've heard.) However, having seen the boys at Red Rocks and at Telluride kinda puts a different spin on the statement 'great place to see them play', and no matter what you say, you can't beat those places with an Alpine Valley. When it rains there, it becomes a mud bath. When it rains out at Red Rocks, you get wet. . .That's all I'm saying. Even the Greek Theatre where it's very intimate, and the band loves to play, it still doesn't really compare to seeing them in Telluride where you're surrounded by mountains. But again, this is an opinion from someone who has never seen them at The Greek either. I'll accept that.

Back to the road. The owner of Chubb's Pub was running another bus trip, this time up to Saratoga Performing Arts Center. The SPAC. June 28th was the date and that's the only show I saw on that run. I wouldn't have seen that one either if not for the bus trip. Being selective was dragging me down, but it was necessary. The owner of Chubb's provided the bus, but no tickets. He did however, throw in a keg of beer for the ride. I think everybody on this bus trip was dosed too, including me, and it made a weird show even weirder. We had horrible seats, at the very top of the venue. SPAC is an Amphitheater like PNC Arts Center, in Holmdel and the Blockbuster Arena in Camden, both in N.J. It was raining at Saratoga and we were in the middle of the woods. We made our way up towards the venue and realized that although the music hadn't started yet, they were on stage already. We were really far away and I hate that feeling. The last few shows that I saw, I was at least close enough to see faces. Watch them play. If I could settle for just hearing the music, I could stay home and put on whatever tape I would want to hear, you know? The only thing that stood out at this show for me was that Weir's hair was really long, swinging around like he hadn't had it cut in a while. (thats the only thing that stood out?) Too long to stay in place, but not long enough to tie back maybe? I guess he was going for the ponytail. Whatever. Who Cares? This show was broadcast on W-PYX FM. It was mostly forgettable for me, but that may have been due in part to the self inflicted mind buzz. The set list was very good though, I was just too far away to really enjoy it.

Toward the end of 1988 the band tried something new. Instead of touring ten cities playing two in each, they played a few shows in each of three cities. They did four shows at the Capital Center in Maryland, four shows at the Spectrum in Philly and finished up with nine nights at Madison Square Garden in New York City. This may have happened because they weren't allowed at certain venues anymore, Hampton for one, but I'm not sure about that. The shows at the Garden were widely publicised for another reason that I'll talk about in a minute.

The shows at the Capital Center were usually interesting, but the sound in that place was never really good. I don't understand why they played there on any kind of regular basis. It was like Nassau Coliseum, but more hollow sounding. Nassau had actually improved over the years, but I never really had good seats at the Cap Center either so that makes it a tough comparison. The show that I decided to go to was September 3rd 1988, for good reason. It was the 11th anniversary of Englishtown, my first show. In fact, it was a lot of people's first show. Of course it would've been nice if it had been 10 years to the day, but you can't have everything. It was a Saturday Night and I went with my friend Joe from work. In the parking lot I ran into a bunch of friends and I told them about the significance of the show and most didn't realize it. Someone had some blotter acid, so a bunch of us indulged. The last time I did acid was at Saratoga, but before that it had been very long time, and this show at the Cap Center was absolutely the last time. For this particular show, we had decent seats. We were on the second level, just above the stage on the right side. We had a great view of the band and pretty decent sound. First set opened with Let the Good Times Roll > Feel Like a Stranger > Franklin's Tower> Red Rooster. Really, really nice stuff. Second set opened with Box of Rain and Victim or the Crime, which I never liked. I thought it was too eery and depressing. Recently, I've revisited it and I think it was Weir's tribute, if you will, to his friend Jerry and his addiction. Maybe I'm wrong, but I still don't like the song much. Next on the agenda was Foolish Heart > Women Are Smarter > Eyes of the World, ending the night with a great combo; Goin Down The Road > I Need a Miracle > Morning Dew. For the encore they played the expected and highly anticipated, at least for me, One More Saturday Night. Remember, I didn't get Saturday Night at Englishtown, so I was really happy to hear it. Within minutes the song was over, but it was very obvious that something else was up. The lights didn't dim right away, and Jerry, with a big grin on his face (probably) hit the opening notes for *Ripple* and I'm not lying when I say that I heard it before he played it. It was a genuine roof raiser. Blew the place apart. The Grateful Dead last played Ripple at the Radio City shows acoustic, but the last electric Ripple was played on 4-29-71 at the Filmore West in San Francisco. On the way out as we were still celebrating the Ripple, I ran into a few taper friends of mine and asked them how it all went. They were of course, still flipping out about it, as I would've been had I been taping. Hell, I was flipping out without a tape of it, but I realized the significance of the show for me and that was all I needed.

David Gans' Grateful Dead hour, which I was still taping every week at the time, always included snippets from amazing shows. He would explain the origin of a certain old Dead standard and then play it with some other songs from a particular show that was recent or, not necessarily so recent. One week shortly after the Cap Center shows David played a soundboard copy of the encores from this show. That's the only SBD copy of it that I've ever heard. I also heard a rumor that they played it as a request from a little boy that was in a hospital. I had that confirmed recently by David Gans on 'Tales from the Golden Road' on The Grateful Dead channel on Sirius Satellite Radio.

Rainforest Benefit 1988

Due to their recent commercial success, the Grateful Dead was unnaturally thrust into the media spotlight and this would be the part of this tour that needs it's own chapter, and the reason is in the title; Rainforest Benefit. Through a series of events out in San Francisco, Bobby and Mickey wound up doing interviews, so much that the band was summoned into the role of Rainforest Savior. The Rainforest Action Network, as it became known, had been in touch with the band and they were asked to make people aware of the world wide destruction of the Tropical Rainforests. The Rainforests, unbeknownst to the world as a whole, were being cleared at an alarming rate, being used for cattle grazing and for timber. The plant and animal life that would be, or is being destroyed, is a vital resource for experimental medicines and nutritional advances. Essentially, the balance of nature was in danger. To this end, the Grateful Dead played an unprecedented nine night stand at the Garden and chose to lend their support for this cause during their final performance there.

I went to seven out of the nine shows at the Garden and it was quite literally spectacular. I tried to get up there early enough every day to hit The Good Ole Days Tavern. This was a great pre-show hangout, where we would grab some food and a few drinks before the short walk across the street to see Jerry. I had taper tickets for the first two shows, the 14th and 15th, Wednesday and Thursday respectfully. I ordered all of my tickets through the Dead's ticket office so the 16th, 18th, 22nd and 23rd were also Dead Office tickets, but those were not taper seats. Saturday's show didn't come from the Dead's Ticket Office. That ticket came from Ticket Bastard. That was the nickname that we gave to Ticketmaster, the agency that controlled every ticket sold on the East Coast for a very long time, and charged crazy service fees for every purchase. (Not as crazy as online convenience fees though) The boys were in the mainstream media because of the new album, Jerry's come back (yup, still enjoying that ride) and the hype revolving around Saturday's benefit show. These shows were all fantastic, and knowing that we were coming back every night for the week was so comforting.

On the final night the Grateful Dead donated their time to the Rainforest Action Network. Although this was certainly not the first time the Dead had performed a benefit show, it was most definitely one of the most widely publicised events they had ever participated in. Jerry didn't much like having to be the spokesman for anything, but when asked about their participation, in an interview published in High Times magazine in 1988, he said, "It seems pathetic that it has to be us, with all the other citizens of the planet, and all the other resources that are out there, but since no one else is doing anything about it, we don't really have a choice."

This happened because the need in this particular situation, was worthy of their attention, and they believed they could help the cause. This was one of the few times that I actually noticed people showing up in suit and ties and evening wear. It's never out of the question for people to be dressed up because some Deadheads have to come right from work and sometimes court gets out late or you just can't get out of the office soon enough to get changed. Any number of other scenarios are definitely possible. I was actually wandering around the walkway between the upper and lower level seating and heard somebody yell my name. I thought it could've been for me, but I dismissed it and kept walking only to hear my name very clearly once more. I stopped and looked up toward the nosebleed section and saw a friend of mine from work, (Tom B) whom I knew was not a Deadhead. He was out to dinner in the city on this night (dressed to the nines) and someone in the restaurant offered him 2 pairs of tickets for the benefit show at the Garden. He accepted the tickets and told his three friends that he would probably see his friend Jim (that would be me) at the show. Pretty freaky huh?.

The guest list for this show was very impressive. The event was Sub-titled 'Benefit for the Rainforests: Cultural Survival, Greenpeace & Rainforest Action Network'. It was broadcast on W-NEW FM in New York and W-MMR in Philadelphia. Bruce Hornsby and the Range opened the show and the cast of characters were seemingly endless. Suzanne Vega played two songs, Mick Taylor helped out on a couple, and Daryl Hall and John Oates were on hand to sing, *Every time you Go Away* and *What's going on??*, with Jack Casady from Hot Tuna on bass. Tom "T-Bone" Wolk played on a couple of tunes and Mark Riviera played Sax on a couple of tunes as well. It was a huge group effort, and what group effort would be complete without Mickey's old friend from Egypt, Baba Olatunji and his Drums of Passion. The highlights of the nine night run are just too numerous to mention. (But I'll try) There were 125 different songs played with a total of 155 songs with repeats. On the fourth night they opened the second set with a rousing Not Fade Away > Scarlet > Fire> Women R Smarter> drums > Other One > Wharf Rat > Throwing Stones > Not Fade Away. A very peculiar opening since, but if I remember correctly it was actually a request by the audience. They just started the NFA chant on their own and the Band came out and started playing it. More than likely they had planned to do Scarlet Begonias, but it was overwhelmingly vetoed in favor of some 'real love'. . .We also got our Tom Thumbs Blues and our Foolish Heart along with Memphis Blues, Hey Pockey Way and Dear Mr. Fantasy with some Hey Jude thrown in. We got some Samson and some Franklin's Tower and of course one of my all time favorites, Dire Wolf....The Box of Rain and the Morning Dew, and It Must've Been The

Roses. . .I also got to hear Jack Straw and Shakedown Street with a little Touch of Grey and some Bertha, Cumberland Blues...The funny thing about Touch was that it was only played once during the entire nine night run, and it was the current hit! On Tuesday the 20th they played eleven songs that were one time only for the run, and on Thursday the 22nd they played eight songs that were only performed once the whole week and a half. These shows were all kickass and we knew they were going to be because this week, they had a purpose. Also, they were playing the same venue for a week and a half without having to travel beyond a few blocks so they must've been loving that as much as we were, if that be possible.

So, what was I saying? Oh, 155 songs over nine nights averaged out to 17 songs per night, not including the drums and space sequence that is played every night. They played a different encore every night but one, when they repeated U.S. Blues, seven shows apart. The final night we were treated to a double encore, Good Lovin > Knockin on Heaven's Door, with just about every one in attendance joining the band on stage. Of those songs that were played, 55 of them were only played once, and 95 were played only twice. Five songs, which included My Masterpiece, Victim or The Crime, Foolish Heart, I Need a Miracle and the final Not Fade Away were all played three times. Remember Not Fade Away was actually played twice in the same night. The songs that were repeated were never played on consecutive nights, in fact they were played at least three nights apart. We all know already that when the Grateful Dead comes to any city and plays two or three shows in a row, there is usually no repetition. Given that the Boys were in NYC for nine shows, there would almost have to be some repeats, as with most bands, but they served up some very nice surprises and played a lot of material. This has nothing to do with the following that they've attracted though. Since the beginning they have always varied their repertoire, if only for the sake of performing. They love playing the music so much that to repeat the material would be, in and of itself, non productive. So they couldn't just repeat the same stuff over and over again...Lucky for us..(all the info garnered for the above stat fest was obtained partially from Deadbase VII and partially from my master recordings)

1988 Road Trips

As the celebration at the Rain Forest shows came to an end, word had spread that they were planning a small tour down south including three shows in Florida and then off to New Orleans and Texas from there. They wouldn't be back around by us again until next summer. Seeing as how I had never been to Florida to see the boys play, as I was talking to my friend J. Bones about it, we decided to hit Miami and St. Petersburg together. These shows were set for October 14th in Miami and the 16th and 17th in St Petersburg. The 16th is Weir's birthday, so I thought that might be an interesting reason to go as well. Joe had some family down there so we were able to stay pre-shows for free and then pick up a hotel afterward. We flew into Daytona Intl. Airport and took Rt. 4 South to 275 West to get to Clearwater where Bones' family lived. We arrived two days early and caught up with my friend and frequent touring buddy Bob later in Miami. Three other friends joined us at that point. It's real backwoods down in Clearwater. Not right where his sister lives, but getting to the area was like driving through the Everglades. Not that I've ever driven through the Everglades, but I've seen Flipper so I have an idea. (Can't believe I just said that) After Clearwater, Miami was another road trip in and of itself. We had to get back onto 275 South, which goes right past St. Petersburg, and take that to 75 South for about five hours until we hit the East Coast to pick up 95 south to the Dixie Hiway. That took us right into Miami.

For me, these shows were more about going to Florida at first, because after seeing six out of the nine shows at the Garden what could I possibly be missing if I didn't go?. . . Ahhh, but that is exactly the point, isn't it? You never know what they're going to do on any given night, so this really wasn't just about going to Florida after all, was it? It *was* an excuse to *go* to Florida though and it turned into an exciting little road trip for us. Much like going to Red Rocks for three shows, except that we weren't staying for a week. It was also very exciting, flying down to Florida to catch Jerry and the boys again so soon after the Garden shows. In fact, anytime we can all get together (me, my friends, Jerry, Bob, Phil, Billy and Mickey) it's a good thing.

We discussed the logistics of the show in Miami before we left though, about how Miami was considered the drug trafficking capital of the world. Maybe not the world, but probably our country. I just figured it would be like every other place we've ever gone to. We go in (to the city) see the show and get out. What I wasn't counting on was the very obvious police presence. This wasn't meant to intimidate us though, it was meant to protect us. We were actually parked in a gated lot and the gate to the lot was kept closed. We were let out on a 'need to be let out basis' and that was it. I honestly didn't involve myself in that scenario, I just went into the show and sat down and enjoyed myself. I did bring my tape deck with me and patched into some nice Neumann mics. I hadn't seen them around much, so I was happy to check them out again. The Miami opener was the first Touch of Grey played since that one time at the Garden. How funny is that? Granted this is only the 4th show since the last Garden shows, but still, that's a long time to not play your big hit, right?? I'd have to say that the highlights of the show for me were Brown Eyed Women and All Over Now. They also played a sweet China > Rider for the second set opener and a nice long rollicking He's Gone in the middle of the second set. Overall the first of three was very good and very energizing. I said before how much more fun a show can be, just knowing that you're going to see another couple over the next two days and man is that ever true. So here we are in Miami and guess where we have to go now?? Straight back up to St. Petersburg, four and half hours away, for the next two nights. Up in St Petersburg we were meeting up with a few more friends. One that I've known since the early 80's, and her girlfriend, who actually lived down in Florida.

The band played at the Bayfront Center Arena in St. Petersburg. The Bayfront is a Basketball arena with bleacher seats on each side and in the back. The feeling in this place was very relaxed. No feeling of hype like that of the Garden shows. This was a just another stop on tour to see one more show. The surprising thing about this night was the Music Never Stopped opener. This is mostly a set closer, especially since the time when a set structure was noticeable. When something like this happened though, you had to believe that it would make for an interesting evening. Once they throw the structure off, it becomes anybody's game. In other words, since nothing generally follows this song because it's a set closer, they would now have to actually think about something to play next, instead of it being automatic. It was followed by Sugaree, which is arguably Garcia's favorite tune to play.

The second set also held a nice surprise. The band was fiddling around for a bit on stage and it turned into a spacey jam, which lasted about 5 or 6 minutes and then slipped into One More Saturday Night. (Remember I said earlier to watch for the Sat. Night opener) Again, not a usual opener by any means, but now that they've done that one, what will the encore be??. They followed Saturday Night with Crazy Fingers, which doesn't get nearly enough stage time, and the encore was U.S. Blues. That's ok too, because we got a great show along the way.

After this wonderful show we went back to the hotel, to our suite, and tried to get some rest. The suites in this hotel were above the floors where the regular rooms were so we had to have an access card to make the elevator go up far enough. Bob thought that was the coolest thing about the room. The first time he took me for the ride, the day before he was so excited. Like a kid that just stole candy and got away with it!!

Everyone was hungry so we tried to order room service—I know. . .expensive, right?. . .we didn't care too much at that point—but we found out that room service was closed at midnight so decided to order out. The only thing we could all agree on was pizza. Dominoes Pizza. I wasn't all too thrilled about the choice myself, but I was hungry too so I settled for it. After the munch, we all got some much needed sleep and then woke in the morning in time for the Continental Breakfast. To partake in this hotel event, I would have to get up way earlier than I really ever wanted to, but you know there's always one or two in the bunch that are up way too early anyway, spoiling the snooze time for the rest of us. This particular Sunday night show would be our last on this tour. No one from our crew was going to New Orleans or Texas from here so for tonight, one more show to look forward to. Tonight is Weir's birthday and we are all aware of it. It should make for a great time, although they may not even mention it.

Weir did a *Memphis Blues* in the first set and Jerry ended it with *To Lay Me Down* into *Deal*. No matter what the mood is, To lay me Down is always a welcome tune for me, for everybody really. The second set opener was *Box of Rain*, which I hadn't heard in a while. Victim or The Crime, which I can mostly do without, was next and then Unto a Foolish Heart, off the newest release. After, they played a really nice Terrapin into Gimme Some Lovin into The Wheel > Watchtower > Morning Dew... When they came out for the encore, guess what??. . .

Happy birthday to you...Happy birthday to you....Happy birthday dear Bobby! . . Happy birthday to you. !!!. Bobby turned 41 that day and the whole crowd sang to him. . .Then they played *The Mighty Quinn*.. What a treat! In December, 1988 Bob went out to California with our friend Steve, to see the Dead for New Years. I met Steve through Sally's brother Bruce a few years earlier. Bruce was the same guy that stood on the fire in Virginia Beach, "Only in Virginia!!" remember him? They were among a whole new crop of friends than we had met in probably '82 or '83. They grew up in Hoboken, but also had a house down by the Shore. Steve grew up in Bradley Beach and was longtime friends with them. Anyway, the Grateful Dead were playing in Oakland that year, and they saw three shows including New Years. Bob and I had always talked about going out for New Years shows, but being in retail I could never take a week off at that time of year. Along with that, of course is the family aspect. I really liked being home for New Years with the rest of my friends, and the shows were broadcast nationally (for a few years anyway) so that worked just fine for me. Still, I would have loved to have been able to go, even once.

While they were out there, probably January 3rd or 4th I got a phone call from my credit card company asking me to approve a large purchase on my card. I had loaned my card to Bob for his trip so he could pick up the rental car that he had charged, using my card. The operator told me what the charge was for and apprehensively I said, "Yes, of course". . . .Right after I hung up from her, Bob called me to say he was really sorry, but the tickets went on sale and he just had to buy them. He said that if I couldn't make the shows, he'd take the tickets and pay me back, but he just had to get them. I asked him when the shows were and he told me the first week in February. So I decided right then that I was going to California to see the Dead in February, an easy decision really. Come to think of it, after these shows I planned a vacation week in February every year.

February is a great month to take a week off because here in New Jersey it can either be winter weather, with a chance of snow that I won't have to deal with commuting to work in, or it could be a week of beautiful weather, which has happened more than a few times. One time about five years ago during my February week off, we had 70 degree weather for most of the week with a little cooler weather closing the week out. (I took my Christmas lights down off my house with a t-shirt on) Then, I think it was the following year, we had the snowstorm from Hell, or Antarctica, depending on your perspective. We got about three feet of snow overnight, with drifts climbing fences and the sides of the house up to 7 feet deep. I didn't have to shovel the driveway for a couple of days because I was off. Of course, that was a mistake because by that time the snow had melted a little and frozen overnight twice and it was real difficult to move. (A learning experience) We had a paved driveway though, so it wasn't all that bad. The next year during the Fall, I went out and bought a snowblower, the best insurance you can buy against a snowstorm. Once you have one, you may not see significant snowfall for a season or two.

By this point in time, my friend Rick, whom I had known for years now and have been to countless shows with, had amazingly fun times with, had moved out to California with his parents. His Dad was retired and his Mom moved with her job out to Calaveras County. Rick was working with a video crew for the Lakers. He did Laker games and most any other event that was held there. When I was planning my trip he told me I was more than welcome to stay there with him and his parents. His parents and I got along very well. They loved me. . . I would sit and talk to his Mom for a while any time I was at their house when they lived in Avon. She could talk and talk and talk and laugh. She had a great sense of humor and she was a very funny lady. His Mom and Dad have both since passed away. . . .(RIP Mr. And Mrs. C. Good people) I let Rick know that I would be catching up with Joe first in San Diego and would see him just before the shows. I took my vacation this time from Tuesday to Tuesday because these shows were Friday, Saturday and Sunday. I arrived in 'Sandy Eggo' on Tuesday afternoon and met up with Joe at the airport. He has a business in San Diego, doing marble restoration, so he was able to take a day off to hang. I rented a car the next day and we drove up the Pacific Coast Hiway, (a.k.a. Route 1). When we made it to Malibu Beach, we drove up Malibu Canyon Road and you would never guess what we saw. It was snowing and we drove right into it. I stopped the car and got out just to take it all in. It was actually snowing hard, like New Jersey snowstorm hard and Joe couldn't believe it. Neither could I, but I'm from New Jersey where it's actually supposed to snow. (Joe is from New Jersey too, but not for quite sometime now) This is Malibu fucking Beach! Granted we were in a semi mountainous region of Malibu for the snow, but still, it was snowing in California!

We drove back down to Route 1, and continued our journey north. When we hit Beverly Hills we stopped for a drink. We looked around for the coolest place we could find where some celebs might be hanging out, but the best we could do was Carol O'Conner's Place. Carol O'Conner played Archie Bunker on the break through series All in The Family. We were both aware that he had a bar out there, so we went and stayed there just long enough to have a drink or two and bullshit about scripts we were reading, and what other projects we were working on. No one gave a shit, but we were laughing anyway. We left the bar soon after and headed up the hills into the private sector. Joe knew where some famous people lived, so he showed me some houses. We drove past Ronald Reagan's house, which was on the top of the hill in this development. Later we were driving along another main strip where there were a lot more regular sized homes and found some mail on the sidewalk belonging to Mel Blank— he was responsible for voicing hundreds of cartoon characters including the loveable classics Bugs Bunny, Porky Pig and Daffy Duck— it was a picture envelope, but it did have an address on it so we opened it to see whose it was and there was a picture of Mel in it. I don't remember if Joe recognized him, but I know I did. We walked up to their door and rang the bell. A young lady opened the door, but she was on the phone so she wasn't real talkative. We just handed her the envelope and she thanked us and we went our merry way. Not a great story, but a story none the less.

Next we drove past Lucille Ball's house and I was very tempted to go knock on her door. I have always loved her work and I believe that there'll never be another true female comic talent like her. There will be imitations, but it'll always refer right back to her. My 'good friend' Joe talked me out of it.'Fucker!'. Something about guard dogs and trespassers, I don't know. . . Carol Burnett was in her league of course and I think that Gilda Radner was well on her way, had she lived to see it. I read a story about Lucy shortly after her death that made me regret my decision not to approach the house. She said that she didn't mind when fans stopped by her house to say hi. She thought that the admiration was sweet and as long as it didn't get out of hand it was fine. She passed away about six months after that. It was a very sad day for me and the for the world.

Our next stop was The Beverly Hills Hotel. This place is a very, very nice Hotel. Not only is that an understatement, but we felt a little out of place even checking it out! We walked in (obviously tourists) hoping to run into somebody, . . .Anybody! . . .Guess what! . .Nobody! The movie *Beverly Hills Cop* was really big at the time and I have to admit I felt like Eddie Murphy as I went running down the front side of the Hotel, jumping into my rented Chevy Malibu. It was a Classic moment, even if it only lives in my head.! We went behind the hotel to check out the bungalows that are there. For some strange reason we both thought that this was where Belushi had died. We even took pictures of ourselves outside room # 2 where we thought he was found. It wasn't there at all of course. It was actually at the Chateau Marmont on West Sunset Blvd. in West Hollywood. (Dumb asses!)

When we were done there we headed down Route I, back toward San Diego. It was a really nice drive, something I had never done before, and at this point, I wondered how many people have ever taken the time. Probably not the people that lived there because it's there and so are they, so why bother, right? It's certainly not the same as taking the Parkway in New Jersey. We stayed at his place for the rest of the day, which was almost over anyway, had a few cocktails and some dinner while watching the sun set off in the distance. Watching the sun sink into the ocean is weird when you're from New Jersey. That night we watched the Tonight Show with Johnny Carson, and he mentioned that Malibu had snow for the first time in 30 years. Funny thing is that not every one got to see it, but we did!

Well now, after this fun filled day trip, we were now ready to go to The Great Western Forum to see the Grateful Dead. We would meet up with Rick at the Forum with no real plan, except that we would be staying with him for two days. I've said it before, and here I'll say it again. Seeing the Grateful Dead out in California is a different experience from seeing them anywhere else. The mood is casual, but just as exciting. There aren't a lot of people without tickets out there either. (Not that I noticed anyway) The Shakedown Street flea market was in full swing, just like everywhere else, but there was one obvious problem. These shows were in Inglewood, where gang violence is considered a problem. (This is what I was told) There were fences all around the arena like any other, but there was definitely a feeling of 'let's get our butts inside sooner rather than later' kinda thought process going on.

The first night opened with Feel Like a Stranger> Franklin's Tower and when Weir said, "You know it's gonna get stranger....so let's get on with the show..." The crowd was really feeling it. The second set opened with Brent's tune, Just a Little Light. I happen to love this song. It's really well written and makes a person think about themselves.

"I had a lot of dreams once, some of them came true. The honey's sometimes bitter, when fortune falls on you." *

Maybe he was singing about himself. Anyway, for some reason Weir wasn't on stage for that tune, but it was followed by Truckin. You know sometimes Truckin is a huge highlight for the night. I know, you wouldn't think so because it's the radio hit and some Deadheads might not like it for that reason. The one tune that everybody knows. You ask someone in any crowd if they like the Dead and 60% of people who say they don't like the Dead will say they like Truckin and Casey Jones. Ironically, some of those same people will mention those same songs as the reason they don't like the Dead. Anyway, Truckin gets the full audience participation every time. *"What a long strange trip it's been"* Right? And when they sing *"Sometimes the lights all shining on me"* they could just turn off the stage mics and let the audience's voices fill the arena. It's just fantastic being a part of that every time. Jerry played Crazy Fingers next and the rest was typical. Bobby closed the show with a rocking Sugar Mags...Then Baby Blue was the encore.

It was really nice spending the next couple days with Rick. I hadn't seen him in a long time. We spent part of our time trading tapes in a very non particular way. We never traded tape for tape, it was always 'what's mine is yours, yours is mine'. Considering how many shows we've seen together it was only right. It was a shame that we lost touch almost completely when he moved out to Cali, but he was having the time of his life.

The second night we saw some familiar faces from back East which, to me was surprising as hell. Some of the girls that used to hang with our crew now lived out there and had come to see the boys, so of course we all ran into each other. Jerry played a new tune called *Built to Last*..., which we love because we're all hoping that the Dead are still Built To Last. It's a peculiar love song;

"There are times when you offend me, and I do the same to you. If you can't or won't forget it, I guess we could be through"

"There are times when I can help you out, and times when you must fall. There are times when you must live in doubt and I can't help at all." Hunter/Garcia

Bobby did Dylan's Queen Jane next and then Brent's very environmentally friendly, We Can Run followed that. This is a tune about everything that has happened, and that can happen, to our home, Planet Earth, and it's very moving and disturbing at the same time.

The lyrics: *"Dumping our trash in your back yard / making certain you don't notice really isn't so hard / you're so busy with your guns / and all of your excuses to use them. Well, it's oil for the rich and babies for the poor / you got everyone believing that more is more / before reckoning comes maybe we'll know what to do then.."**

Tell me that doesn't make you think.

My favorite is, *"Today I went out walking in the amber wind / there's a hole in the sky where the light pours in / I remember the days when I wasn't afraid of the sunshine. But now it beats down on the asphalt land / like a hammering blow from God's left hand / what little still grows/ cringes in the shades of the night time.."* *

With the refrain; *We can run, but we cant hide from it...Of all possible worlds we only got one, we gotta ride on it....What ever we've done, we'll never get far from what we leave behind, baby we can run, run, run, but we cant hide..."**

**music and lyrics by Brent Mydland.*

It was such a great song it was picked up by Planet Earth Network as the theme song for an episode. The second set gave up the Chinacat

>I Know You Rider opener and followed with Women R Smarter and Standing on The Moon. 'Standing', another new song off Built to Last, which actually describes brilliantly, the sight of the Earth as seen by someone from the moon. I just had a really strange thought. From a Distance by Bette Midler is more or less about the same thing, but not nearly as cool. . .ahem. . .

The next song was Estimated Prophet, and that usually means Eyes of the World is coming up next, but not this time. This time Brent took the reigns with his tribute to his kids called I Will Take you Home and that went into drums and then came Eyes of The World. Now that was sweet. Miracle > Black Peter> Lovelight closed the set. . . Lovelight really took on a life of it's very own when Weir brought it back. It used to be a standard for the Dead in the 60's, when Pig Pen would jam it out for 25, sometimes 45 minutes and bring down the house, just rapping all the way through it. (Way before there was rap) Weir took it for his own in 1981 at the Melk Weg in Amsterdam for the first time without Pig Pen. That must've been fun for them. The encore for the evening was Box of Rain. Another song that I always love to hear. (Considering how long it eluded me, right?) The third night. The final night. The night that ended a great run of shows at a venue in beautiful California, is best described as "What the hell is going on here tonight??"

First Spencer Davis came out to close the first set for the last two songs, How Long Blues and Gimme Some Lovin...(The rest of the set was pretty much inconsequential). The last time the Dead played How Long Blues was August 19th, 1970. (Thank you Deadbase) Rick got us some VIP passes for the lounge upstairs, so during the set break we went upstairs to have a very expensive beer and meet and greet whomever might happen to be hanging out up there. The only person of interest was Spenser Davis who we ran into on our way out. That was cool though.

The second set brought about an even bigger surprise though. The Boys came out on stage with...Wait, who is that??. . Bob Dylan is here? Who knew about this??. .This was really gonna be a treat (little did I know). They opened the set with Aiko-Aiko and Dylan was just hanging out playing, not doing much of anything. . . Just playing. This song is over and the band was just kinda hangin back. . .Waiting. . .Then Garcia plays a couple of key notes, which I recognize right away as Monkey and The Engineer. They stop for a second and then Weir steps up and checks the mic 'woooo'. . . and then they played Monkey and The Engineer. After that catchy little number they played Alabama Getaway, then Dire Wolf, then Cassidy, then Memphis Blues. Drums came up next and Mr. Dylan left the stage. Then they played three songs after drums and then the encore, which was Not Fade Away> Knockin on Heaven's Door, and Dylan once again graced the stage with his presence.

So to recap, the boys came out with Bob Dylan for the second set and played five, first set songs including an electric Monkey and the Engineer to open the second set. The rumor on the street was that Dylan selected those songs because they they were his favorites. . . That's really not so hard to believe, right?

The Summer Solstice show.
Ping Pong Palace June 21st 1989.

The Grateful Dead was celebrating the Summer Solstice (longest day of the year) with a show at the Shoreline Amphitheater in Mountain View Ca. In the beginning of June they announced that the event was going to be televised on Pay-Per-View. The idea of PPV was still a very new concept then. We were told to go to our Cable Company and buy a converter box to unscramble the signal, and I was struck with yet another brilliant idea. Why not have a party and an open house? The funny thing about this is that Bobby and Jerry did a commercial for the broadcast. They were sitting in two seats next to each other asking one another questions, "Hey Bob what are you doing for Summer Solstice this year?" "I don't know Jerry what are you gonna do?" "Well, I thought I might have a party at my house, but it's way too small, what about your house Bob, could we have it there?" "Ah. No. My house is way too small too. Hey I have an idea, why not have it at your house." as they both looked and pointed toward the camera.

It was a pretty damn funny concept for a commercial and it worked for me. I made some calls, went out and bought a keg and started setting up the gizmos to make it possible to watch the broadcast. Of course this included connecting a VCR between the converter box and the TV so I could record the concert on Video, which after some trial and error was definitely a go. The show started out with a jam called Hideaway, then Touch of Grey into Minglewood Blues. Then there was a mid set Box of Rain, a Dire wolf and a Masterpiece. The second set opened with Scarlet into a Bucket, Ship of Fools, Estimated Prophet, Eyes of the World, drums Truckin, Other One, Morning Dew, Lovelight and Brokedown Palace for the encore. The greatest thing about the show itself was the presence of Clarence Clemons on Sax through most of the second set.

I had people coming from all different directions for this one. Close friends, friends of friends, and even neighbors of ours who weren't Deadheads stopped in for their dose of Grateful weirdness. All were welcome, open house with no cover. The keg was flowing with ice cold beer and everybody enjoyed the hell out of it for an evening. It was such a great feeling for me, because I felt like I was making this show happen for all my friends. (The Producer, as it were) The show was cool because it started in the early evening when the sun was still shining and the song selection was great. A really, perfect night. If I could go back to re-live a moment in my own lifetime, this would be in my top five.

1989; Pittsburgh Road Trip

This was a time in my life when Brian and I were going to Grateful Dead Night at Chubb's Pub every Tuesday with tapes in hand. But a lot of people were bringing tapes now, so we were forced to take turns. Some of the stuff that was being played sounded like crap, but most was really good. The guy who had taken over the mix wasn't allowing anything to be played that didn't sound amazing, but something unique could be listened to for nostalgic reasons and then we would move on.

Hanging at Chubbs was a really good time, but we hadn't had a road trip in quite a while so there was one brewing. When I say we hadn't had a road trip in a while, I'm talking not much longer than a month or two. That was usually about it. As far as touring was concerned, I wasn't really into going to any great lengths at this point After having been down South and out West so recently. The shows out at The Forum in L.A., were more than enough to keep my buzz going for a bit. That being said, I got a phone call at work one afternoon from Shelly, one of my Chubb's friends, to see if I was going on the bus trip to Pittsburgh. I told her I didn't think I was going, but she said I had to go. Gerry (the owner of

Chubb's) had tickets for the shows, with really great seats and the bus was filling up. A lot of our friends were going and we were gonna have such a great time and yada, yada, yada. . .So I said fine, I'll go. My next move, I decided to call Brian and convince him to go as well. I said, "Come on Bri. We'll go, just me and you. No girls, just a guy thing and we'll have some fun. Just relax and enjoy. . .What do ya think...??" Sounded great to him. We met at the bus station, picked a couple of seats, sat down and enjoyed the six hour ride. (If I can really say that we enjoyed the ride) As we were getting ready to leave we noticed a blonde chick sitting up in her seat in front of us, like she was sitting on her legs, which she was. We both noticed. . .very cute. . .nice smile. . . .laughing out loud. . .tight jeans. . .nice tight jeans, and there was a girl sitting next to her with her back to the window, but all the way down in her seat so we couldn't really see her very well. Later on Brian was checking her out again, but I paid no mind. I was having a guy weekend. . .That was it. When we got to the hotel, got our room assignments, all on the same floor, which was great. There were eight rooms that covered both sides of our long stretch of hallway. There was alot of us.

The first night the party started with Aiko-Aiko, Rooster, Dire Wolf, All Over Now, We can Run, Brown Eyed Women...Finished off with Queen Jane, Tennessee, and Music Never Stopped. For the second set we got our Shakedown Street and boy was it appropriate in this case. The weather was great. The crowd outside was thick and lively and spread out over at least three parking lots and drenched in tie-dye.. *'Don't tell me this town ain't got no heart, you don't even have to poke around'*. All you got to do is stick your head out the window and you'll see how much heart this town has. In fact, as I learned later in my life, the city of Pittsburgh has got more heart than most any other city in America. It's the home of the Pittsburgh Steelers and although I hadn't discovered them yet, I was destined to be a huge fan. Next in the line-up was Women r Smarter into Foolish Heart, The Wheel > Gimme Some Lovin> Hey Jude Finale> Round and Round > GDTRFB > Lovelight and the encore was Baby Blue. . .

All in all, it was a great show amongst the shows that I've seen up to this point, but I had to continue being choosey about the shows I was going to and at least mentally avoid extensive road trips. I was loved traveling to different places more than anything and that's why I went to Florida so quickly. That was a quickie jaunt to meet up with a some old friends that I rarely see anymore. This trip here was about going to a couple shows with my friend Brian, someone that I really haven't gone to a lot of shows with overall, and having some me time with no worries about rides or how much I was drinking or anything else. It's also my first trip to Pittsburgh, but it wouldn't be my last. . . I found it very funny that the Steelers world and the Dead world overlapped so nicely. There is a lot of mutual love for both out there. The difference between tailgating for the Dead and tailgating for the Steelers is at Dead shows the air is filled with music and tie dyes are everywhere. At Steelers games the common thread is playing sack toss and/or flip cup (drinking game) and wading through a sea of Black n' Gold, rather than tie-dyes. By the way, the Pittsburgh Steelers have the largest female fan base of any team in the NFL, so there are Babes everywhere. I mean the BABES are every where. (I capitalized babes for a reason) Obviously another huge plus. After the shows, we caught the bus back to the hotel. Now, a little hallway party developed, on it's own. The rooms were all together and everyone was feeling great, so we just wanted to drink some more and maybe eat a little. . .

Dooo. Yoouuu...Miiinnnnd...!!!! That's all we could hear off in the distance for about five minutes and we were wondering what the hell that was all about. One of the guys from the bus trip was on his way back to the party and this catch phrase followed him. . . I never got the complete story but I could make one up. This guy, we'll call him Dirk, was waiting in the never ending non-moving line to get out of the arena and some wasted chick in front of him said, "Do ya mind? Hello! Do ya mind?... Like to get the hell outta here...like ...today maybe.", and Dirk was just high enough, probably on mushrooms, to make that statement resonate in his head and turn it into, dooo yooouu miinnnd. . .and the two of them came back with it just like that..

While we were hanging out there in the hallway, I did notice something that struck me funny. There was a girl sitting across the hall from me that was not dressed like a Deadhead. She was very noticeably observing everything around her, much like I do, or would be doing in a situation where I felt out of place and was looking for a fit somewhere. She was wearing a sweater and jeans and her socks were very noticeably the same color as her sweater. I found it slightly amusing, in my own state of 'mush' mind, and I got up from where I was and went over and sat down next to her and said, "I just noticed something pretty amusing and I was wondering if you were aware of it." She asked me what it was that I had noticed with a grin on her face and I said. "I wondered if you were aware that your socks match your sweater?"

She said, "Yes I am, and I did it on purpose." Then I got back up and went back to where I was sitting and went on with my evening. A few minutes later I noticed that she was now sitting next to me. Not talking to me mind you, just sitting.

I said, "Look, it's the girl who wears socks to match her sweater on purpose." and she laughed. I said, "You wanna see something pretty cool. Watch this. Hey Brandi, could you bring me a slice of pizza? Watch, she'll bring it to me. Do you want a slice?"

The girl told me she was not hungry, and that it wasn't nice to just expect this girl to do this for me. I said, "Brandi loves me and I know she doesn't mind." Five seconds later, out she came with the slice and she asked me if I needed a beer. I said I was fine, but maybe my new friend would like one. She said she was ok and that was that. A few minutes later Brian sticks his head out the door into the hall and gives me a look that says 'come in here', with an overdramatized wave of his hand. A few seconds later he gives me another stronger look and says, "Hey! Get in here!...Now!" To which I sprang up away from the wall I'd been sitting against and flew into the room. Once inside he told me that the cops, actually hotel security, were making their way down the hall at that very moment and he just thought I needed to get inside. Thank you very much my friend. . . Didn't give the hallway another thought.

JIM DALEY

About five minutes later there was a knock at the door and there she was, the sweater girl, whose name I still didn't know. I told her to come in and she said she had to go get her friend real quick and she'd be right back. She came back, but she was alone. Her girlfriend didn't want to come out anymore. She was done. So we hung out for a while with my other friends in the room, about six of us. We were all talking about the shows we had seen and about how cool this one was and she was saying how she only came out to Pittsburgh to protect her girlfriend from the hippies. Protect her from who? From us? Ha! We had to laugh about that. She said she really had a good time so far and didn't see the element that she had expected. We were having this really long conversation about the music and song selection and I made some crazy observation about 'Dark Star being in everything that they do'. What I was talking about was the jamming that takes place in a lot of their songs is the same kind of fluid jamming that occurs during Dark Star, but even my friend Bob, who knew what I meant, started laughing at me. It seemed like I was trying to get really deep and I realized that too, so it was kind of funny. I wasn't just spouting though, because I had heard this interview years earlier with Jerry, when he made the same reference to Dark Star in the same context that I had, but I didn't remember hearing Jerry say it until recently when listening back to some of my old tapes and I heard the actual interview where he was discussing the Dark Star reference.

Anyway, the night ended and she went back to her room. The next morning, as I was getting my stuff together to leave for the bus, the sweater girl showed up and said hello. She told me that she didn't really want to leave the night before, but she was with her girlfriend and she thought it was the right thing to do. I told her it was fine and that I'd be down (for the bus) in a minute and I would see her then. When Brian and I got to the bus the girls were sitting in different seats in front of one another so we sat with them, which was the plan apparently. Now I realized that this was the girl that was sitting down in her seat and her girlfriend was the one that Brian and I had noticed the day before when we first got on the bus in Shrewsbury.

We four spent the day together, and started something that wouldn't end for a while. The girl had several large decorative bandana's with her and while we were standing around chatting she wrapped two of them around my head and I let her, proving to her what a great sport I was and she liked that. Then we started walking around town together. It was a beautiful day for a walk in the city of Pittsburgh, again not realizing that we were in a "Drinking town with a football problem", which is the way it is most often described by football fans.

We were headed up toward the "Shakedown Street" flea market and her girlfriend split with another one of her friends. We were searching for stuff, just looking around and I came across a pair of blue, feathered earings that were made from peacock feathers with some naturally occurring weird design in the middle of it. Much like an eyeball surrounded by brilliant colors. She really liked them so I bought them for her. As she was putting her other earings back in her purse she realized she didn't have her tickets with her. Her girlfriend, who had just taken off, had both of them. We now had to stop everything and track her down, which took us up to show time. That kinda sucked, but it could've happen to anyone. The show that night was really good and we hung out together for most of the evening. We drove home on the bus together and we exchanged phone numbers, (before the advent of the cell phone) which was also weird because her number and mine were very similar except for the area code. We kept in touch a lot over the next couple of weekends. She was fun to hang with so that's what we did.

This story is significant in my touring life because I married this girl a year later and have my only son from that marriage. It was an interesting meeting to say the least and at that time in my life, I don't think I would've met someone any other way.

A Stadium Tour

*I*n late '88 and '89, the shows were longer in comparison to earlier on, and the set lists were interesting enough. Jerry was headed for unhealthy ground again and sometimes, granted not all the time, he seemed to be going through the motions on stage. Some of us were painfully aware of it, and others were simply in denial. Even though I wasn't in the touring frame of mind anymore, I was interested to see where this new relationship was headed, so that being said, I thought it would be interesting to show her exactly what was going on here. For the next tour, I bought two tickets for each of the five local shows, and took her to all of them. We went to JFK Stadium in Philly, then to Giants Stadium in East Rutherford for two shows, and then RFK Stadium in Washington DC for two shows. I wanted to show her very quickly how much fun it was and that it was safe. She had a great time and she was surprised that so many of the same people were at all these shows, and that a lot of them were friends of mine.

In the Summer of 1989 we had ourselves a Grateful Stadium tour here on the East Coast. It started in Foxboro Mass., at the Sullivan Stadium on the second, then stopped in Orchard Park NY, on the fourth, (Truckin up to Buffalo, DVD release) and then JFK. This show stands out for several reasons. For one, I was taping from a prime spot in front of the board, which by now is a definite no, no. I had my gear set up with nice Neumann mics. (This was the first time I had used those mics in a very long time) It was a sweltering hot day with was no relief in sight. This concert, according to reports I've read, was nearly canceled because the stadium was almost condemned before we got there. It was literally falling apart as we were approaching the building. Deadheads were picking up pieces of concrete (from the collapsing structure) and putting them in their back packs as a keepsake.

Dan Healy had microphones set up in different spots throughout the stadium, on the stairways, to pick up random conversations that were replayed throughout the stadium. All in all, it was a great day for a show despite the heavy heat and the band played like they were having a really good time. . .This was the third of a seven show stadium tour that the Grateful Dead were doing with Bruce Hornsby and the Range as an opening act. Though I missed the first two, I did catch the last five with the aforementioned friend. What makes this show really special though, was the out of this world, show stopping rendition of Brent's latest original, Blow Away. The rest of the show deserves some attention though. The opener was Bucket into Aiko. Weir then pulled out the Memphis Blues Again, and then Jerry did Loser followed by Let it Grow before Brent's inspirational sermon about how good love goes so bad. . .

So, as I was taping the show and Brent started playing this song I looked down at my deck and thought I had plenty of room left for this song. In fact, I remember thinking, "No problem at all."

Then it happened. As Brent started sliding into the climax of the song, that's when we heard it. The indicator that he was by no means finished with this song. In fact, he had a lot more on his mind today than he normally did, and he was going to take all the time he needed to get it off his chest. He wanted to tell us a story. He wanted us all to feel his reasons why he wrote this song in the first place. And that's when we heard it, "Wait a minute!"

The band completely stopped playing for a few seconds, like someone had pulled the plug, and then slowly, Weir starts to strum. Just a few chords to bring the song back up again. Very slowly the rest of the band comes back in, as if they had all been ready for this moment and we were the only ones who were unprepared. At this point, all of us in the taper's section were bent over looking at our tape decks to see our tapes spinning. I thought everything was gonna be ok, but it was already really fuckin long when Brent stopped the action, and then I knew I was in trouble. It would take a little bit of subtle jamming to build the song back up to where it was and then Brent's gotta figure out a way to end it.

My tape ended about two and a half minutes too early and I watched as the tape neared the end and then had to accomplish the necessary flip as smoothly as I could possibly manage it. I would say that maybe half the tapers had flipped this when Brent started singing, because in my experience, a lot of newer tapers would never pause between songs, so their tape would've been closer to the end and therefore be a more accurate decision maker at the time. My master ended up getting cut, which really sucked because it was an amazing version of the song, maybe the best ever. Thankfully though, now we can all enjoy the video, released by GD Productions as Crimson, White and Indigo, and see Brent's intense look during this song. Thank you GD Productions.

The Grateful Dead's concert here was the last public event held at JFK Stadium. It was built in 1925 and was the host to many rock concerts and other significant events. The building was torn down in 1992 to make way for the Wachovia Center.

The next show on our tight little schedule was Giants Stadium. July 10,1989. It's funny to me the references that I make in my head pertaining to all things Grateful Dead. Meaning? July 10 translates numerically to 7-10, which to me is the Dead's address in the Haight. 710 Ashbury Street. It always rang a bell with me whenever I heard it. Is that ridiculous or very common? I don't know for sure, but it's definitely me.

The Sunday show was very crowded, as one would expect for a weekend show. Very few tickets were available outside, but still there were a few. The lot at Giants Stadium was always a good time and although there was a Shakedown Street Market here, there were also a lot of people just walking around selling stuff. The t-shirts that Deadheads were selling in the late 80's were all really nice and fairly inexpensive compared to what was inside. The designs were made by artistic Deadheads that either wanted to spread around some great art or needed to make money for tour or both. Fifteen or twenty bucks could almost always get you a really nice quality shirt with an original design outside the show. Inside they were closer to $35 bucks and some of the designs were really far out.

The thing is though, that I'd had my fill of t-shirts at some point, so now in order to entice even $15 bucks out of my pocket for a shirt, it would have to impress me. Over the years I've gotten some very interesting shirts and I didn't wear them alot so they are still in pretty good shape. Out at Red Rocks in 1979, way before there was Shakedown Street flea market, there were some Deadheads selling shirts in the campground. That year I bought a Cosmic Charlie t-shirt that was silk screen printed on a regular white t-shirt, (the kind I never wear) and it had all the Peanuts characters on it, hand painted, in wide circle. There was Linus, Schroeder with Lucy leaning on his little piano, Pig Pen, and Nancy. Snoopy and Woodstock were in the middle dancing and Charlie Brown was running through the group. Above in Bold print were the words COSMIC CHARLIE and below that it says 'how do you do'. Then underneath Charlie was written 'truckin in style along the avenue'. At Brendan Byrne Arena in '86, I found a really cool Trekkie shirt. I was not into Star Trek at all, but this was definitely a keeper. On the front there were three of the main characters from the show, Spock, Kirk and Bones, flanked by Deadheads on either side, looking pretty spaced and the quote was, "They're Dead Jim" On the back was a statement that sold the shirt for me.

Space......The final Frontier,
Their ongoing mission.

To be Seeked out by Strange Life forms.
To change Civilization.
To Boldly go
Where No Band Has Gone Before.

Now, isn't this the greatest shirt ever if you were a "Trekkie". Another favorite of mine was the Dr Seuss shirt. I found it at Giants Stadium in 1992. The Cat in the Hat was on the front with the crowd and the Dead playing in the background, and on the back it read in large, wildly colorful letters.

What a score !
I'll Tell you more,
I Got Great Seats,
They're On The Floor !
Think That I Will Go On Tour,
And Lose My Head,
'til Ninety Four !

One more favorite was my Cats Under The Stars shirt. It was a light blue t-shirt with a rainbow colored air brush of the Garcia Album Cover. That one is a medium so I know I got it a long time ago, probably '79 or '80 This is the one shirt that I can't find. Maybe some day I'll find it again.

Anyway, back to Giants Stadium. The highlight of the first show was Shakedown into Jack Straw. When Shakedown started a bunch of fans jumped the wall onto the field, but security was all over them. I was in no mood to be jumping anything, plus I was not on my own and I wasn't gonna make my girlfriend jump the wall. A nice Chinacat > I Know You Rider > Samson opened the second set, then Built to Last and Truckin followed by Gimme Some Lovin and GDTRFB. This show was a great example of what can happen at any Dead show, but the next night was even better.

The next day we left a little earlier and along the way, made a quick stop at a friend's house. He was a guy that I had worked with on the night crew shift. Lenny was his name and he just happen to be on disability leave at the time. It took us about 45 minutes to convince him that he was coming with us, so although I would like to say that we kidnapped him, he actually came willingly. I told him that we would hog tie him if we had to, but he wasn't getting out of it. "Oh so you have a ticket for me right? What, no ticket?" "No. We don't have a ticket for you, but no worry"

Once we got there, we went for a walk around the stadium under a dark threatening sky and found a ticket for him within 10 minutes. So that part worked out. I brought my deck with me because I had seats on the field, which basically meant that we didn't actually have seats at all. I set up in front of the board, which if you remember wasn't really allowed anymore. It was very casual here though, and there were already several people lined up with mic stands so it was fine. After the first two songs we felt a light rain starting, which was a relief actually, because it was so hot and humid we were drenched in our own body fluids. (Eeww! That sounds gross, huh?) Looking up into the sky, lightening could be seen off in the distance and there were reports of tornadoes touching down in the area as well. Random puddles were forming all throughout the field, and really became intrusive in the taper section. At one point promoter John Scher was encouraging everyone to leave the field area for their own safety, due to the lightening. The rain did let up a little during the second set, but continued on steadily. The one thing that stands out for me was the Music Never Stopped. During this song the rain was coming down really hard and I had to cover my deck pretty well. Not a problem. I looked over at my friend Lenny at this point and he was just taking it all in, enjoying the hell out of it. Playing a little air guitar, helping Jerry along. During the drums segment of the show the Neville Brothers came out and jammed with the Dead, leading them into Iko Iko > Watchtower > Morning Dew > Sugar Magnolia. . .The encore was Knockin on Heaven's Door and the Neville's were on stage for that too. By the end of the show we were thoroughly drenched, to the skin, but it was very comfortable. We made our way out to the car and headed home in a traffic jam that was backed up like a parking lot for several miles. But that was to be expected.

For our next two shows we were solo again, just the two of us, in Washington D.C. at RFK Stadium. The drive down to D.C. is not an easy one and it's also confusing. It's really tiresome because you really have to pay attention when you get close, as there a million different ways to go in three different directions, relatively speaking. Seriously, heading down that way is like driving down a funnel of highways until you get to exactly where your particular exit is and then you have to be ready cause, it's right there!!!... and then it's gone. Same with getting out of D.C. and getting back on the damn interstate. Luckily, we were heading for the stadium, which is right outside of the mess. 295 pretty much takes you right to it. Getting out of the RFK 'mess' is different than getting into it, but it's still not as bad. The White House, is only 4.7 miles from the stadium.

The second show was great. Bruce Hornsby opened again and this time we got to see him play. He also came out and played piano and accordion with the Dead. Bruce liked to play accordion on Sugaree. I think Jerry got a kick out of it too, because he was always beaming when Bruce came out and put that thing on. All these shows in 1989 were exciting and well played, what with Brent's new musical contributions and Mr. Garcia feeling better. I was still shying away from the full touring schedule, even though it doesn't seem like it as you read on.

Regrettable

The Grateful Dead came back around in October and played Hampton again, but this time due to the overwhelming demand for tickets of late, the band was billed as Formerly the Warlocks. The billing change was supposed to keep crowds to a minimum, but as far as we could tell, anyone that followed the Dead's touring schedule found out about it anyway. Ironically, there was a much bigger reason for the billing on the horizon than we ever could've imagined. I brought my girlfriend and went with a bunch of my friends including Brian, Steve and Bob. The first night they did the first Help on the Way > Slipknot > Franklin's Tower since September 12th 1985. They also did an amazing Eyes of The World and a show stopping Morning Dew. I suppose the highlight of the night was the encore though, because they played We Bid you Goodnight. They brought this tune back from the depths of the 70's at the Alpine Valley shows in July of this year, but this was the first time most of us got to hear it. My girlfriend had to work in the morning so we left after this show. I really didn't mind leaving, but I would have rather stayed. We hit major traffic on the way home so we didn't hit the N.J. Turnpike until 6 am. By that time she wound up calling out sick anyway, so we really should have stayed.

All this being said, the second night in Hampton was the show to see. Of all the shows to miss, this was not the one. Before I left for home I loaned my deck, for only the third time in my life, to my friend Steve. He said he would take care of it and I trusted him implicitly and unconditionally. The next day, after sleeping through half of it, I got a phone call from Steve. He was just barely able to speak. First he asked me if I was sitting down. Apparently, Jerry and the Grateful Dead played the show of all shows that second night. The show that, if you're a Deadhead, you would be talking about for the rest of your life. The second set started off with Playin in the Band > Uncle John's Band > Playin which in and of itself is not so extraordinary, but then they slipped into Dark Star, which hadn't been played since the Greek Theatre in 1984, and that slipped into drums into some really wild and weird space > Death Don't Have no Mercy > Dear Mr. Fantasy > Hey Jude Finale > Throwing Stones > Good Lovin. Then they played Attics of My Life, for the encore. The wild and weird space to which I refer was mind blowing. I had never heard anything like it, even played back from the tape it was unimaginable

Before the show while walking around looking for a set of mics to patch into, Steve ran into our friend Arney. He told Steve that he was taping in a small group with Sennheiser mics that he had used the night before and that he'd be happy to run the deck for him for the night. Steve told him of our agreement regarding the deck and Arney told him it wasn't a problem and that he was sure that I wouldn't mind either. So Steve handed my deck off to Arney for the night and went about enjoying the rest of his evening. So far. . . So good.

After the show, people were literally spellbound. I've been present at a lot of shows where people just stayed and took their sweet time getting their shit together before leaving, but Steve told me that people were literally not moving from their seats. They were just hanging out, waiting for the buzz to subside I guess. Maybe trying to figure out what just happened. 'Did they really just play the most amazing show ever, and was I really here for it?' Who knows? I've been in many a situation where I did not feel like leaving, but did so because that's the protocol. In this particular situation though, they really didn't know what to do. It was like they were just 'hit by a bus', left to linger in thought about the crazy musical experience that our boys just shared with them. State Police and Security Guards were called in to move the crowd toward the exits. It was like the scene in a bar after the lights come on, last call is over and it's time to leave, but no one is walking toward the door. He said it took an hour and a half for the crowd to actually gather up and finally split.

This situation was so crazy, but on top of that bizarre experience inside the show, it was not over for Steve. He had made his way over to toward taping section to see Arney, but the section was kind of empty. He actually had to meet up with Arney outside the coliseum and that was when the mind game really began. Arney didn't want to part with the tapes or the deck. He told Steve that he was better friends with me and that he'd known me longer and he just needed to make copies of the show real quick and then he would return the tape deck to me himself. Steve let him take the deck back to his hotel room to make copies, because he happened to be staying at the same Hotel. When Steve showed up at the room, Arney gave the deck back to him, but as they were discussing the point, he grabbed the deck and the tapes away from him again and told him that he still needed to make those copies, and couldn't wait. (Seriously?) The thing is here, that Deadheads that hadn't tripped in years had done acid for these shows, in celebration of the "Warlocks" reunion. The Warlocks played these amazing songs that hadn't been put together in the same show since the 60's and the tapers and everyone else felt that 'heaven had opened up and the answers to all the questions of the universe could suddenly be understood' (can you imagine the over-reaction? Ha ha.). . .

I mean, I totally get the importance of the show in terms of the Grateful Dead lore, but people were losing their minds, if only temporarily, after this show. Now obviously, I have heard these tapes since then, and I have to agree that the music on these particular tapes will not be duplicated, especially by any current incarnation of the band that we are now being treated to. (anything since Jerry died) The jam leading up to and including 'Death Don't Have No Mercy' is mind boggling for sure, and I do believe that if I had been there, in that state of mind,

I would have been blown away too. The Midi effects that the band was using far surpassed anything that they were able to do at most any other time in their performing career prior to this, so there was 'wind whipping' around the coliseum and 'glass breaking' what sounded like 'moans and groans' and all kinds of shit going on. I understand why people were losing it, but my friend Arney needed that tape, so he took my deck out of Steve's hands again and actually held it over the balcony right outside the hotel room. . . What the Fuck ??. . . Yea, he used the 'I've known him longer' argument again and that he would make sure that the tapes and the deck got back to me safely.

Steve said, "That's all well and good dude, but that's not the agreement that I had with Jimbo, so I think that you, being his good friend, and all, should respect his wishes and not put me in this particular situation. It's not fair to me and it's certainly not fair to your friend Jim. Is it?"

He eventually talked him "down off his ledge" and he gave him the deck back, but it was a weird moment to say the least. The antics continued in the hotel room with fighting and screaming and only after a lamp was broken, did cooler heads prevail. He has since been forgiven for his actions, by me and Steve, in fact no hard feelings at all because I 'get' the mind trip that he was on. At the time I was a little weirded out by it, but I was more pissed that I missed the show than about the story that Steve had to tell me. The story actually seemed surreal to me and totally unbelievable, so I guess that made it easier for me to dismiss.

Now back to the fun! Cause that's what it's all about, right? The next five shows in a row were at the Meadowlands in New Jersey. I went to the first two and the last two, but the middle night, which was a Saturday, I couldn't find a ticket for. This was only the second time I was shut out of a show, ever. That Friday night when they were off Bob and Jerry made an appearance on the Late Show with David Letterman.

The first show opener was Let the Good Times Roll > Bertha > Greatest Story. Good Times Roll seemed to be a favorite opener for 'the boys' lately. A Chinacat > Rider second set opener led to an awesome Estimated Prophet > Terrapin >drums >The Wheel >Watchtower > Black

Peter >Lovelight. The encore was Baby Blue. The second night was part two of five parts. No repeats of course, and a Cumberland Blues and a rockin Sugar Mags. . .Weir also did a Queen Jane and a Jack Straw, which is another true favorite of mine. My girlfriend didn't come with, for the first two nights but she joined me for the last two.

On the third night, that Saturday when I didn't get in, I ran into my old friend Andy, that I met in Colorado in 1983 with the guys from Matawan. (Went to Lone Star Café with him for Hunter after the Caldwell show) Andy had been hanging out with the son of a very famous saxophone player by the name of Clarence Clemons, and he had the 'inside scoop' that the Dead was going to play the Dark Star and everything else from Hampton on Weir's birthday, which was the last show of this run. I was very relieved to hear about it, but I also felt at the time that he was being really smug and boastful about it. You know how you can tell sometimes that someone is full of shit but can't stop themselves?, that's how I was feeling about it. Honestly though, thinking back now, he really was just being helpful. I was really bumming out about not being able to find a ticket that night so he gave me the best consolation he could. "You have tickets for Weir's birthday show? Then it's all good Jim. That's when they're playing the Darkstar dude. No worries." Having run into him at other shows since then, I appreciate his friendship. He was a really nice guy when I first met him in Colorado and it was really cool that he told me what was going on. I was very happy that I wasn't gonna miss the Warlocks' stuff on the night that I didn't get in. My girlfriend was there with me for these shows too, when the classic stuff was pulled out. I couldn't believe it. She saw exactly nine shows before seeing this shit, and it only took me 141. Wow!...

Sporadic Touring in 1990

uring the first week of July, 1990, I got a call from my friend Tom about the Dead playing at RFK Stadium. I didn't have a ticket, but he said that wouldn't be an issue. He picked me up along with our friends Donny and Willis and we were drinking Heinekins for the whole ride down. (very hidden inside the windowless van) They started the show with Let the Good Times Roll, which had been in rotation since 1988 and went into Feel Like a Stranger right into Bertha. Nicely done and they were sounding great. Brent did Just a Little Light, which is a favorite of mine and then Queen Jane, Stagger lee, which I hadn't heard in a long time followed by Cassidy, Tennessee Jed > Music Never Stopped. This set was so much fun I was having such a great time with the very real exception of being in nosebleed heaven (Don't know why they call it heaven) and the fact that I was developing a bad, behind the eyes, headache that I could not shake off. I don't remember ever having this type of headache at a show before, but I've had them plenty of times at home. Lay down with a hot compress over the eyes for half an hour or so kind of headache. I think because I hadn't eaten anything up to that point and I'd been drinking for three hours, and then stopped, my body reacted to it. Plus, we had these horrible seats, sitting with the pigeons, which I was not cool with at all. The one thing I didn't liked was being too far away from the band. I like watching them play as closely as possible. Not everybody concerns themselves with that, (hallway spinners) but it's pretty important to me. As the second set started, my headache got a little worse. There was a vise around my head and it was tightening with every note that was played.

The second set started with Box of Rain (yeah!)> Victim or the Crime (boo!)> Foolish Heart (alright!) > Dark Star (wow!). . . Boy, what a bad time to have a headache. I tried to talk myself out of it; 'This could be the last Dark Star you'll ever see, what the fuuuuck'. . .

Unreal! I couldn't believe this slamming headache I had. It lasted through the rest of the set and got worse on my way out of the show. I started searching for Advil right away. I looked around for a little Deadhead chick that might have something for a headache with her. (What else do they carry around in that little bag?) I started tapping shoulders and asking questions, frantically. After only couple of shoulders, I had my Advil. I watched the Advil drop into my hand and I was so thankful I hugged her, told her I loved her (got a look, and a smile) and then continued walking very happily. I had to take it with a Heineken, but you gotta do what you gotta do.

The last show of this tour was July 23, 1990 at Chicago's Soldier Field. On the afternoon of July 26, I came home from work to find my wife sitting with her girlfriend V, and as I walked in they told me that someone in the Grateful Dead had died.

I said, "NO WAY, who???. . . It wasn't Jerry was it???

"No." They said, "It was the keyboard player."

"Holy shit! . . Another keyboard player? Ok, well what happened to him?"

"They were saying drugs, but we'll have to listen for the report again"

I have to admit I was immensely relieved that it wasn't Jerry or Phil or Bobby...

Sorry Brent. Rest in peace man. Brent was an amazing musician. I loved the guy, but I also knew that the band would go on with out him. No doubt. . .The core members of the band were still there, so I was certain that they would go on. They almost had to. So many people depended on the band to do exactly what they do. The 'machine' couldn't just stop. It was the reason why they still toured so much during the year. Sure they loved to play, but first and foremost in Jerry's mind was the family behind them that depended on them so much. I don't mean to speak as if I know Jerry's thoughts, but it is what I'd been hearing in recent years. During the course of his life on the road, Brent's drug problem caught up with him. I heard it was one last taste that got him. Accidental overdose. . .The concoction was cocaine and heroine. A speedball. The same thing that took John Belushi. It's a real shame that everybody can't just learn from each other. But it is about addiction, so what else is there to say.

In these recent months (June 17) my son had been born, but I still had a little time to jump back on the bus once in a while. The Grateful Dead put their heads together and agreed to replace Brent by adding, sometimes sit in, Bruce Hornsby (almost an official member of the band for a time) and Vince Welnick of The Tubes became the new guy. I don't know that this was the greatest of choices for a replacement, but Hornsby couldn't or wouldn't commit to the idea, so I guess it worked for the band. Can you imagine this scenario; Pig Pen to T.C. to Kieth to Brent to Bruce to Vince? It's always the Keyboard player.

I made plans for a small Fall tour. I went to one show at the Spectrum, September 12th 1990 mostly because it was convenient. The first set was somewhat uneventful, opening with Mississippi Half Step into Walking Blues. I was feeling like Walking Blues was getting a little too much stage time at this point. Then Jerry pulled out They Love Each Other, then Uncle, River, High Time. The second set was much better for my frame of mind though; Aiko and Playing in the Band, also getting over played, but was really, really good. Then Jerry played Crazy Fingers into Uncle John's Band; Great combo, very welcome. Drums and space followed and then Morning Dew, which had the crowd raptured, and rightfully so. The crowd was literally singing along with Jerry almost all the way through it. During the space jam Jerry pulled out Handsome Cabin Boy. This song is listed as Two Soldiers Jam on Dead.net, but if you go ahead and listen to the Garcia /Grisman track, it's more than obvious what the song title is. They closed the set with Lovelight and then Brokedown Palace for the encore.

I went to two shows at the Garden the following week, one with the wife since it was her birthday, and the next with Tom and some other friends. The shows were all great, but Jerry didn't seem to be very consistent on stage. He didn't appear to be as healthy as he had been, even a year ago. His diet was apparently slipping, but I have no insider info on that one. (no diet is gonna be foolproof on the road anyway) To the average Head the shows were just great and generally there were no complaints. We are, after all is said and done, a very forgiving audience and that would explain, or forgive any disappointment.

At this point, I had stopped taping altogether. My deck had slowly begun to break down mechanically, and now was not working at all. The first thing I noticed was that the battery power was depleting too quickly. There is a button on the front of the D-5 that lights the LED meter, so you can see the recording levels. When the light button was pushed to check the levels, it pulled power directly from the tape motor, which slowed the recording. When I would play the tape back, it would play faster at those times. If I happened to leave my deck with somebody, even for a few minutes, I would have to explain, "Look, don't push the light meter button ok.? Seriously." "Ok, cool." I'd say, "No really, because if you push the button it will fuck up the speed of the tape." And whomever it was would never take me seriously, so every time the master was getting fucked up. Then the input and output jacks were loose, so the channels would go in and out. I had the deck checked out by two of the best in the business, the Oadey Brothers from Georgia and it was too pricey to get repaired, so I shelved it.

Now after doing some personal research through my tapes, I see that I don't have a lot of tapes from the last four years. In fact I have fewer than 60 tapes covering the years 1990 through 1995. I had one or two exclusive sources for these shows. My friend Dave was getting sound-boards from people all over the country through the mail and he would hand them off to me. Mostly, I was interested in these shows when something out of the ordinary was played. New Speedway Boogie, Ruben and Cherise, Black Throated Wind;

Here are a few a good examples;

University of Las Vegas in Nevada April 28, 1991. Bruce Hornsby on keyboards, first set Bird Song, featuring Carlos Santana on guitar. The second set featured a typical space, Other One, Wharf Rat, Round and Round, but as the Round and round ended Weir kinda woke everybody in the band and the audience up, with an out of nowhere Sugar Magnolia 'ending'. Just the jam at the end mind you, not the whole song, into Sunshine Daydream. I guess he just wanted to play it.

Cal Expo, Sacramento Ca., 5-4-91 because of a first set New Speedway Boogie and The Race is On Oakland Coliseum, Cali, 12-28-91 because it opened with One More Saturday Night into Jack Straw, two of my favorites, plus a great first set over all, featuring Fennario, Minglewood, Dire Wolf, Queen Jane, (a new favorite of mine) a nice Loser and Cassady. Some great stuff.

Orlando Florida 4-7-91 with a Black Throated Wind, Rubin and Cherise, Promised Land.

Albany N.Y. 3-23-91 Cassady, New Speedway.

Chapel Hill North Carolina 3-24-93, which is kinda funny really, because I got this one because of the filler on side B, check it out; So Many Roads a great new Jerry tune, followed by Lazy River Road, another great new Jerry tune, Friend of The Devil and Liberty. This last song here is another great one that came from the genius of Hunter, that he actually released on his latest album at the time called Liberty. I'm a firm believer that this song could've been the next big hit for Jerry and his band of merry music makers but. . . anyway.

Some shows I would take just because they were soundboards and were incredible, but mostly I'd pick 'em just for song selection.

Ok, so the best I can figure at this point is that my last tour with my deck was the mini tour from Hampton through the Meadowlands 1989,

Formerly the Warlocks shows. Even though the whole tour was not billed that way, I'm just saying. I don't remember the exact moment of clarity and realization that my deck wasn't working anymore, but I do recall picking it up one day and finding out that it was definitely shot. I held on to it for at least 12 years in that state before I revisited it and set about to get it fixed. I love my D-5

My decision not to record shows anymore was ok really, because the tapes were literally everywhere. And anytime there was an outstanding show, (in anybody's opinion) there would almost always be a sound board recording circulating soon after. This sometimes made the audience copies obsolete, or unnecessary as it were, so essentially there was no real need to worry myself about any of that. I still had my Nakamichi home deck too, so whenever there was a show that was really great, or one that I was there for and wanted a copy of for myself, I was able to make that happen.

Of course, these days I wasn't going to a lot of shows anyway, so what was I going to tape?. I saw one show in 1991, at Giants stadium on June 17th and that was it for me. This was my son's first birthday and we had a small family party for him at our house. The Dead played the same weekend, not the Saturday but Sunday and Monday. We had our little party on Sunday, which was a little tough because it happened to be Father's Day. All of my family was there plus my buddy Tom with his new baby boy, who was six months older than mine. Tom and I went to Giants Stadium the next night, which was my son's actual birthday. But as I pointed out to my wife, it really made no difference to him, he was only one. The show opened with a nice Eyes of the World and included a great Dark Star jam in the middle of the second set and a New Speedway Boogie in the second set, which the Boys had just recently dusted off for public enjoyment again.

The next run was at The Garden, in New York City again. They scheduled nine shows there this time and by now they had the record for the most sold out shows by one rock band in this venue. Even though I was staying away from the full tilt touring, who am I to stay away from the

Garden of all places? I have seen so many great shows at Madison Square, I couldn't possibly just not go. (It is, after all, still the Grateful Dead) Nine shows, lots of great music, but not all nine for me. I most certainly went to the first two; Sunday and Monday, skipped Tuesday, went Thursday and Friday, couldn't get a ticket for Saturday and then I went Monday. The third show, which was the Tuesday that I skipped, featured Branford Marsalis and was probably the best show of 1991. They opened the show with Shakedown > C.C.Rider > It Takes a lot to Laugh, a Train to Cry. The latter is a Dylan tune that Jerry would most often play during an acoustic set. The Dead played it only twice that I'm aware of. Then Bobby played Black Throated Wind, which I hadn't caught yet. The second set opened with Help on the Way > Slipknot > Franklin's, Estimated Prophet > Dark Star> drums> Dark Star> I Need a Miracle > Standing on the Moon> Lovelight. The reason I even bother to list a show that I wasn't even there for is for Branford's performance. Listening to him play his sax throughout; the soft melodies surrounding this particular set list was pretty incredible, to say the very least. I don't think that a lot of musicians would be able to handle the constant changes that the music goes through when the music is playing the band, (as it were) but he was just amazing. These shows were very high energy as they always were in the city, but Jerry wasn't looking healthy. I know that it's gotta be tough to stay with a health regime when you're out on the road, when the element is all around, but I always thought that the music was important enough to make that difference.

The shows at the Garden were sprinkled with some previously mentioned Hampton/ Warlocks song selections. We had a pre drums Dark Star jam the first night and a full Dark Star drums Dark Star the third night, an Attics of My Life encore the first night and a later set Attics during the seventh night, but there was no sign of Death Don't Have No Mercy. Guess they weren't so inspired. But they did pull out the New Speedway Boogie and A lot to Laugh, a Train to Cry. This Will be the Last Time even got some stage time here at the Garden.

Normally we consider the option of taking the train into the City for shows at the Garden, but the train was just not feasible this time.

Because of all the stops being made on the way home and the lay-over in our Eastern NJ Transit town of Long Branch, we never really knew how long it might take to get home, but the thing of it is, we found a better way. The Metro line in Iselin was the way to go. Drive forty-five minutes up the Parkway to Metro-Park and take the shorter train ride into Penn Station from there. It cuts dramatically, the amount of time spent on the train and still puts the traveling Deadhead in the basement of Madison Square quite conveniently. I wasn't taking any time off work specifically for these shows, so this way we would be home on any given night by 1:45, which is way better than 3:30 right?

On October 26th I was watching an episode of Saturday Night Live when I got a shocker I wasn't ready for. Bonnie Raitt was the musical guest (which is probably the reason I was watching in the first place) and when she came out for the second time she dedicated the song to the memory of Bill Graham. "Holy Shit! I hadn't heard anything about that". I went to get the paper the next day and the obituary said that he had been killed in a helicopter accident with two members of Eric Clapton's band. Thank God (I thought) that Clapton wasn't on that copter too. That would have been horrible. I mean it was already horrible, but you know.

On November 3rd a tribute concert was organized and billed as "A benefit for Laughter, Love and Music" Among the bands and celebrities present were; The Dirty Dozen Brass Band; Bobby McFerrin, Jackson Brown, Aaron Neville, Tracy Chapman, Santana, Robin Williams, Journey, Crosby Stills Nash and Young, Joan Baez, Kris Kristofferson, John Popper and John Fogerty. It was an amazing afternoon, and it was broadcast over KSAN FM in San Fransisco and everyone celebrated Bill Graham's life and his contribution to the history of Rock 'n Roll. The encore for the day was Forever Young into Touch of Grey and everyone was on stage for it. The Grateful Dead had become very friendly with Bill over their many years of association with him. He was family. He was the main reason why the boys played New Years Eve for so many years and the reason they almost always, with very few exceptions, opened with Sugar Magnolia. It was Bill's favorite song. Rest in peace Mr. Bill Graham. It was a pleasure meeting you. . .and being yelled at by you. . .

Road Trip To Albany 1993

I hadn't been going to many shows in these recent years, so with the wife's permission, I planned a trip to see two shows in Albany, N.Y., with a couple of friends. The show dates were the 27th and 28th of March. It was a Saturday and Sunday. It's funny though that when I asked my wife if it would be ok with her she told me that I had to tell or ask, or let my son know first. It's only funny that she asked me to do this because he was only two and a half at the time. It was a full month away and she insisted that I tell him first. So, (to humor her) I went to his room and sat him on my knee and told him what the plan was. He acknowledged it and told me that he would miss me and gave me a real heartfelt hug. It was really, really cute actually. He seemed to understand what I was telling him and that was kind of unexpected. It was still a month away though and that was the funny part. It would be like asking a 6 year old to remember his first birthday party. You wouldn't expect, it right?

When it came time to go, I drove my car and I brought my friend Leon, from the Chubb's family, and Christine, whom I had just met who was the sister of another old friend of Tom's. The drive was quite a long one, as I remember. It was a whole lot longer than I had bargained for. Three and a half hours up the Garden State Parkway to route 87 north straight up to Albany. None of us had tickets to these shows either. (did I mention that before?) Remember how I feel about going to shows without tickets?. . . It's not a good idea, especially when all of us are in the same boat. If we only needed one ticket between the three of us, that would be Ok for the most part, but at this point we needed three in our car alone and then there was the other car load to worry about. There were only two people amongst us that had tickets. . .

We started out by checking out the parking lots in town, but that sucked. Everyone in town already had their tickets and had no extra's. Leon had this really crazy idea (actually turned out to be the best idea ever) to go right outside the city, where the cars were coming in and just hold up a finger. We had done this at Red Rocks in 1979 and it worked out well for us. After about 20 minutes he had tickets for himself for Saturday and Sunday and one extra for Sunday. We were all looking for tickets, but he was having the best luck. After a couple hours we had to give up, sort of. We all agreed that the tickets were spoken for and Chris and I were the only ones that didn't have any for the first nights show. (Only the third show that I was unable to find a ticket for) The Saturday night show was certainly the hardest to get so we had to be content to hang out in a local bar until after showtime. It's kind of a funny thing when you're hanging out in a bar with a very cute Deadhead chick and you're a married man. Sometimes your wife 'gets it', and sometimes she doesn't. She called me at about 7:30 that night wondering how I was doing and what was going on, and I had to tell her that I didn't get into the show and that I was hanging out with Christine. She didn't know Chris, so she was unaware of the situation I was in. Very cute Deadhead chick. Nobody else around. Really?

I was very aware of the situation I was in. I mean, should I hit on her or should I just leave it alone? Seriously, I'm kidding. I never gave it a thought and it never became an issue. We just talked and drank. We didn't drink to get drunk either, just a social. She was really a nice person, really sweet and great to talk to and we were already friends. It was all good. Not that it mattered to my wife at all. She knew it was all innocent, but she never let me forget that phone call or the laughter in the background at the bar. Enough said.

The first night, the one that we missed, was the show. Not because the set list was so amazing, but they did play Casey Jones for the last time, to end the first set, and then I Fought the law, for the encore. This tune was originally recorded by the Crickets after Buddy Holley died with Sonny Curtis on vocals, but the Bobby Fuller Four had a hit with it.

The first time I heard them cover this tune, I wondered what it was that made them choose it, because I had always liked it. Green Day and the Clash had covered it, so it was getting a some attention on the radio. Sometimes there was an interesting story surrounding the addition of a new cover tune. I figured they probably heard it on the radio one afternoon and decided they wanted to play it. That's actually exactly the way it happened this time. I heard the story a few years after the show and it was confirmed by David Gans on Tales From the Golden Road. (Grateful Dead Channel; Sirius Satellite Radio) Apparently the boys were in a limo on the way to a show shortly before Albany and they heard it on the radio. They enjoyed hearing it again, and decided to start practicing it.

The next night we all had tickets so it was a stress free afternoon. We made our way to the Coliseum for the parking lot gig and entertained ourselves while the time passed by. Once we were inside and the show started the song selection was descent, but that wasn't even the best part. After the show while walking to the car, Chris mentioned that she heard some people talking about a hotel close by where the boys were staying. She didn't remember the name of the Hotel, but she said it was right down at the end of the main strip and then. . . It was, like, right there. So being the adventurous Deadheads that we were, we decided to take a chance on sketchy directions to a nameless Hotel that the the band may, or may not be staying at. . . Ok. . . I'm game.

We drove about 3 ½ miles to the end of the block, where we came to a 'T' in the road. Was there supposed to be a 'T' in the road? We didn't know, but we all agreed, in unison, "Screw it." We turned around, making a very wide U-turn, (no traffic for miles, 2 am) to our left. As we did so, we saw the Hotel we were looking for right in front of us. We were psyched! We pulled into the lot and found a parking spot very quickly. We casually walked in the front entrance, trying to look like we belonged, not like we were lost, and slowly walked past the front desk. We didn't want to talk to anybody about why we were there just in case everybody was doing it. We looked to our left and saw the sign for the bar lounge. Great, it looked casual enough. We walked over and entered the lounge and straight in, to our right, was a very large bar area. It was a long bar that stretched to the far wall, about fifty ft. away and it was as crowded as it could get. About five or six people away from where we were standing was Dan Healy, talking to someone that I didn't recognize. Knowing him it was probably a fan and he was just entertaining his questions. I have seen him do that a bunch of times right by the soundboard at shows. Hell, he's entertained my own questions once or twice as well. To our left there were three large booth type table settings. The middle one was where all the action was happening. There was no table there, but there was a fireplace against the wall and a coffee table in the middle. We saw Jerry and Steve Parish on one side. Another roadie, whom I didn't recognize across from him and then Bobby was sitting and the end closer to us. There was also another girl sitting between the roadie and Weir, but that's another story that I also know nothing about.

Christine and I stood there discussing what we were going to do, for a minute or two and then I pushed myself (gently) past this big dude, that I was certain was just a presence for crowd control, just far enough to say hi to Jerry, "Hey Jerr, great to see you again, (Jerry looked puzzled, 'have we met?') thanks for another great show. You look great." and I shook his hand and he said, "Hi, how ya doin. Thanks man." Wow, how cool. This man is my rock n' roll idol. A 60's icon. A revolutionary guitar god (in a lot of people's eyes) and he's thanking me. Holy shit! Pretty cool. Though, if he had said, "You're welcome", it would've sounded weird. Right? He was really very receptive and cordial. It musta been very difficult for him to have a drink in a bar with his friends without the eventual intrusion, but he seemed to be genuinely relaxed and at ease, if that's not too redundant.

Then I turned to face Weir on my left and said, "Hey Bobby, great show." And shook his huge hand. (Very long fingers) he said thanks as well. I walked away and went back to see Chris, who was waiting in the wings and I told her she should really go say hi. She told me that she was really nervous and she didn't have anything to say.

So I said, "Come on Chris, you're a cute little Deadhead chick and they'd love to talk to you, even just for a second".

She said, "I don't know. I don't even know what to say." I said, "Just say hi and say thanks. What more is there really, and when do you think you'll ever get a chance like this again. You have to."

After that she agreed and stepped forward. I convinced her that this would probably be the one and only time she would ever have an opportunity like this. So we both made our way past 'the big guy' again and Christine managed to slip her little tiny self into the area where Jerry and Bobby were hanging out.

She reached over to Jerry and said, "Hi Jerry, can I give you a kiss, on the cheek?"

He leaned over just enough for the peck and she said, "I really love you. You guys are so great."

Jerry looked at the rest of the guys in the group and grinned like he had just won the lottery and he laughed at Bobby.

I whispered to Chris, in her ear, that she should say something to Weir as well, and she said, "Oh Bobby, you're really great too!"

Jerry had a field day with this one. He joined in saying, "Oh Bobby, you're really great too!" in a really high shrill voice, totally busting Bobby's balls. Everybody in their small circle laughed and even Chris got a real chuckle out of it.

Then I turned to Bobby and asked, "Hey Bob, you think you guys will ever play 'Walk in The Sunshine', the only song left on Ace that you haven't pulled out of the dust." It was the only song off of his solo album, 'Ace' that hadn't been played by the Dead. As if he wasn't already aware of that.

He just looked at me and said, "No, I don't think we'll be playing that one."

At this point I noticed that at the next table over, Vince Welnick was sitting by himself just looking around, taking in the crowd. He seemed very content just sitting there, so I walked over and very abruptly sat down on the booth bench and slid in close enough to shake his hand and hang out with him for a moment. It was just like I had been in the bathroom and was coming back to my seat. I sat with him and welcomed him into a very chaotic, but familiar situation. He was genuinely happy to have the company so we talked about "stuff" for a few minutes. After that I left him to the crowd that had now started to gather. It was very cool to see the smile on his face as the Deadheads gathered around him.

After that, Chris and I both settled into the scene without making too big a deal about the whole thing, but we were very happy to have had a few words with the boys. Chris and I had already decided that we were going to drive back home right after the show so that's what we did. We were going to share the drive, but I took the wheel and drove the whole way home. Chris and I talked and laughed so much that the ride went by very quickly and I wasn't tired at all. We were back by 5:30 or 6 the next morning. By then I was quite exhausted and was happy to be back home.

My Last Grateful Dead Show

The Grateful Dead played two shows at Giants Stadium in East Rutherford N.J. June 17 and 18, 1995. I went to the second of the two with my later years, touring buddies Tom and Donny. Giants Stadium was never one of my favorite places to see the Dead play, just because it was so big and any seat that wasn't on the field overpowered the intimacy that makes the Grateful Dead so enjoyable on any given night. I bring up this show for a special reason though, because it was my last Grateful Dead show.

Not my last by choice mind you, because like the Grateful Dead, I don't think I could ever have planned my last Dead show. This happened due to an outlandish positioning of the universe in it's most destructive form, the waves of which being out of our control in the way they usually are that lead to the end of the "Long Strange Trip" that we had all become accustomed to.

That being said, I don't remember much about this show, so through the miracle of the internet, I am re-acquainting myself with what everybody is calling a horrible performance by Jerry, who for the most part, needed the rest of the band to hold him up. I know there was a situation going on with him for a long time, which is one tenth of one percent of the reason I cut back my touring in recent years. I don't want this to turn into a review of the show though, so I'm only gonna touch on a couple of things.

Oh yes, first we have the ever popular six song first set. Oh, how great is that? You go to a stadium show to see a band like the Grateful Dead that you've seen over a hundred times and they play six songs and take a break. There's something wrong with that already, right? Yes. Weir sings 'The Same Thing' and then a song called 'Eternity', which from my standpoint feels like an eternity.

Feel Like a Stranger was the opener and not so bad, jammed out well, but not intense by any means. Bertha actually sounded real good. Stagger Lee was definitely not strong vocally, but of late Jerry seemed to be straining to sing out even basic tones, so for me Giants Stadium is not a stand out. Nothing had really peaked my interest in a long time on tour though. (Keep in mind that for us, a long time would be just longer than three or four months) I'm going to shows now (speaking in terms of the early nineties) because it's been a part of my life for so long that I couldn't just blow it off. I didn't want to blow it off really, because you never know how good it might be; It's still the Grateful Dead, and that's still always the case, no matter how it seems to be. I didn't see myself flying out to California so much anymore, especially since my son was born and my priorities shifted drastically, but God knows that if Jerry had cleaned up his act and things had gotten better, I would've eventually taken my son to those places where I had been and had experiences that far and away, surpassed my expectations. All this being said, I was content to hit only local shows for the last three or four years (except Albany, my last road trip) and even in 1994, I only went to Giants Stadium, that was two shows and I'm still trying to figure out or remember whether I went to both of them or not. It's confusing to me that I really remember those earlier Grateful Dead road trips better than those toward the end.

Anyway, the Giants Stadium show was in June 1995, and it was only one month later, on July 9, 1995 the Grateful Dead played their last show. This wasn't planned either. If it could've been planned, I would guess that it would've been on a grander scale. Probably part of a fair-well tour or at least a lengthy run at a favorite venue or two. But that wasn't to be. What happened was so wrong. It made the world sad. It made my world sad. It was another month later, August 9th that the sadness hit and everything changed. The memory is still so clear to me that it could've happened yesterday. You know that story that everyone has, "Where were you when." Everybody has one. Mine kinda sucks. I ran into a guy who was a casual friend, known only to me through work and even then on a very limited basis. He had news for me that could've been anything other than what it was. Most times we had limited two minute conversations that consisted of meaningless jabber, and then the work continued and I wouldn't see him for another month. But this day, that split second conversation included four little words that made everything else I was supposed to be doing in that moment seem so trivial. Those four words made me feel slighted at first, and coming from this guy, I was a true non believer. I hardly even reacted to it initially. Who the hell was this guy to tell me something so personal? To me this was actually like a death in my extended family. Not the kind of family that I saw during the Holidays, or that I called when I needed help moving. This was a family however, that I felt every bit as close to as those I was related to by blood and I could feel my heart beating stronger as I sought out confirmation for this sad news.

Oh, and those four words? "Jerry Garcia died today." I stopped what I was doing and went outside to listen to the radio in my car for as long as it would take to confirm.

The first song I heard was Friend of the Devil. . . Not a good sign. Then, right after that, I heard 'Truckin' and my heart sank. . . I felt my feet and my hands get a little numb as the blood rushed from them, as I tried to grip my steering wheel a little tighter and push away the bad news. The Grateful Dead doesn't get a lot of air play on our local station. Hell they don't get a lot of air play anywhere, but this station had a gimmick called Doubleshot Tuesday. This was on Tuesday when they would play two songs from each artist played; The problem?, this was a double shot on a Wednesday. I figured with the news that I just heard, this couldn't be a good sign. Next, I distinctly remember 'Mr. Marty' Martinez, coming on right after Truckin saying, "That was Friend of the

Devil and Truckin from the Grateful Dead, and we are celebrating the life, and mourning the sudden passing this morning, of Jerry Garcia, who died this morning at the Serenity Knolls Drug Treatment Center. We will be talking about Jerry and playing his music all day long and taking your calls to see how you feel."

The cause of his death was not immediately known, but they were saying right away that it was not an overdose. I was so taken aback by this news, I sat there in the seat of my car and stared at the radio in disbelief. What was going on? I can't believe what I'm hearing. Jerry is really dead? I sat there for what seemed like hours trying to piece together the rest of my day in my head. I didn't have the luxury of leaving for the day like thousands of other Deadheads that I heard about later. I rested my head on the steering wheel for a few moments until I was able to hear the radio talking to me again. As I did, my mind began to wander. . .

The conversation that took place just moments before, caught me completely off guard, but has played over in my head a million times since that day;

I saw him walking through my work area when he stopped and said, "Hey, I have to tell you something. You're the first person I've run into that I knew would really care."

I said, "Ok, what is it that you think only I would care about?". .

"Jerry Garcia died today." He said.

I said, "Yea. . . I doubt that very much."

He said, "No really, it's all over the news and I remembered that you're a big Dead fan and you're the only person I knew that would really care."

As I thought about the way in which, I received this dis-heartening news, I really felt it was such a pitty that of all the people in and around his world, I was the only person that he knew of that would care. I thought, "What a limited existence." I mean on that day, August 9, 1995 the whole world, for at least a few minutes, was reminded of the life of this incredibly gifted musician and compassionate human being. People all over the world stopped for a moment to think about him, and a lot of people cried for a lost friend. All of this being said, I hold the distinction of being the only person that he knew that would care. Well, thankfully I knew a hundred (thousand) more people that cared, that cried, and felt a real loss that day. Thankfully, my world consisted of a lot of shoulders to lean on and a lot of emotional support that I could depend on. I Thank God for that. I still thank God for that. He took Jerry Garcia from all of us way too soon, but He left us with each other for comfort, to mourn the passing of our friend. Could've just left Jerry with us and saved the need for all the comfort. Sadness. . .

I left the radio on for a few minutes longer than I should have because I couldn't turn it off. I wasn't on a break or anything, but I just couldn't go back inside. I did have work to do, but I just couldn't leave right away. This really sucked for me because, as I said, unlike most of the other people that I spoke to later, I didn't have the option on this particular day, to just go home. I had to stay the rest of the day because there was no one there I could pass the buck to. . .

I went back to my job feeling kind of numb. Just like that guy who had just given me the news, I felt there was no one I could tell that would care. (No Deadheads at my job) There was no one I could talk to that would understand the sense of loss that I felt, but I needed to talk to someone. I needed to talk to someone right away that would get it, without me having to say anything. I called my friend Tom. He wasn't at home, but I talked to his wife for a few moments and could tell that she understood. She spoke to me in her soft vooice, as if we had both lost someone special. She knew the pain that my friend, her husband, was feeling. She said she had just spoken to him, and she would relay my message. This was way before the age of 'everyone has a cell phone' but he did call me back after a few. When I spoke to him we decided that we should have our own Memorial for Jerry that weekend. We would make phone calls and get everyone together that we could think of, and just listen to music and tell stories and share our feelings. A lot of Deadheads are very huggy people and hugs, in this case, are way better than drugs. Anyway there were a lot of drugs. . .I mean hugs available there. Enough hugs to go around for everyone, with no worry of hug withdrawal.

After my conversation with Tom, I returned to my work and shortly thereafter, my wife walked in. She came walking toward me and told me something about my son. She had made arrangements for a day care situation or something for him and I honestly didn't hear a word she said. I asked her if she had been listening to the radio at all and she told me that she hadn't. She asked me what was wrong because now she saw the look on my face.

I said, "Jerry Garcia died this morning."

Now, I'm not sure if she said 'are you sure?' or 'are you ok?' But I said, "He died this morning at a rehab center in California. I'm not sure what happened yet, but I'm pretty sure it wasn't drugs. I'll know by the days end." Then she asked, "Are you ok?" and my only response was, "I don't know." I couldn't be sure how I was feeling. I was definitley in a state of non-belief, for sure. Even after listening to the radio for confirmation, I really just needed to be around people or even one person whom I could talk to, that knew what the deal was. Just the thought that I didn't have this extension of my life to reach out to anymore was a strange feeling for me. For everyone I'm sure. This was going to take some time. Some reflection.

Jerry's gone? No more Grateful Dead tour? That was certain. Hard to comprehend that idea. That concept. I knew what the other people were going to think. The people outside our "bubble". . . Drug addict.

I'm just thankful that the official cause of death wasn't drugs. Drugs were most certainly a contributing factor, but at 53 he was finally trying to clean up and be healthy. I have to believe that. . . I will continue to believe that.

Bob Weir was scheduled to perform in Hampton, New Hampshire on this very day. He kept to his schedule and dedicated his performance to his friend, "Our departed brother." He played Amazing Grace and dedicated it to Jerry. I got a copy of this show not long after and I wrote my thoughts at the moment, on the inside label;

This is the day life as we know it changed forever. Although we all knew it would eventually happen, we somehow figured we'd go first or something. I never expected it to affect so many people, as it did. Quite a pleasant surprise. Made it all a little easier to deal with. . . Rest in peace Jerry. . . You'll always be loved, and thought of in the nicest possible way!

Yes. I said before, the world did seem to stop and take a long look at our pain on this day. More attention was paid to Jerry and the Grateful Dead than I ever expected there would be. Little did I know how much this event would affect the lives of other people around the world. Even President Clinton was moved with emotion by Jerry's passing. He remarked that Jerry was "a great talent" and that he had "his demons" that were part of the legacy of the life that he lead. Al and Tipper Gore were actually seen at the Greek shows after the election year and Tipper was quoted as saying that it was not her first show. It seemed as though our generation was finally in the White House, and as strange as that seemed to be. . . It was true.

Certain events were taking place on both coasts and around the world on this day. People were gathered in Strawberry Fields by Lennon's Imagine Mosaic to mourn with each other and leave pictures and flowers, showing their love and respect for the music that was created by this special man. For the first time in history a tie-dyed flag was flown above City Hall in San Francisco, and the Stock Exchange in New York City stopped trading and paused for a moment of silence for our beloved guitar hero, on this very sad day.

I left work for the day at 4 pm and was home eight minutes later. I received three phone calls that afternoon. My friend Joe from California called to talk and reminisce. Joe said he had decided that he was going to move back home because at times like this he was thinking about how much he missed living here with all his old friends. I told him right away that I wouldn't hold him to that because of the circumstances of the time. I knew as well as he did that his life was now in California and no matter how much he missed his life back East, his life was truly out West now.

My friend Rick called and we spoke for a very long time. He and I went to a lot of shows together. The two of us brought a family of friends together that would never have met without either one of us. We had lost touch with each other over the years because he moved out to California with his parents and then chose to live in upstate New York where his wife grew up. Through it all though, we have stayed good friends.

Next I spoke with my best Grateful Dead buddy. The guy that I've known since I was crawling around my back yard. My friend Mike and his wife Patty. When I first started getting live tapes from my friend Dale in high school, Mike was the first guy I went to with them. Listening to tapes from the Filmore West in 1971 with Pigpen wailing on Lovelight, was what started my taping obsession. Late night parties at Mike's house would also include Reflections by Jerry Garcia Band and Tiger Rose by Robert Hunter. Later on that night I heard from my friend Tom again and plans were set in motion for the Memorial on Friday night.

Now for another perspective. Some observations from outside of our little bubble. Before I get into this next story I have to explain that for more than half of my life I have been a fan of two of the most mis understood entertainers possible. My love for the Grateful Dead is beyond explanation for the most part, ("They're a band beyond description") which by now doesn't bother me in the least, but I've also been a huge fan of Howard Stern for a very long time. Trying to explain my love or my interest, or my appreciation for that matter, for Howard is even more frustrating sometimes. It especially cracks me up that people who don't have satellite radio and can't listen to him anymore don't think he's relevant. This brilliant human being who happens to have millions of listeners across the country, is probably more mis understood than Deadheads and he doesn't get us either. In a room full of guys and girls the one subject that gets judged worst than being a Deadhead (relatively) is being a fan of Howard. So I have to ask. Where the hell are all these listeners hiding out? I have to believe that it couldn't be just strippers and perverts that listen, because I listen and I'm neither. I also know for a fact that he has a female fan base because I listen religiously and girls call in all the time. Years ago he used to get a lot of hate callers who were women, (also listening) but not so much in the last ten or so. It cracks me up when people say that they don't like him because he degrades women. He actually has a huge amount of respect for women, he just also happens to have a sexual sense of humor that would rival that of a 5th grader. I switch back and forth between the Dead channel and Howard all day long. I followed Howard to Satellite Radio before the Grateful Dead had their own channel, so now when Howard does leave (I couldn't imagine) I would keep my Sirius.

My infatuation with Howard Stern began in September of 1982, when his afternoon drive radio show arrived on W-NBC in New York City. I was listening to the show one afternoon on my way home from work and I couldn't believe the shit that was coming out of his mouth. Mostly, it was trash talk about his bosses at NBC. My first thought was; 'This guy is fuckin funny as shit, but he's crazy talking about his bosses this way. He's not gonna be on the air too much longer talking like this.' I went inside the house and asked my brother if he had heard this guy, Howard Stern on NBC yet, and that if he hadn't he had better check in quickly, cause he wouldn't be on long.

So, all this being said, the man can talk, talk, talk and while he is brilliant and interesting and hilarious most of the time, he is not a Grateful Dead fan at all. I tuned in to his show the next morning, August 10, not really thinking about what the topic of conversation might be and I got a surprise. About two minutes after tuning in, someone called in to talk about Jerry dying and to tell Howard how saddened she was by it. . .

Oh boy.

Howard starts in, "Oh big surprise, Jerry Garcia is dead. . . Only problem now is, what to do with all these stupid Deadheads that'll be wandering the streets looking for something to do."

She followed that comment with, "Howard, why are you so mean spirited?"

Howard said, "Look. Don't you guys get it! He was a drug addict and he was gonna die soon anyway, I mean Jesus, go out, get a life, get a job, and grow up!"

She continued, "But Howard it's not about growing up, it's about loving the Grateful Dead. Jerry meant so much to so many people. Stop being so mean!"

Now watch out, cause here it comes.

"Stop!. . . Stop your belly aching and grow up for Christ's sake! Listen to me. Those of you who know me for years, know that I hate the Dead, and I've always hated the Dead, and quite frankly I don't care that he's dead. I really don't. It doesn't affect me in the least.", and then he hung up on her. He did continue to talk about it for a few minutes with Robin and his other 'compadres', but it was more of the same bashing amongst them as well. No Deadheads on staff at the Stern show. . .Sorry

It felt weird listening to him bad mouthing Deadheads the way he did, but I had to listen. It actually made me laugh a little bit listening to him cause I already knew how he felt about the whole thing and it put a reality spin on it for me. It wasn't a moving tribute, it was real life, out of our circle, if you will. A recounting of the event by somebody that really didn't care about it. It wasn't really so bad. After a while I had to turn it off anyway, because I had to work, but not because I couldn't listen. Howard has always been about the truth and about real life. It's part of his appeal, for me anyway. His show has been a regular part of my day since that broadcast on NBC when I heard him blasting his bosses. He has always been honest and forthright with his audience and he's always given a shit about people. Suffice it to say that being a fan of the Howard Stern Show and being a Deadhead has been roughly the equivalent of being a member of the Ku Klux Klan or a Hari Krishna. Impossible to explain or defend, but extremely important to the believer.

When Friday came, I needed to bring my son with me to Tom's house. He was very happy to join me because he and Tom's son had become friendly. I called the wife at her work to let her know that she could pick him up that night or better yet, I could just bring him home in the morning. It seemed like a good idea at the time. When she showed up to get him that night, she had a really bad attitude about it. Gave me a look like she had caught me cheating on her or some such nonsense. I never understood why she reacted that way that night. She was always very nice to Tom and his wife and I really needed this memorial, like anyone would need a Wake to say good bye and properly mourn the loss of a friend. Well that's done. Since none of us could be involved in the actual service, this is what we had to do. Denis had just turned five in June and Tom's son was just six months older. When they were both younger they had birthdays and such together, so they were happy to be spending time together.

There were so many people there. Old friends with a bunch of kids and loud music, and stories and hugs and free flowing tears. . .It was more special than any of us could possibly have hoped for. We've had parties with a lot of these same people before, but the mood there that night was like that of a celebration with Jerry's life at the forefront. I hope that when it's my time, all the same people are there and it goes somewhat the same way.

A Life After Jerry

For the next few weeks, as I ran into people that I hadn't seen since Garcia's passing, I was offered condolences like a family member had passed. This is how I felt about Jerry's death. It struck a nerve very deeply, like John Lennon's death affected millions before him. The outpouring of love and support that was shown him during the weeks following his murder were replicated for Jerry.

My mother-in-law joined my wife and my son and I, on a day trip to The Museum of Natural History in N.Y.C. It was about a week after Jerry died, so along the way we made an impromptu stop at Strawberry Fields to visit the Imagine Mosaic. As we walked toward the Dakota, past the gateway and the doorman stand, my wife and I looked at each other and she said very quietly to me, "Don't say anything." I understood why and complied. When we crossed the street I told her that I was going to walk to the Mosaic real quick just to check it out. It was still partially covered with pictures and flowers and mementos that were left by mourners. I knelt down next to it myself and thought of all the amazing, unforgettable times that I'd had with many friends at the hands of this very special musician. (Jerry, not John at this point)

At the time, I remember thinking to myself that when all was said and done, the thing I would miss most besides Jerry's magical moments on stage, was seeing Phil play again. Bobby always had a side gig going, and I figured that would most likely continue to roll on, but over the years, as early as 1985 there were strong rumors spreading throughout the Dead community that Phil wanted to take some time off. Whether it be to clear his own head or simply to spend more time with his own family. Then of course, because of the financial expectations of the Grateful Dead Organization these things never happened. Then the Touch of Grey phenomenon gave the band a renewed spirit, so that was all good. Now, with Jerry gone, there would be the freedom to do just that. Take as much time off as you want Phil. We love you and you deserve it.

The first rumor to circulate regarding the surviving members was about Billy Kreutzman skipping off to Hawaii, not wanting to be bothered with any reunions or special tours of any kind. Billy was the rock n' roll drummer that Jerry first met when he was hanging out at Morgan's Music Shop, teaching Banjo, so arguably he knew Jerry longer than anybody else in the band. I remember hearing an interview, or a piece of an interview with Billy when he said, "Hanging around Jerry was so interesting and exciting. I knew that if I wanted to be a drummer and play in a band, that I should stay with this guy. He was so cool to be around." Next was Pig Pen and right after that was Bobby, on a New Years eve in 1964 I think.

The week after Jerry's death Bill Graham Productions organized a public memorial service in Golden Gate Park. It was on August 13th 1995, and everyone who was any part of the rock n' roll scene in San Francisco was present. The guests were numerous. Each of the surviving members stood at the podium and said a few words to the crowd of well wishers, mourners, and Deadheads. Robert Hunter wrote a eulogy for his friend;

'Jerry my friend, you've done it again. Even in your silence the familiar pressure comes to bare, demanding that I pull words from the air. . . Now that the singer is gone where shall I go for the song?. . . So I'll just say I love you which I've never said before, and let it go at that my friend, the rest you may ignore.' Words written and spoken by Robert Hunter.

It was much longer than this, but you can look it up.

Within just a few weeks the band made the decision to drop 'Grateful' from its name forever, in memory of Jerry. In October, during Halloween week, I was checking out an episode of Rosanne on NBC. She always did great Halloween shows. This particular one had Rosanne and her sister messing with an Ouija board. It's supposed to help the player(s) to contact dead people. The players all have their fingers on the game piece and they're supposed to just follow where it goes, not giving it any help at all. The game piece is actually a large pointer. While it travels around the board it points to letters to spell out answers. While they were playing, it directed them to spell out G-a-r-c-i-a. The last segment of the show they contacted a guy they had dressed up like Jerry, but didn't really look like him at all. Rosanne told him how much she missed him and how sorry she was to hear of his passing. He told her that all was well and not to worry about him. I thought it was a nice little tribute. During the same episode Rosanne gave birth to her son and during a dream state sequence and all the hospital staff were dressed like dancing bears, adorned with masks and tie-dyes, and she named her new son Jerry.

Trying to Find The Magic Again

At this time there were quite a number of Deadheads who refused to go see the boys in any incarnation after Jerry's death. I must say that I was not amongst that crowd. I looked for ways to see the band in any configuration possible. The only thing I didn't participate in was lengthy travel, except for the first year. On the anniversary weekend of Jerry's passing, several bands got together up in the Pocono's area for a festival type of concert that was called The Gathering on the Mountain. It was set up on two separate fields about the size of a football field. The crowds weren't very big, which made it totally manageable. There were about ten bands there that included The Strawberry Alarm Clock and Juggling Sun's. Also on the bill was The David Nelson Band, an expanded version of Hot Tuna and The JGB Band, which included all the regular members of the Jerry Garcia Band along with Steve Kimock and Mark Karan on lead guitars. Mark Karan eventually joined Bobby's Rat Dog.

They had the whole Shakedown Street flea market going on there with t-shirts tie-died skirts and the usual fair. They had food available and plenty of room for camping. It was a great day for feeling the music, and the celebration of Jerry's life. This was the reason for the festival. There were no members of the Grateful Dead in attendance this first year, but the feeling was still emotional and the music heartfelt. This was the last festival that I went to. I can't seem get it together to go to a festival. It just doesn't appeal to me to sit through a full day of bands, even if they are all Dead related. There has been a Gathering of the Vibes every year since this first one, and they seem to have gotten better every year, but I still haven't gone.

The following year Bob Weir participated in a concert festival type of thing geared for Deadheads called the Further Festival. M.O.E. opened the show, the Bob Weir band, currently dubbed Rat Dog played next and the current jam band hit maker, Black Crows headlined the show. I couldn't figure why the Black Crows would be the headlining act for a Dead related festival, but now I'm thinking that maybe the promoter wasn't banking on our presence to sell enough seats so they grabbed the closest thing possible, slightly related to our scene (their current hit was Hard to Handle) and figured that would do it. The only thing that did for me was vacate one seat at just about their third song in. Luckily, or obviously, my friends were of the same mind set. None of us made the connection between the Grateful Dead audience and the Black Crows fan base. Though one thing that stood out for me at this show was during M.O.E's set, Bob Weir came out and sang Me and My Uncle with them. This choked me up a little since it was the first time I'd heard the song played without seeing Jerry on lead.

Bob toured with Rat Dog again the following summer as part of what was once again known as the Further Festival. So, where did the Further moniker come from? Tom Wolfe wrote a book some 40 years ago, that was published in 1968, called The Electric Kool-aid Acid Test. The book chronicled the cross country road trip embarked upon by Jerry's friend and LSD guru/participant Ken Kesey and his band of Merry Pranksters. The bus was painted from end to end in psychedelic colors and the destination sign on the front of the bus stated Further, which is exactly where they were all headed.

The Further Festival this particular year consisted of Los Lobos, Hot Tuna, and Bob's band. I took my wife and my son to the first Further Festival in Camden N.J., and we had great seats. We were sitting at about 12th row in the center. My son was real excited because he really liked La

Bamba, which was Los Lobos' hit single from the year before. They opened the show with Bertha and followed it with a bunch of songs, some of which we were familiar with and some not. The bummer was that they didn't play La Bamba. I wanted to hear it too, dammitt! The next band to play was Hot Tuna. This band consisted of Jorma Kaukonen and Jack Cassidy, both formerly of Jefferson Airplane. People all around us were yelling out 'Hot Fuckin Tuna', because that's what you do at a Hot Tuna show. My wife kindly asked them to edit that and say Hot stinking Tuna for the benefit of all children within ear shot. . . And surprisingly, they listened.

Over the course of the next couple years we were witness to Phil's new band, which consisted of musicians that he hand picked for reasons only he was aware of and this he called, Phil and Friends. It was comprised, most consistently of John Molo on drums and Jimmy Herring on lead guitar, but we were treated to some other amazing players through the continuous evolution of this band. The first time I saw Phil and his friends play was at the Convention Hall in Asbury Park on April 29, 2001. I was with some of my best friends for this show. Actually, anybody who ever claimed to have any interest in the Dead at all was at this show. Phil opened with a very long jam into Eyes of the World. As Phil started to sing I felt exhilarated. Phil Lesh was up on stage, with musicians that he respected, playing his bass, doing what we Deadheads had been begging him to do for the last half dozen years, singing. The big news for this tour was that Warren Haynes had joined the band on lead. Wow, I've got to say now that before this I wasn't real familiar with Haynes as a player in any respect, but my eyes were opened wide after this show.

Over the course of the following nine years, we were treated to several versions of Phil and Friends that included a handful of excellent musicians. Rat Dog also continued to tour with pretty much the same group of musicians, but the two never played together until February of 2008, when the core members of the Grateful Dead got together again to support Obama's campaign. I saw Rat Dog at the Paramount Theatre in Asbury Park N.J. and at the Count Basie Theatre in Red Bank N.J. just about a year apart from each other and they were too completely different shows. I saw Phil two or three times over the years. Once with Warren Haynes and Jimmy Herring another time with Jackie Green and Larry Campbell. I thought that Warren Haynes provided some amazing jams for the band, but his most important contribution for me was his vocal. Warren sang Built to Last like he wrote it. Oh yea, I heard Warren sing that song when 'The Dead' toured in 2003. I also heard him sing Stella Blue around the same time and it was phenomenal. Warren also played lead, in what was called The Other Ones, which was actually formed before 'The Dead'. Joan Osborne found her way into the lineup for a tour, and to me, sounded amazing on songs like Stella Blue, Sugaree and Brokedown Palace. Jackie Green's performance with Phil was another unexpected surprise for me. He says he was not a Deadhead when approached by Phil, but you wouldn't know it from hearing him play, except that he had his own unique style with all our favorite tunes.

In more recent years the core group has been whittled down to just Phil and Bobby, accompanied very successfully by a new drummer, Joe Russo and two backing vocalists, Sunshine Becker and Robin Sylvestre, mainstay Jeff Chimenti on Keys, and John Kadelcik was added in the impossible to fill, Jerry spot. This band is called Furthur. They are definitely the best incarnation of those post Jerry attempts at making Grateful Dead music. Most everybody reading this probably knows where John came from, but briefly, he was responsible for co-founding the most successful Grateful Dead tribute band ever conceived. Having recreated 100's of Grateful Dead shows over the twelve years they have been together, they were a phenomenal group of musicians who happened to be Deadheads. They devised a plan to learn every song the Grateful Dead played by simply playing set lists from shows that the Dead had played in their past. They were amazing with John at the helm and now with Jeff Mattson, formerly of the Zen Tricksters, they're still rocking. I have traveled some distances to see these guys play and it has always been worth the trip. There are actually four venues in my area that have hosted the DSO and if every time they came around they would hit those four, I would be hard pressed to not 'do the tour'.

The Final Word

As far as the Grateful Dead touring scene was concerned, I did feel like a member of their extended family and although I never held a laminate (backstage pass) and was never backstage at a show, (also never got into a show for free) there was always a personalized feeling involved because of the time spent on the road seeing them play. When you travel to as many shows as we did, consecutively, you feel like you're part of something really special. Add to that, taping most every show that I went to and it becomes something bigger. It's an absolute part of being a touring Deadhead. Yes, here I make that distinction between being a Deadhead and being a touring Deadhead. I don't think that someone has to go to hundreds of shows to be a Deadhead.

My only regret regarding Grateful Dead touring is that I never saw them play on New Years Eve. For as many shows as I've seen, in as many Cities and as many different venues, I never really pushed the idea of a New Years show. I even said, "Nah" once. I have to admit that I'm a little partial to being home with friends for that particular National Holiday. In as much as it is celebrated throughout the world as a new beginning, it's not really a national holiday at all. It's recognized as a drinking night for amateurs and as a night when you wouldn't want to be on the road after dark whether sober or not, cause it's a national 'party night'. I have always enjoyed being with close friends on New Years, with food and ice cold beer and the Grateful Dead as background music, be it a live broadcast or a taped fun-fest.

For reasons that are very obvious, the Grateful Dead ceased to exist without Jerry on lead. He was an irreplaceable player in the line-up. Pig Pen died, they went on; T.C. sat in and then left, they continued; Keith Goddchuax left, the band continued; Brent Mydland died, the band continued. Brent and I got on the bus at about the same time, and although I felt that the band would survive without him, it did leave a hole and force a major change in the band. The incarnations that we've seen since Jerry's death have been rough copies at best, with the aforementioned Furthur 2010-'13 being the closest thing to the Grateful Dead that we will ever see, I believe.

This year, 2015, will be 20 years since we lost our brother, Jerry Garcia. Doesn't really feel like it's been that long. He was not a guru, though he was perceived by many, including the Press, to be just that. It was expressed by Robert Hunter best, at the Town Hall show that I went to with my friends Mike and Patty. "Jerry was pretty much a genius and an ordinary guy all rolled up in one."

I always thought "My landscape would be empty if you were gone" was a very accurate lyric for Deadheads, but those lyrics mean so much more now. Will we ever listen to Black Peter the same way again? That song took on a whole new meaning since December 1986, for Jerry's coma comeback. Black Muddy River is now a very different, more poignant song. When Touch of Grey comes on and I hear "We will survive" I will always think of the amazing times I had going to see Jerry and the Boys play whatever their hearts desired.

Thinking back to the moment when I was told of Jerry's death makes me very sad, every time. Bertha, Samson, Eyes of the World, Not Fade Away. . .The band played these songs the first time that I saw them and again at the last show that I saw. No real significance at all, just a thought at the moment. . . . .

My final thoughts concerning a man that I had a great deal of respect for, but didn't really know.

"Jerry, our landscape has changed since you've been gone. But Phil and Bobby and Bill and Mickey have continued to carry your torch. Your love for music has touched many and the music is still alive. It has changed as you would have wanted, it has evolved as it should, and it has taken a turn as many different players have had a hand in keeping it alive.

What's really important though, is that it's being played and it's being danced to and enjoyed by many. . .

Thanks Jerry, for your inspiration. It has moved us brightly and you are missed."

My name is Jimbo and that's my story.

All The Grateful Dead shows that I recorded

Nassau Coliseum LI.	10-31-79	I Realistic Stereo Mic > Sony TC-158SD Tape Deck
Hampton Coliseum Va.	5-2-80	I Realistic Stereo Mic > Sony TC-158SD Tape Deck
Baltimore Civic Center	5-4-80	I Realistic Stereo Mic > Sony TC-158SD Tape Deck
Hartford Civic Center	5-10-80	I Realistic Stereo Mic > Sony TC-158SD Tape Deck
Nassau Coliseum	5-16-80	I Realistic Stereo Mic > Sony TC-158SD Tape Deck

College Park, Cole Field House

University of MD	3-7-80	Realistic Mic > Sony TC-D-5M

College Park was my first show with the new D-5. All the following were recorded with the Sony D5-M, different mics will be listed

Hartford Civic Center	3-14-81	I Realistic Stereo Mic > Sony TC-D5-M
Hampton Coliseum Va.	5-1-81	I Realistic Stereo Mic > Sony TC-D-5M
Spectrum Philly Pa	5-4-81	Nakamichi 700's > Bass Box > Sony D-5M

Glens Falls Civic Center	5-5-81	Nakamichi 300's >Side of stage
Nassau Coliseum, LI.	5-8-81	Sony Mics FOB
Nassau Coliseum, LI.	5-9-81	AKG 1000's
Buffalo War Memorial	9-26-81	AKG 1000's
Capital Center, Landover Md..	9-27-81	AKG 1000's
Scope Coliseum Norfolk Va.	4-3-82	I Nak 300 mic plus 1 Shure SM58 mic
Spectrum Philly Pa.	4-6-82	1 Realistic Stereo Mic
Nassau Coliseum, LI.	4-11-82	1 Realistic Stereo Mic
Nassau Coliseum, LI.	4-12-82	Sennheiser 421's
Glens Falls Civic Center	4-14-82	Nakamichi 300's w/ shotguns & Bass Box
Providence Civic Center	4-15-82	Sound Problems...Nak 300's w/guns Bass Box
Hartford Civic Center	4-18-82	Nak 700's w/guns & Bass Box
Hampton Coliseum Va.	4-9-83	Sennheiser 421's
Brendan Byrne Arena East Rutherford, N.J	4-16-83	w/Steven Stills Sennheiser 421's
Brendan Byrne Arena East Rutherford, N.J.	4-17-83	w/Steven Stills Sennheiser 421's
Spectrum Philadelphia, Pa.	4-25-83	Sennheiser 421's
Spectrum Philadelphia, Pa.	4-26-83	Sennheiser 421's
Madison Square Garden N.Y.C	10-11-83	"St. Stephen" Sennheiser 421's
Madison Square Garden N.Y.C	10-12-83	Sennheiser 421's
Hartford Civic Center	10-14-83	Bouer Mics
Hartford Civic Center	10-15-83	ennheiser 421's
Hampton Coliseum Va.	4-13-84	Sennheiser 421's
Hampton Coliseum Va.	4-14-84	Sennheiser 421's
Niagara Falls Convention Center	4-17-84	Nakamichi 300's
Philadelphia Convention Center	4-19-84	Audio Technica 813

Philadelphia Convention Center	4-20-84	2-421's w/ Senn 441 blend
Philadelphia Convention Center	4-21-84	2-Sennheiser 441's
Worcester Civic Center, Mass.	10-8-84	2-421's w/ Senn 441 blend
Worcester Civic Center, Mass.	10-9-84	Nak 300's
Augusta Civic Center, Me.	10-11-84	Nak 300's
Augusta Civic Center, Me.	10-12-84	Nak 300's
Hartford Civic Center	10-14-84	Nak 300's
Hartford Civic Center	10-15-84	Nak 300's
Brendan Byrne Arena East Rutherford, N.J.	10-17-84	Nak 300's
Brendan Byrne Arena East Rutherford, N.J.	10-18-84	Nak 300's
Portland Civic Center Me.	3-31-85	Nak 100's w/ shotguns
Portland Civic Center Me.	4-1-85	Nak 100's w/ shotguns
Providence Civic Center	4-3-85	Nak 300's
Providence Civic Center	4-4-85	Nak 300's
Spectrum Philadelphia, Pa.	4-6-85	Nak 300's
Spectrum Philadelphia, Pa.	4-7-85	Nak 300's
Spectrum Philadelphia, Pa.	4-8-85	Nak 300's
Richmond Coliseum Va.	11-2-85	Senn. 421's
Worcester Civic Center, Mass	11-4-85	Senn. 421's
Worcester Civic Center, Mass	11-5-85	Senn 421's
Rochester Community War Memorial	11-7-85	Senn. 421's
Rochester Community War Memorial	11-8-85	Nak 700's
Brendan Byrne Arena East Rutherford, N.J.	11-10-85	Senn. 421's
Brendan Byrne Arena East Rutherford, N.J.	11-11-85	Senn. 421's
Spectrum Philadelphia, Pa.	3-23-86	Nak 300's
Spectrum Philadelphia, Pa.	3-24-86	Nak 700's w/ guns

Spectrum Philadelphia, Pa.	3-25-86	Sennheiser 441's
Oakland Coliseum	12-15-86	Senn. 441's
Oakland Coliseum	12-16-86	Senn. 441's
Oakland Coliseum	12-17-86	Senn. 441's
Hampton Coliseum Va.	3-22-87	Sennheiser 421's
Hampton Coliseum Va.	3-23-87	Sennheiser 421's
Hampton Coliseum Va.	3-24-87	Sennheiser 421's "Godzilla Straw"
Hartford Civic Center	3-26-87	Sennheiser 421's
Hartford Civic Center	3-27-87	Sennheiser 421's

Battery Problem during 1ˢᵗ set. The start of deck issues

Red Rocks Morrison, Colorado	8-11-87	Nak 300's
Red Rocks Morrison, Colorado	8-12-87	Nak 300's
Red Rocks Morrison, Colorado	8-13-87	Nak 300's
Town Park Telluride, Colorado	8-15-87	Nak 300's

Most definitely one of the all time greatest places to see the Grateful Dead play...

Town Park Telluride, Colorado	8-16-87	Nak 300's
Providence Civic Center RI.	9-7-87	Nak 300's w/ guns
Capital Center Landover Md.	9-12-87	Nak 300's
Capital Center Landover Md.	9-13-87	Nak 300's
Madison Square Garden N.Y.C.	9-19-87	Nak 300's w/ guns
Madison Square Garden N.Y.C.	9-20-87	Nak 300's w/ guns
Spectrum Philadelphia, Pa.	9-22-87	Nak 300's w/guns
Spectrum Philadelphia, Pa.	9-23-87	Nak 300's
Spectrum Philadelphia, Pa.	9-24-87	Sennheiser 441's
Hampton Coliseum Va.	3-27-88	Sennheiser 421's
Hampton Coliseum Va.	3-28-88	Sennheiser 421's
Brendan Byrne Arena East Rutherford, N.J.	3-30-88	Senn. 421's plus FM feed

Brendan Byrne Arena East Rutherford, N.J.	3-31-88	Senn. 421's
Hartford Civic Center Conn.	4-3-88	Senn. 421's
Worcester Civic Center, Mass	4-7-88	Senn. 421's plus FM feed
Worcester Civic Center, Mass	4-8-88	Senn 421's
Spectrum Philadelphia, Pa.	9-9-88	Sennheiser 421's
Spectrum Philadelphia, Pa.	9-11-88	Sennheiser 421's
Spectrum Philadelphia, Pa.	9-12-88	Sennheiser 421's
Madison Square Garden N.Y.C.	9-14-88	Sennheiser 421's
Madison Square Garden N.Y.C.	9-15-88	Sennheiser 421's
Madison Square Garden N.Y.C.	9-16-88	Sennheiser 421's
Miami Civic Arena Miami, Fla.	10-14-88	Sennheiser 421's
Bay Front Center St Petersburg, Fla.	10-15-88	Sennheiser ME-80
Bay Front Center St Petersburg, Fla.	10-16-88	Sennheiser ME-80
Pittsburgh Civic Arena Pittsburgh, Pa.	4-2-89	Neuman Mics
Pittsburgh Civic Arena Pittsburgh, Pa.	4-3-89	Nak 300's
Great Western Forum LA, Ca.	2-10-89	Nak 300's w/ guns
Great Western Forum LA, Ca.	2-11-89	Nak 300's w/ guns
Great Western Forum LA, Ca.	2-12-89	Nak 300's w/ guns
JFK Stadium Philadelphia Pa.	7-7-89	Neuman mics

I think this is the last show I taped...

Bibliography

1. John Barlow interview, 11-25-82;
From conversations with the Dead by David Gans. Last three paragraphs of that chapter page 177-78. Da Capo Press.com Special Market Dept. Perseus Groups Group II Cambridge Center Cambridge, Mass.

2. David McQueen story; Kids following Jerry down the street. From Garcia; An American Life by Blair Jackson. Penguin Putnam Publishing 375 Hudson Street NY, NY. 10014 Page 42, paragraph 4–6.

3. Jerry Traveled cross country taping bluegrass music with hopes of being hired by Monroe. From Garcia; An American Life by Blair Jackson. Page 61.

4. Garcia Drug Trouble and Diabetic Coma; Page 322– 323 – 345 – 416

5. Garcia drug intervention; Page 335

6. Garcia drug bust in Golden Gate Park; Page 335

7. Garcia / Rothman Broadway shows; page 371– 372.

8. Garcia/ Grateful Dead Use of Persian; Page 289

9. Bill Graham Killed in helicopter; Page 409

10. Information on LSD; Wickapedia Encyclopedia

11. Information on some Grateful Dead Set lists; www.dead.net

12. Other information on Grateful Dead set lists ; DeadBase VII by John W. Scott, Mike Dolgushkin and Stu Rixon.

Made in the USA
Middletown, DE
04 April 2015